T0212970

Communications in Computer and Information Science 703

Commenced Publication in 2007
Founding and Former Series Editors:
Alfredo Cuzzocrea, Dominik Ślęzak, and Xiaokang Yang

More information about this series at http://www.springer.com/series/7899

Leszek A. Maciaszek · Joaquim Filipe (Eds.)

Evaluation of Novel Approaches to Software Engineering

11th International Conference, ENASE 2016
Rome, Italy, April 27–28, 2016
Revised Selected Papers

 Springer

Editors
Leszek A. Maciaszek
Wrocław University of Economics
Wrocław
Poland

Joaquim Filipe
INSTICC and Instituto Politécnico
  de Setúbal
Setúbal
Portugal

ISSN 1865-0929   ISSN 1865-0937 (electronic)
Communications in Computer and Information Science
ISBN 978-3-319-56389-3   ISBN 978-3-319-56390-9 (eBook)
DOI 10.1007/978-3-319-56390-9

Library of Congress Control Number: 2017937151

Printed on acid-free paper

This Springer imprint is published by Springer Nature
The registered company is Springer International Publishing AG
The registered company address is: Gewerbestrasse 11, 6330 Cham, Switzerland

Preface

The present book includes extended and revised versions of a set of selected papers from the 11th International Conference on Evaluation of Novel Software Approaches to Software Engineering (ENASE 2016), held in Rome, Italy, during 27–28 April.

ENASE 2016 received 79 paper submissions from 28 countries, of which 14% are included in this book. The papers were selected by the event chairs and their selection was based on a number of criteria that include the classifications and comments provided by the Program Committee members, the session chairs' assessment, and also the program chairs' global view of all papers included in the technical program. The authors of selected papers were then invited to submit a revised and extended version of their papers having at least 30% innovative material.

The mission of ENASE is to be a prime international forum for discussing and publishing research findings and IT industry experiences with relation to the evaluation of novel approaches to software engineering. The conference acknowledges necessary changes in systems and software thinking due to contemporary shifts of computing paradigm to e-services, cloud computing, mobile connectivity, business processes, and societal participation. By comparing novel approaches with established traditional practices and by evaluating them against systems and software quality criteria, ENASE conferences advance knowledge and research in software engineering, including and emphasizing service-oriented, business-process driven, and ubiquitous mobile computing. ENASE aims at identifying the most hopeful trends and proposing new directions for consideration by researchers and practitioners involved in large-scale systems and software development, integration, deployment, delivery, maintenance, and evolution.

The papers selected to be included in this book contribute to the understanding of relevant trends of current research on novel approaches to software engineering. In particular, the contributions in this book address, inter alia, such fundamental topics as software quality management, model-driven engineering, user-centered engineering, formal methods, software process improvement, and software development and integration.

We would like to thank all the authors for their contributions and also the reviewers who helped ensure the quality of this publication.

April 2016

Leszek Maciaszek
Joaquim Filipe

Organization

Conference Chair

Joaquim Filipe   Polytechnic Institute of Setúbal/INSTICC, Portugal

Program Chair

Leszek Maciaszek   Wrocław University of Economics, Poland and
Macquarie University, Sydney, Australia

Program Committee

Marco Aiello	University of Groningen, The Netherlands
Frederic Andres	Research Organization of Information and Systems, Japan
Guglielmo De Angelis	CNR–IASI, Italy
Oscar Avila	Universidad de los Andes, Colombia
Paul Bailes	The University of Queensland, Australia
Maria Bielikova	Slovak University of Technology in Bratislava, Slovak Republic
Jan Olaf Blech	RMIT University, Australia
Ivo Blohm	University of St. Gallen, Switzerland
Rem Collier	University College Dublin, Ireland
Rebeca Cortazar	University of Deusto, Spain
Massimo Cossentino	National Research Council, Italy
Bernard Coulette	Université Toulouse Jean Jaurès, France
Patrick Cousot	New York University, USA
Mariangiola Dezani	Università di Torino, Italy
Tadashi Dohi	Hiroshima University, Japan
Schahram Dustdar	Vienna University of Technology, Austria
Angelina Espinoza	Universidad Autónoma Metropolitana, Iztapalapa (UAM-I), Spain
Vladimir Estivill-Castro	Griffith University, Australia
Anna Rita Fasolino	Università degli Studi di Napoli Federico II, Italy
Maria João Ferreira	Universidade Portucalense, Portugal
Martin Gaedke	Chemnitz University of Technology, Germany
Stéphane Galland	Université de Technologie de Belfort Montbéliard, France
Frédéric Gervais	Université Paris-Est, LACL, France
Paolo Giorgini	University of Trento, Italy
Cesar Gonzalez-Perez	Institute of Heritage Sciences (Incipit), Spanish National Research Council (CSIC), Spain

Markus Schatten   University of Zagreb, Croatia
Josep Silva   Universitat Politècnica de València, Spain
Michal Smialek   Warsaw University of Technology, Poland
Ioana Sora   Politehnica University of Timisoara, Romania
Andreas Speck   Christian Albrechts University Kiel, Germany
Maria Spichkova   RMIT University, Australia
Witold Staniszkis   Rodan Development, Poland
Miroslaw Staron   University of Gothenburg, Sweden
Armando Stellato   University of Rome Tor Vergata, Italy
Gunnar Stevens   University of Applied Science Bonn-Rhein-Sieg,
                                  Germany
Chang-ai Sun   University of Science and Technology Beijing, China
Jakub Swacha   University of Szczecin, Poland
Rainer Unland   University of Duisburg-Essen, Germany
Olegas Vasilecas   Vilnius Gediminas Technical University, Lithuania
Stefan Wagner   Universität Stuttgart, Germany
Krzysztof Wecel   Poznan University of Economics, Poland
Bernhard Westfechtel   University of Bayreuth, Germany
Jack C. Wileden   University of Massachusetts, USA
Martin Wirsing   Ludwig-Maximilians-Universität München, Germany
Igor Wojnicki   AGH University of Science and Technology, Poland
Michalis Xenos   Hellenic Open University, Greece
Kang Zhang   The University of Texas at Dallas, USA
Alfred Zimmermann   Reutlingen University, Germany

Additional Reviewers

Lorenzo Bettini   Università di Firenze, Italy
Thomas Buchmann   University of Bayreuth, Germany
Mario Coppo   Università di Torino, Italy
Mohamad Gharib   University of Trento, Italy
Claudia Di Napoli   C.N.R., Italy
Jan-Peter Ostberg   Universität Stuttgart, Germany
Laure Petrucci   Université Paris 13, France
Elvinia Riccobene   University of Milan, Italy
Luca Sabatucci   National Research Council, Italy
Sven Verdoolaege   Polly Labs, Belgium
Fabian Wiedemann   Technische Universität Chemnitz, Germany

Invited Speakers

Sergio Gusmeroli   Engineering Ingegneria Informatica SPA, Italy
Wil Van Der Aalst   Technische Universiteit Eindhoven, The Netherlands
Ernesto Damiani   EBTIC-KUSTAR, UAE

Contents

Advancing Negative Variability in Model-Driven Software Product Line Engineering

Thomas Buchmann[(✉)] and Felix Schwägerl[(✉)]

Applied Computer Science I, University of Bayreuth, 95440 Bayreuth, Germany
{thomas.buchmann,felix.schwaegerl}@uni-bayreuth.de

Abstract. Model-driven software product line engineering aims at increasing the productivity of development of variational software. The principle of negative variability is realized by a multi-variant domain model, from which elements not needed for specific product variants are removed. The application of negative variability is impeded by two factors: First, metamodel restrictions lead to limited expressiveness of the multi-variant domain model. Second, unintended information loss may occur during product derivation. In this paper, we present two conceptual extensions to model-driven product line engineering based on negative variability, being alternative mappings and surrogates. Alternative mappings virtually extend the multi-variant domain model. Surrogates repair unintended information loss by context-sensitive analyses. Both extensions have been implemented in FAMILE, a model-driven product line tool that is based on EMF. Alternative mappings are defined in a dedicated mapping model. Surrogate rules may be defined in a declarative domain-specific language and are taken into account during product derivation. The added value of alternative mappings and surrogates is demonstrated by a running example, a UML-based graph library.

1 Introduction

1.1 Background

Software engineering aims at increasing the productivity of computer programming by providing powerful methods and tools for software development. Among others, model-driven software engineering and software product line engineering have emerged as complementary disciplines contributing to the achievement of this goal.

Model-Driven Software Engineering (*MDSE*) [13,29] puts strong emphasis on the development of high-level models rather than on the source code. Models are not considered as documentation or as informal guidelines how to program the actual system; in contrast, they have well-defined syntax and semantics. Moreover, model-driven software engineering aims at the development of *executable* models. Ideally, software engineers operate only on the level of models such that there is no need to inspect or edit the actual source code (if any). The *Eclipse Modeling Framework* (*EMF*) [27] has been established as an extensible

© Springer International Publishing AG 2016
L.A. Maciaszek and J. Filipe (Eds.): ENASE 2016, CCIS 703, pp. 1–26, 2016.
DOI: 10.1007/978-3-319-56390-9_1

platform for the development of MDSE applications. It is based on the Ecore metamodel which is compatible with the OMG *Meta Object Facility* (*MOF*) specification [22].

Software Product Line Engineering (*SPLE*) [11,25,30] deals with the systematic development of products belonging to a common system family. Rather than developing each instance of a product line from scratch, reusable software artifacts are created such that each product may be composed from a library of components. Basically, two different approaches exist to realize variability in SPLE: (1) In approaches based upon *positive variability*, product-specific artifacts are built around a common core. *Composition* techniques are used to derive the final products. (2) In approaches based on *negative variability*, a *superimposition* of all variants is created in the form of a *multi-variant domain model*. The derivation of products is achieved by removing all fragments of artifacts implementing features *not* being contained in the specific feature configuration for the desired product. In the remainder of this paper, we assume negative variability, without intending to discuss the advantages and drawbacks of these two coexisting approaches.

1.2   Model-Driven Software Product Line Engineering Process

In the past, several approaches have been taken in combining both techniques to get the best out of both worlds, resulting in the integrating discipline *Model-Driven Product Line Engineering* (*MDPLE*). Both software engineering techniques consider models as primary artifacts: Feature models [17] are used in product line engineering to capture the commonalities and differences of a product line, whereas *Unified Modeling Language* (*UML*) [24] or domain-specific models are used in model-driven software engineering to describe the software system at a higher level of abstraction.

As shown in Fig. 1, product line engineering consists of *domain* and *application engineering* [11,25]. *Domain engineering* is dedicated to analyzing the domain and capturing the results in a model which describes commonalities and differences thereof. Furthermore, an implementation – the so called *platform* – is provided at the end of domain engineering. The platform is then used during *application engineering* to derive specific product variants, i.e., instances of the product line.

Domain and application engineering differ from each other also with respect to required processes: Domain engineering requires a full-fledged *development process*, while application engineering is ideally reduced to a simple *configuration process* executed in a preferably automated way. The activities belonging to the entire engineering process are described below:

1. ***Analyze Domain.*** A *feature model* describing mandatory, optional and alternative features within the product line captures the result of the domain analysis. Typically, *Feature-Oriented Domain Analysis* (*FODA*) [17] or one of its descendants – like FORM [18] – is used to analyze the domain.

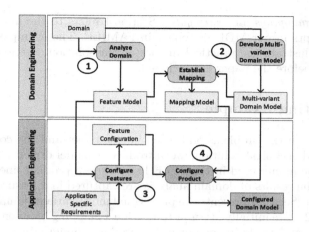

Fig. 1. Model-driven product line engineering process as supported with FAMILE (reproduced from [9]).

2. Develop Multi-variant Domain Model. Afterwards, a *multi-variant domain model* is developed, which realizes all features determined in the previous step. A connection (*mapping model*) between the feature model and the domain model is established, e.g., by annotating model elements with *presence conditions*.

3. Configure Features. In order to build a specific system with the reusable assets provided by the product line, features of the feature model have to be selected. The selected features constitute a *feature configuration*, describing the characteristics of the product variant to be derived.

4. Configure Domain Model. According to the selection of features made in the previous step, the domain model is configured automatically. This is done by selecting all domain model elements which are not excluded by feature expressions evaluating to false. The outcome is an application-specific *configured domain model*.

1.3 Contributions

In this paper, which is a revised and extended version of [9], we address two issues which have been neglected so far in research on MDPLE using negative variability: *limitations in variability* and *unintended information loss*. We have identified these problems (among others) in a large case study [4] which had been performed using our old tool chain for model-driven product line engineering [10]. To overcome the identified issues, we provide the conceptual contributions *alternative mappings* and *surrogates*, which have been implemented as extensions to the MDPLE tool FAMILE [5–7].

The paper is structured as follows: In Sect. 2, we motivate our contributions by introducing a running example. Section 3 explains the conceptual foundations of *alternative mappings* and *surrogates*. Section 4 refers to the implementation of these concepts in our MDPLE toolchain FAMILE. The example is revisited in Sect. 5 to illustrate the practical impact of our solution. Section 6 discusses related work, before the paper is concluded.

2   Motivating Example

To illustrate both the problems addressed in this paper and the corresponding conceptual and technical solution, we introduce a model-driven adaptation of an example commonly used in the SPLE literature—a product line for a *graph library* [20]. The results of domain analysis are captured in a feature model (see Sect. 2.1). Next, Sect. 2.2 presents the provisional multi-variant domain model. In Sects. 2.3 and 2.4, we initially attempt to provide a mapping between domain and feature model, and to derive one example product configuration, respectively. During these attempts, we encounter the conceptual obstacles addressed in this paper, *limitations in variability* and *unintended information loss*; the example is revisited in Sect. 5, which explains how these obstacles can be removed.

2.1   Feature Model

The outcome of domain analysis is shown in Fig. 2 using the concrete syntax proposed in [17]. A graph consists of *Vertices* and *Edges* (mandatory features). Edges may optionally be *labeled, weighted*, and/or *directed*. Furthermore, search algorithms may be provided: depth-first (*DFS*) and breadth-first (*BFS*) search. Last, additional algorithms may be applied to graphs. In case the feature *Algorithm* is selected, at least one of *Transitive Closure* and *Transpose* must be selected. A cross-tree dependency, which is not shown in the diagram, ensures that a transpose is applicable for directed graphs only.

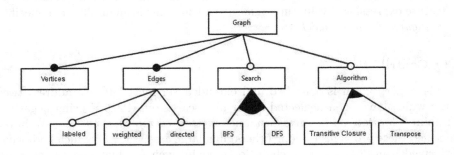

Fig. 2. Feature model for the graph product line.

2.2   Multi-variant Domain Model

The platform of the product line is modeled using a UML class diagram, which is refined with the help of eight UML activity diagrams. The diagrams have been created using the UML modeling tool *Valkyrie* [3], which is based on the *Eclipse UML2* metamodel. Assuming negative variability, the diagrams serve as *multi-variant domain models*. The class diagram shown in Fig. 3 provides the structural view on the platform. The optional features *labeled, weighted,* and *directed* have been realized using the attributes label, weight, and two associations starts at and ends at, respectively.

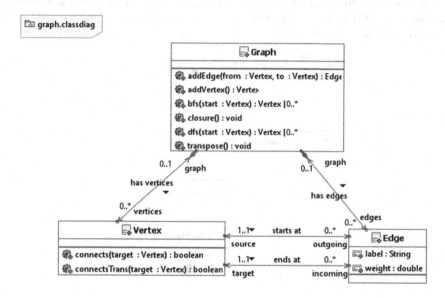

Fig. 3. Class diagram forming the core of the multi-variant domain model.

For the behavioral part of the platform, eight operations have been declared. Four of them (bfs, dfs, closure, and transpose) realize the corresponding features arranged below *Search* and *Algorithm* in the feature model. Operation closure uses the auxiliary operations connects and connectsTrans. Due to space restrictions, we consider only two of the operations, namely addEdge, which is refined in the activity diagram shown in Fig. 4, and bfs (see Fig. 5). The statements contained in the activities are written in the *Action Language for Foundational UML (ALF)* [23].

In the operation addEdge, the values defined by the parameters from and to are assigned to the properties source and target of a new instance of the class Edge. Then, the edge is added to the graph (by instantiating the association has edges) and returned.

The breadth-first search in bfs has been implemented using sequential first-in-first out auxiliary data structures. The sequence of vertices to visit is initialized by the vertex start specified as parameter. Then, in a loop, all successors of the current vertex that have not yet been visited are added to the result list, until no more vertex remains. The set of vertices to be added in each iteration is calculated by the complex expression prev.outgoing.target → difference(res).

2.3 Mapping

In approaches based on negative variability, the connection between the multi-variant platform and the feature model is provided as a so called *mapping*. We may view the mapping tool-independently as a table, where the left column references an element from the multi-variant domain model, and the right column contains a condition for its inclusion in a specific product, represented as a propositional logical expression.

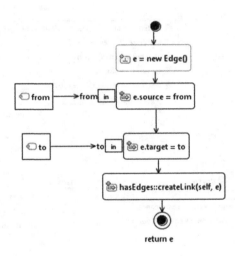

Fig. 4. Activity diagram for the auxiliary operation addEdge.

Table 1 shows the mapping for the three diagrams presented. So far, the activity diagram from Fig. 5 does not contain any variability.

In contrast to the other optional features, the realization of *directed* is much more difficult. Following our domain analysis, in case *directed* is deselected in a given variant, we want to combine the associations starts at and ends at to one single association connects, having multiplicity [2..2] at the Vertex end. Furthermore, the operation addEdge must be adjusted to carry only a single parameter. This must also be considered in the activity diagram for addEdge: Parameters from and to are supposed to be combined into a single multi-valued parameter, which is added to the adjacents of the newly created edge. Table 2 summarizes all changes to the multi-variant domain model intended to be connected with a deselection of the feature *directed*.

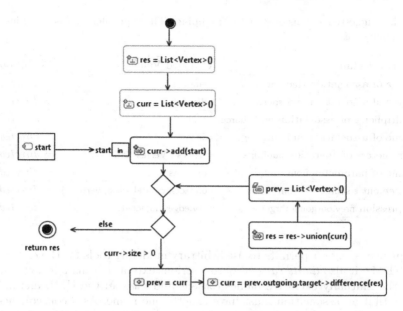

Fig. 5. Activity diagram for the operation bfs (breadth-first search).

Table 1. Initial mapping for the running example referring to elements of the presented class and activity diagrams. For simplicity, mappings for mandatory features have been omitted.

Diagram	MVDM Element	Condition
Figure 3	Operation bfs	*BFS*
	Operation dfs	*DFS*
	Operations closure, connectsTrans	*Transitive Closure*
	Operation transpose	*Transpose*
	Attribute weight	*weighted*
	Attribute label	*labeled*
	Association ends at	*directed*
Figure 4	parameter to	*directed*
	Activity e.target ← to	*directed*
Figure 5		

While most of the state-of-the art MDPLE tools support the basic mapping shown in Table 1, the contents of Table 2 are impossible to express without destroying the syntactical and semantical correctness of the model (in particular, it is forbidden to connect an activity by several incoming and/or outgoing edges). Yet, it is required that the multi-variant domain model must be a valid instance of its respective metamodel. Although this has several desirable practical

Table 2. Suggested extensions to the mapping. The equivalent division (Figs. 3, 4 and 5) applies.

MVDM Detail	Changed Value	Condition
Name of association starts at	connects	¬ *directed*
Name of association end source	adjacents	¬ *directed*
Multiplicity of association end source	[2..2]	¬ *directed*
Name of association end outgoing	edges	¬ *directed*
Parameters of operation addEdge	vertices : Vertex [2..2]	¬ *directed*
Name of parameter from	adjacents	¬ *directed*
Statement e.source ← from	connects::createLink(e, vertices)	¬ *directed*
Expression prev.outgoing.target	prev.edges.adjacents	¬ *directed*

consequences – e.g., it permits to use arbitrary modeling tools for the creation of the MVDM – it also *limits variability* to a serious extent. For instance, we cannot model the mutually exclusive names connects and starts at; the UML metamodel requires that an association must have exactly one name. As a consequence, in many places in the platform, we cannot specify realization details of both variants, *directed* and ¬*directed*, in the superimposition. The problem of *limitations in variability* will be formalized in Sect. 3.

2.4   Product Derivation

For the remainder of this section, let us assume that an adequate solution has been found to overcome limitations in variability, and we are able to adequately express the multi-variant domain model from which specific product variants may be derived.

Nevertheless, unexpected behavior may occur during product derivation. As negative variability is implemented by removing parts of the MVDM not needed in a specific product, there exists a risk of losing more information than intended. An example is provided in Fig. 6, which shows the activity diagram of addEdge for a variant which does not include feature *directed*. After filtering out the activity e.target ← to, its incoming and outgoing control flows remain dangling.

In this example, the information loss can be repaired adequately by removing both dangling edges and by connecting the adjacent activities. This repair strategy, however, takes into consideration knowledge about the semantics of the model and cannot be applied generically. In Sect. 3, we will detail this problem and propose a conceptual solution to automatically derive semantically meaningful repair actions.

3   Conceptual Extensions to Negative Variability

Before detailing the contributed solutions *alternative mappings* and *surrogates*, let us briefly reproduce the problems identified in Sect. 2 in a more general form.

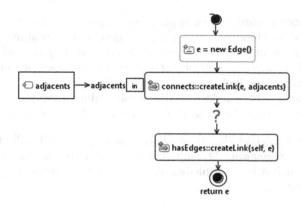

Fig. 6. Configured activity diagram for addEdge affected by information loss.

Problem: *Limitations in Variability*. As approaches relying on negative
   variability use a multi-variant domain model, the respective meta model is a
   limiting factor for variability. In particular, single-valued structural features
   can hold only one value, e.g., a UML association may have only one name.
   Furthermore, each model element must have exactly one container (except
   for the root, which has none).

Solution: *Alternative Mappings*. The concept of alternative mappings
   allows for variability in values of single-valued features of domain model elements (e.g., UML association names). Technically, this has been realized by
   virtual extensions to the multi-variant domain model, physically located in a
   dedicated *mapping model*.

Problem: *Unintended Information Loss*. When products are derived from
   the multi-variant domain model, context-sensitive information stored within
   cross-references, e.g., a transitive control flow, may get lost; state-of-the-art
   tools only take context-free information into account when deriving products.

Solution: *Surrogates*. Unintended information loss is addressed by means of
   surrogate rules. During product derivation, these rules are interpreted such
   that the product variant is repaired; to prevent information loss, reference targets are replaced by appropriate substitutes. Our technical solution provides
   SDIRL, a declarative OCL-based language where domain-specific surrogate
   rules may be defined.

3.1   Preliminaries

Both conceptual solutions are tool-independent and do not require a specific
technological platform. Nevertheless, our contributions explicitly address model-
driven projects; therefore, we make some minimal assumptions with respect to
the underlying modeling paradigm:

– The multi-variant domain model is defined on the basis of a fixed metamodel;
   therefore, each object occurring in the MDVM is instance of a unique class.

- References must accord to the typing and multiplicity rules defined in the metamodel. Two kinds of references are assumed: containment and non-containment references. Containment references are *acyclic* and *existentially dependent*. Furthermore, each object except for the root object of a model must have exactly one container.
- Object may also carry single-valued or multi-valued attributes, whose types and multiplicities must be defined in the metamodel unambiguously.

Implementing a subset of the *Meta Object Facility* (*MOF*) [22] standard, the *Eclipse Modeling Framework* [27] matches these assumptions. Likewise, our own technical solution has been implemented as extensions to the EMF-based tool FAMILE (cf. Sect. 4).

3.2   Alternative Mappings

When applying the principle of negative variability, a multi-variant domain model constitutes the superimposition of all products. Nevertheless, it is an ordinary model instance which must satisfy the structural constraints imposed by its metamodel. Following the assumptions made above, there are at least two structural constraints that impede the use of an ordinary model instance as the multi-variant domain model without being affected by the issue of *limitations in variability*:

Value Variability. The underlying metamodel defines a multiplicity, consisting of an upper and lower bound, for each structural feature (i.e., attribute or reference). The multi-variant domain model cannot intrinsically represent a number of alternative feature values applicable for different product variants that is greater than the upper bound defined in the metamodel.

Container Variability. According to our assumptions, an object must either be the root of a resource, or be contained by exactly one container object. Thus, the location of an object in the containment tree must be fixed in the multi-variant domain model. This restriction prevents different products from containing a specific object at different locations.

Alternative mappings mitigate these restrictions. They are supplementary domain model elements defined externally (e.g., FAMILE defines them in a dedicated mapping model) and inserted into the configured domain model during product derivation. Conceptually, three different kinds of alternative mappings are distinguished.

Alternative Object Mappings are virtual objects belonging to a given class of the domain metamodel. They are virtually assigned to a container object using a suitable containment reference defined in the metamodel. Multiplicity rules need not hold.

Alternative Cross-reference Mappings allow for the virtual creation of links, i.e., of applied occurrences of existing objects in configured domain models. They are assigned to a source object using a suitable non-containment

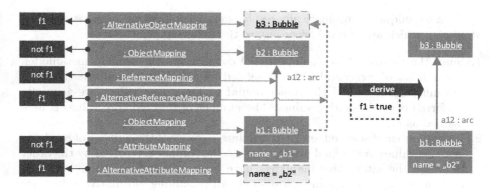

Fig. 7. Abstract example for the application of different types of alternative mappings. (Color figure online)

reference defined in the metamodel. Typing rules must hold for the target object, but multiplicity rules are ignored.

Alternative Attribute Mappings allow for the virtual insertion of atomic data values into existing attributes defined in the metamodel. The attribute type must conform to the metamodel, but multiplicity rules are ignored.

An example for the internal usage of alternative mappings is provided in Fig. 7. The blue elements of the figure represent a cut-out of the multi-variant domain model as object diagram being instance of a simple bubbles-and-arcs metamodel. The green part contains alternative mappings (dashed border) in addition to *core* mappings (mappings that refer to "real" MVDM elements). Both core and alternative mappings may carry feature expressions, which implement the mapping sketched, e.g., in Table 1. In case feature f_1 is selected, the name of b_1 is changed to b_2, and the arc a_{12} is re-targeted to a new element b_3.

3.3 Mutex Conflicts and Selection Strategies

The introduction of alternative mappings leads to *unconstrained variability*: For single-valued features, several values may be defined. As soon as a configured domain model is derived, however, the result is not guaranteed to fulfill the multiplicity constraints defined in the metamodel. In particular, the upper bound may be exceeded, which primarily impedes the derivation of a syntactically correct product.

A *mutex conflict* occurs between a set of domain model elements $\{e_1, \ldots, e_n\}$ whenever the following conditions hold:

- All elements $\{e_1, \ldots, e_n\}$ are values of the same structural feature (attribute, non-containment, or containment reference) of the same object.
- The number of selected elements s, i.e., the subset of E carrying presence conditions that evaluate to *true*, exceeds the upper bound u of the structural feature.

As a technique to automatically resolve mutex conflicts, we propose *selection strategies*, which are applied according to the following priority rules:

1. Since the multi-variant domain model conforms to the domain metamodel, the number of structural features defined by core (i.e., non-alternative) values must never exceed the upper bound u. Thus, *core* values are generally preferred over alternative values. The number of selected core values is here defined as s_c.
2. If the number of selected alternative values s_a exceeds the number of available slots for values in the final product $u - s_c$, the conflict is resolved by the order in which the alternative mappings have been inserted, such that only the earliest $u - s_c$ elements are considered. All remaining alternative values are artificially excluded from the product. The number of excluded values is here defined as e.

Altogether, selection strategies ensure that the effective number of values for the structural feature will not exceed the upper bound defined in the metamodel:

$$s_c + s_a - e \leq u \tag{1}$$

3.4 Surrogate Rules

The derivation of configured domain models in approaches based on negative variability consists in filtering of elements being mapped to a feature expression that evaluates to *false*. Filtering non-containment links, however, can result in unintended information loss, especially concerning context-sensitive information that is encoded transitively by a sequence of links. An example has been provided in Sect. 2.4: Control flows in activity diagrams have transitive semantics; a path from a given source to a target activity may be destroyed by removing an activity in between, resulting in two dangling flows.

Each *link* part of the multi-variant domain model may be expressed as a triple $l = (r, s, t)$, where r denotes the reference defined in the metamodel from which the link is instantiated, s corresponds to the source object from which the link emerges, and t denotes the target object.

Surrogate rules are a conceptual extension to negative variability that allow to repair context-sensitive information lost during product derivation. Formally, we can define a surrogate rule as a tuple $(r, f(t))$, where r denotes a reference defined in the metamodel, and $f(t)$ denotes a *replacement function* that takes as input the filtered reference target, and returns a set of *surrogate candidates* that may replace t in order to prevent information loss in the respective context.

Surrogate rules are interpreted dynamically during product derivation as follows for each link contained in the multi-variant domain model (including alternative mappings):

– If the source object s is selected (i.e., its presence condition evaluates to *true* after applying the selected feature configuration), and t is deselected, continue with the next step. Otherwise, cancel. (Nothing can or needs to be repaired.)

- For each surrogate rule $w = (r, f(t))$ applicable to r, apply its replacement function $f(t)$ to the link target t. Collect all resulting surrogate candidates in a set C.
- Remove from C all candidate objects whose presence condition evaluates to *false* after applying the selected feature configuration.
- If C is empty, there is no viable way to repair the information loss. Thus, cancel.
- If C contains exactly one element c, replace the original link target t with c in the final product.
- If C contains multiple elements $c_1, \ldots, c_n$, choose one of these elements non-deterministically (e.g., by user interaction) to replace t.

To illustrate the definition and application of surrogate rules, let us consider another bubbles-and-arcs model instance. The metamodel defines a reference type *arc* connecting a source and a target bubble. Furthermore, the following *surrogate rule* is defined:

$$w_1 = (arc, f(b) = \text{targets of } b) \tag{2}$$

w_1 applies to all references of type *arc*; the replacement function is defined as the set of successors of the original target t. This way, transitive information, lost by filtering a bubble from a path of bubbles and arcs, may be restored. An application of this rule is illustrated in Fig. 8: surrogate rule w_1 is applicable to arc a_{12}. When applying $f(b)$ to the arc's target b_2, the candidate set is calculated as $C = \{b_3\}$. Therefore, b_3 replaces b_2 as reference target of a_{12} in the configured product. w_1 is not applicable to a_{23} because b_2 is deselected and b_3 is selected; this arc is omitted from the product.

4 Implementation

4.1 FAMILE

Before we give detailed information about the implementation of *alternative mappings* and *surrogates*, let us briefly provide a short description of our tool *FAMILE*. More comprehensive tool descriptions can be found in [5–7].

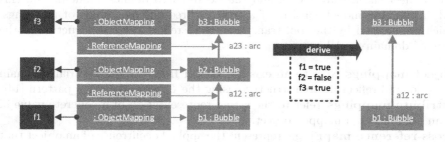

Fig. 8. Abstract example for the application of a surrogate rule.

FAMILE (Features and Models in Lucid Evolution) is an EMF-based MDPLE tool that offers capabilities to capture commonalities and variabilities of a software family using feature models and to map features to elements of arbitrary EMF-based domain models, which contain the realization of those features. FAMILE has been developed itself in a model-driven way, being based on several metamodels. The feature metamodel describes the structure of feature model and feature configurations, respectively, and F2DMM (*Feature to Domain Mapping Model*) is the metamodel for mappings between features and realization artifacts (elements of the multi-variant domain model). For the editing of instances of feature models, mapping models, and feature configurations, corresponding editors are provided. For editing the multi-variant domain model, existing editors may be reused (Fig. 9).

Technically, feature models and feature configurations share the same metamodel. Using the feature model editor, mandatory and optional features may be defined in a tree hierarchy. Furthermore, *cardinality-based feature modeling* [12], a generalization of *or* and *alternative* groups, is supported. The feature configuration editor allows to assign selection states to features and ensures the validity of the configuration with respect to the constraints defined in the feature model. Figure 10 shows screenshots of both editors.

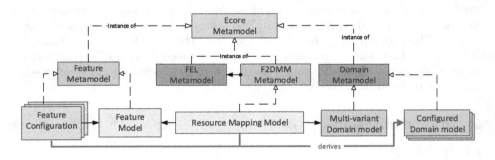

Fig. 9. Architectural overview of FAMILE (reproduced from [9]).

FAMILE's core component is an editor for *mapping models* (F2DMM), which interconnect the feature model and the Ecore-based domain model(s). To this end, a mapping model consists of a tree of three different kinds of mappings, which are created by the tool transparently to reflect the tree structure of the mapped domain model:

Object mappings refer to an existing EObject from the multi-variant domain model and reflect its tree structure using the *Composite* design pattern [14].

Attribute mappings refer to the string representation of a concrete value of an attribute of a mapped object.

Cross-reference mappings represent the applied occurrence of an object that is already mapped by an object mapping.

Fig. 10. Screenshots of the example feature model (cf. Fig. 2) and two example feature configurations (cf. Sect. 5) opened in their respective editors provided by FAMILE.

The connection between domain and feature model is realized by feature expressions specified with *Feature Expression Language (FEL)*, which implements propositional logical expressions on the variables of the feature model. Each element (object, attribute value or reference) may carry a feature expression. Once a feature configuration has been provided, FAMILE may derive the configured domain model by filtering domain model elements decorated with feature expressions evaluating to *false*.

More precisely, the evaluation of a feature expression with respect to a given feature configuration yields one of eight possible *selection states* (cf. Fig. 11). Four selection states immediately result from evaluating a mapping's assigned feature expression: *active* and *inactive* denote that it evaluates to a positive or negative value, *corrupted* means that there are syntax errors in the expression. The state *incomplete* arises in case a mapping has no feature expression assigned or as long as no feature configuration has been loaded. The four remaining selection states indicate that automatic repair actions have been applied to ensure well-formedness (cf. Sect. 4.2), that a *mutex conflict* has been resolved (see Sects. 3.2 and 4.3), or that a *surrogate* rule has been applied to prevent information loss (Sects. 3.4 and 4.4). Once a feature configuration has been loaded, selection states are displayed to the user as overlays of the mapped domain model elements (cf. Figs. 12 and 13).

4.2 Basic Consistency Control Mechanisms

Another feature of FAMILE is built-in consistency checking: Before product derivation, product consistency constraints are applied to ensure well-formedness [5]. To this end, *context-free* consistency constraints are automatically derived from the used domain metamodel: each object depends on its container, if any. Furthermore, the SPL engineer may specify *context-sensitive* constraints using the declarative, OCL-based [21] *SDIRL (Structural Dependency Identification and Repair Language)* [5].

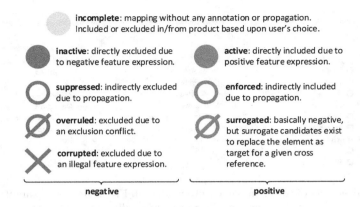

incomplete: mapping without any annotation or propagation. Included or excluded in/from product based upon user's choice.

inactive: directly excluded due to negative feature expression.

active: directly included due to positive feature expression.

suppressed: indirectly excluded due to propagation.

enforced: indirectly included due to propagation.

overruled: excluded due to an exclusion conflict.

surrogated: basically negative, but surrogate candidates exist to replace the element as target for a given cross reference.

corrupted: excluded due to an illegal feature expression.

negative

positive

Fig. 11. Possible selection states for F2DMM mappings and their graphical representation (reproduced from [9]).

Listing 1.1. SDIRL dependency rule for the source of a control flow in activity diagrams.

```
import "http://www.eclipse.org/uml2/3.0.0/UML"
dependency FlowSource {
    element flow : uml.ActivityEdge
    requires action : uml.ActivityNode {
        flow.source
}   }
```

An example of a SDIRL dependency rule is provided in Listing 1.1. The import directive establishes a reference to the metamodel, in our case the Eclipse UML2 metamodel. The subsequent dependency rule, FlowSource, states that each flow in a UML activity diagram (represented by class ActivityEdge) has a context-sensitive dependency on its source activity. Within the body of the requires block, arbitrary OCL expressions are permitted. In this way, dependency rules provide a generalized form of links of the form $l = (r, s, t)$ defined in Sect. 3.4.

When applying a feature configuration to the mapping model and calculating the respective selection states, violations of context-free or context-sensitive dependencies may arise. A *dependency conflict* is present whenever a mapped element is active while a required element, e.g., its container, is inactive.

Propagation strategies [5] have been introduced as an automatic consistency repair mechanism to resolve dependency conflicts. The SPL engineer may choose globally (for each product line) among two pre-defined strategies, being *forward* (exclude the element bound in the variable element) and *reverse* (include the required element) propagation. The application of propagation strategies may lead to two new selection states: Either, an *inactive* mapping can be artificially made positive, i.e. *enforced*, or an *active* mapping can be artificially made negative, i.e. *suppressed*.

4.3   Alternative Mappings

FAMILE implements *alternative mappings* as described in Sect. 3.2. Physically, these supplementary domain model elements are located in the mapping model, such that the multi-variant domain model remains unmodified; during product derivation, they are materialized and integrated into the corresponding product variants.

In FAMILE, the distinction between alternative object mappings, cross-reference mappings, and attribute mappings introduced in Sect. 3.2 applies. For alternative object mappings, two different technical solutions are supported: On the one hand, they may be defined *in-place* in the mapping model; the user has to specify a class to be instantiated at the selected location. On the other hand, a *model fragment* with a dedicated root object may be referenced. This fragment is located in a separate EMF resource and may be referenced multiple times, such that *container variability* is achieved.

The implementation of the detection and resolution of *mutex conflicts* slightly differs from the conceptual description provided in Sect. 3.3. EMF does not directly enforce cardinality constraints, but merely distinguishes between single-valued (upper bound of 1) and multi-valued (upper bound greater than 1) structural features. Accordingly, the problem of *limitations in variability* only affects single-valued features.

Mutex conflicts are detected automatically as soon as a feature configuration has been loaded into the F2DMM editor. For their resolution, the first alternative with a positive selection state is preferred. This is signaled to the user by the selection state *overruled* being assigned to mappings for all artificially excluded elements which had a positive selection state previously (cf. Fig. 11). In case the user demands for a different conflict resolution, he/she may either change the order of alternative mappings or modify the feature expression(s) assigned to the respective elements.

4.4   Surrogate Rules

Surrogate rules (cf. Sect. 3.4) have been incorporated into FAMILE as an extension to the language SDIRL. A dependency rule may include an arbitrary number of surrogate statements, where OCL expressions that must conform to the type of the requires variable can be phrased. The expression may refer to the objects bound to the element and requires variables. Objects that result from evaluating any of the attached surrogate expressions are recorded as *surrogate candidates* for the given cross-reference. Surrogate candidates may replace the element(s) bound to the requires variable as cross-reference target(s). This way, surrogate statements implement *replacement functions* $f(t)$ declared in Sect. 3.4.

An example of a dependency rule containing a surrogate statement is provided in Listing 1.2. Dependencies of control flows to their target activities are defined in analogy to Listing 1.1. The surrogate block states that successors of filtered activities may replace the target activity in order to prevent information loss. In this way, the context-sensitive correctness, i.e., the transitive semantics of control flows, is maintained.

Listing 1.2. SDIRL dependency rule for outgoing control flows, containing a surrogate rule.

```
dependency FlowTarget {
    element flow : uml.ActivityEdge
    requires action : uml.ActivityNode {
        flow.target
    }
    surrogate {
        flow.target.outgoing.target
    } }
```

Both dependency and surrogate rules are pre-calculated during domain engineering and interpreted later on during application engineering after a feature configuration has been loaded. In Fig. 11, the selection state *surrogated* has been introduced for cross-reference mappings being basically *inactive* or *suppressed*, but for which at least one surrogate candidate having a positive selection state exists. Therefore, surrogate rules are applied *after* propagation strategies.

During product derivation, one of the determined surrogate candidates must be chosen by the user to replace the applied occurrence of the mapped object (cf. non-determinism in the description in Sect. 3.4). FAMILE supports three different methods, one of which must be chosen by the user: In a fully *automatic* mode, the first surrogate candidate is selected. In an *interactive* mode the user can select among the set of all candidates. Furthermore, one can choose not to use surrogates at all. In this case, the information loss is intentionally *ignored*.

5   Example Revisited

To demonstrate the added value of our conceptual and technical contributions of *alternative mappings* and *surrogates*, we refer back to the example introduced in Sect. 2.

5.1   Defining Alternative Mappings

The suggested extensions to the mapping sketched in Table 2 can be realized using different types of *alternative mappings* representing the changed values listed in the table. The corresponding conditions are realized by feature expressions assigned to alternative mappings. The default resolution strategy for *mutex conflicts* appears to be counter-intuitive in this example; all changed values are ignored as the respective non-alternative values have a higher priority assigned. Therefore, all original values for which an alternative value is defined must be annotated with the negation of the condition for the alternative; in our example, this corresponds to the feature expression *directed*.

Figure 12 shows the definition of an alternative value that corresponds to the first line of Table 2: the overall goal is to combine the associations starts at and ends at into one association, connects, in case feature *directed* is deselected.

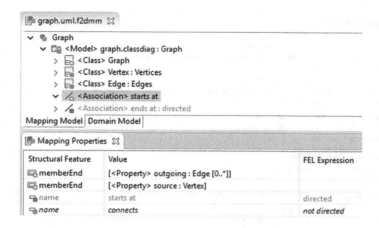

Fig. 12. Definition of an alternative value for an association name using F2DMM.

This is realized in three steps: First, the association ends at is annotated with the feature expression *directed*, making it disappear for undirected graphs. Second, the original name of the association, starts at, is annotated with *directed*, too. Third, an *alternative* (represented in italics) attribute value connects is introduced for the structural feature name, and annotated with *not directed*. Since the feature configuration UndirectedWeighted (cf. Fig. 10) is currently active, the original name is virtually replaced by the alternative name.

5.2 Repairing Information Loss with Surrogates

In Sect. 2.4, the problem of *unintended information loss* was exemplified by a path of subsequent activities being destroyed by filtering an activity lying in between. The problem sketched in Fig. 6 is addressed by the surrogate rule Flow-Target provided in Listing 1.2 (the internal mechanisms roughly correspond to the abstract example of Fig. 8).

Surrogates come into play as soon as elements with a negative selection state are cross-referenced by another, positively annotated, element. Such a situation is present in the activity diagram for addEdge after loading the feature configuration UndirectedWeighted (cf. Fig. 13): The activity e.target ← to is filtered out, but referenced by the control flow selected in the editor. For this control flow, a *surrogate candidate* has been pre-calculated by evaluating the surrogate statement within the SDIRL rule: the activity hasEdges::createLink(self, e). As a consequence, the selection state of the reference becomes *surrogated*. Please note that no surrogate rule has been defined for source activities in Listing 1.1; therefore, the control flow originally targeting activity hasEdges::createLink(self, e) is going to be omitted from the current product.

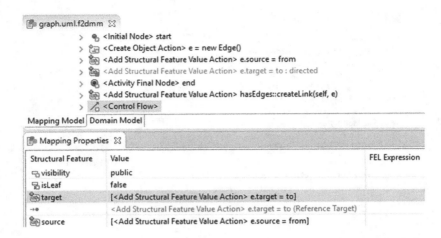

Fig. 13. Inspection of an application of the surrogate rule FlowTarget.

5.3 Deriving Product Variants

The results of deriving the product based on the currently loaded feature configuration, UndirectedWeighted, is shown below. Figure 14 shows that some trivial filter steps have been applied: operation transpose and attribute label have been removed since their corresponding feature is deselected. Furthermore, the associations starts at and ends at have been combined as requested.

Since a single change has been applied, the configured activity diagram for operation bfs is omitted; in contrast to Fig. 5, expression prev.outgoing.target has been replaced by prev.edges.adjacents, as requested by Table 2.

The result of the application of the surrogate rule is depicted in Fig. 15. The activity e.target ← to has been excluded from the product. The dangling flow has been re-targeted to hasEdges::createLink(self, e). This way, transitive control flow information is maintained. Furthermore, some elements have been renamed according to the alternative attribute values defined.

The product derived for configuration WeightedLabeled (cf. Fig. 10) is not shown; there is only a slight deviation from the multi-variant domain model shown in Fig. 3: attribute weighted is missing. No further differences exist since all features except for *Weight* are active, and alternative values are not enabled as *directed* is selected.

6 Related Work

6.1 General Comparison

MDPLE approaches based on *positive variability* require the use of special development tools in order to specify implementation fragments and to *compose* the variable parts with the common core [2]. The language VML* [33] supports both

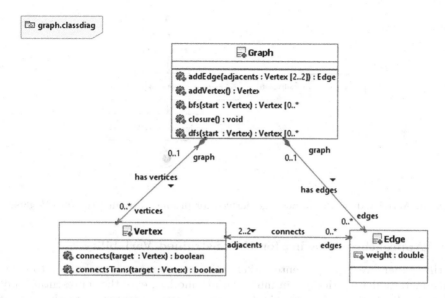

Fig. 14. Class diagram derived for product variant UndirectedWeighted.

positive and negative variability, since every feature is realized by a sequence of small transformations on the core model. MATA [31] allows to develop model-driven product lines based on UML. It relies on positive variability, which means that around a common core specified in UML, variant models described in the MATA language are composed to a product specific UML model. Graph transformations based on AGG [28] which are used to compose the common core with the single MATA specifications.

An essential requirement in tools based on *negative variability* is the mapping between features and their corresponding implementation fragments. On the one hand, the mapping information may be either stored within the implementation, e.g. by using preprocessor directives in source code based approaches [19], or annotations in model-based approaches [15,32]. The tool *fmp2rsm*[1] combines FeaturePlugin [1] with IBM's Rational Software Modeler, a UML-based modeling tool using specific UML stereotypes for features. *MODPL* [10] also uses stereotypes to annotate Fujaba[2] models. On the other hand, the mapping information can be made explicit by using a distinct mapping model. Like FAMILE, FeatureMapper [16] virtually adds variability information to arbitrary Ecore-based domain models.

---

[1] http://gsd.uwaterloo.ca/fmp2rsm.
[2] http://www.fujaba.de/.

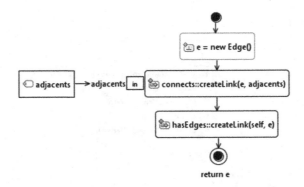

Fig. 15. Activity diagram for addEdge derived for product variant UndirectedWeighted.

6.2   Approaches Allowing for Unconstrained Variability

In this paper, we have presented *alternative mappings* as a technique to over-come metamodel restrictions in multi-variant models, e.g., the representation of multiple alternative values for single-valued structural features. To the best of our knowledge, when considering negative variability, there exists no approach in the literature that corresponds to *alternative mappings* described here, which explicitly stores alternative model elements in separate resources in order to virtually extend multi-variant domain models.

In approaches based on positive variability [2,31,33], alternative values may be dynamically added to the platform using separate transformation specifica-tions. However, during the product derivation process, the order in which the single model transformations are carried out is crucial, since "the last update wins". Thus, a conflict detection and resolution mechanisms corresponding to *mutex constraints* and *selection strategies* presented here cannot be realized upon positive variability.

SuperMod [26] applies a *filtered editing* approach to MDPLE, realizing the *update/modify/commit* workflow known from version control systems. The SPL engineer operates in a single-version view of the model, which is persisted in a multi-variant repository, allowing for unconstrained variability behind the cur-tains. However, in the local workspace, developers are intentionally restricted to single-version editing.

6.3   Approaches to Preventing Information Loss

Surrogate rules, as discussed in this paper, prevent the loss of context-sensitive information stored in, e.g., a sequence of cross references. The concept of *sur-rogate rules*, which are used to calculate target candidates beforehand, one of which is chosen as replacement reference target during product derivation, is unique in the field of MDPLE. As a replacement, we outline one representative belonging to approaches performing context-sensitive analyses *before* product derivation.

The source-code based tool CIDE [19] provides the SPL engineer with a product specific view on the source code, where all source code fragments not part of the chosen configuration are omitted in the source code editor. As opposed to #ifdef-preprocessors, CIDE abstracts from plain text files and works on the abstract syntax tree of the target language instead. The tool is based on a product line aware type system which helps to detect typing errors resulting from applying negative variability to the multi-variant model. Since a general type system for arbitrary languages is still subject to research, a general solution is missing. Thus, for each language, a new grammar and a new product-line aware type system must be supplied by the SPL engineer, whereas in FAMILE, corresponding SDIRL rules must be added. Furthermore, detected errors are not repaired automatically, but product derivation is disabled as long as context-sensitive analysis reports errors.

7   Conclusion

In this paper, we have addressed two issues in MDPLE based on *negative variability* that had been considered as major drawbacks when compared to positive variability, namely *limitations in variability* and *unintended information loss*. To address these issues, the following conceptual contributions have been presented in this paper which have been implemented as extensions to the MDPLE tool FAMILE, without destroying the main advantage of negative variability, namely the usage of arbitrary modeling tools.

Alternative Mappings. Since the multi-variant domain model has to be a valid instance of the domain metamodel, several constraints must hold. In particular, single-valued structural features may contain at most one value. Thus, it is not possible to express variability for those features directly. This restriction is mitigated by our concept of *alternative mappings*. These in turn may cause several values competing for a single-valued feature. To resolve this, we have realized the detection of *mutex conflicts* as well as their resolution by means of *selection strategies*.

Surrogates. In case an element is filtered, it cannot occur as the target of another cross-reference. This way, context-sensitive information may get lost. Using the mechanism of *surrogates*, it is possible to replace filtered reference targets by non-filtered elements of the same type. Corresponding replacement rules may be specified declaratively in the OCL-based language SDIRL.

Using a case study, a model-driven product line for a graph library, we have shown both the motivation for as well as the application of our contributions; the final results match the expectations provided at the beginning of this paper. In a literature review, we have shown that alternative mappings and surrogates advance the state of the art in MDPLE based on negative variability.

Future research addresses evolution of software product line artifacts, round-trip between domain and application engineering, and improved support for maintaining the consistency between model and generated source code [8] in both domain and application engineering.

Resources

The tool FAMILE, including the extensions presented in this paper, may be obtained by using the Eclipse update site provided at:[3]
We recommend a clean Eclipse Modeling installation. The package also contains the example presented in this paper. For a deeper insight, you may import the plug-in project de.ubt.ai1.famile.example.graph2 into your Eclipse workspace.
Screencasts demonstrating the usage of the tool can be found here:[4]

Acknowledgments. The authors want to thank Bernhard Westfechtel for his valuable and much appreciated comments on the draft of this paper. Furthermore, we give thanks to the anonymous reviewers and all attendees of ENASE 2016, who gave important feedback that was carefully considered during the revision of this paper.

References

1. Antkiewicz, M., Czarnecki, K.: FeaturePlugin: feature modeling plug-in for eclipse. In: Proceedings of the 2004 OOPSLA Workshop on Eclipse Technology eXchange (eclipse 2004), New York, pp. 67–72 (2004)
2. Apel, S., Kästner, C., Lengauer, C.: FeatureHouse: language-independent, automated software composition. In: Proceedings of the ACM/IEEE International Conference on Software Engineering (ICSE), pp. 221–231. IEEE, May 2009
3. Buchmann, T.: Valkyrie: a UML-based model-driven environment for model-driven software engineering. In: Proceedings of the 7th International Conference on Software Paradigm Trends (ICSOFT 2012), Rome, Italy, pp. 147–157 (2012)
4. Buchmann, T., Dotor, A., Westfechtel, B.: Mod2-scm: a model-driven product line for software configuration management systems. Information and Software Technology (2012). http://dx.doi.org/10.1016/j.infsof.2012.07.010
5. Buchmann, T., Schwägerl, F.: Ensuring well-formedness of configured domain models in model-driven product lines based on negative variability. In: Proceedings of the 4th International Workshop on Feature-Oriented Software Development, FOSD 2012, pp. 37–44. ACM, New York (2012)
6. Buchmann, T., Schwägerl, F.: FAMILE: tool support for evolving model-driven product lines. In: Störrle, H., Botterweck, G., Bourdells, M., Kolovos, D., Paige, R., Roubtsova, E., Rubin, J., Tolvanen, J.P. (eds.) Joint Proceedings of co-located Events at the 8th European Conference on Modelling Foundations and Applications, pp. 59–62. CEUR WS, Technical University of Denmark (DTU), Building 321, DK-2800 Kongens Lyngby, July 2012
7. Buchmann, T., Schwägerl, F.: Developing heterogeneous software product lines with famile – a model-driven approach. Int. J. Adv. Softw. 8(1 & 2), 232–246 (2015)
8. Buchmann, T., Schwägerl, F.: On A-posteriori integration of Ecore Models and Hand-written Java Code. In: Pascal Lorenz, M.V.S., Cardoso, J. (eds.) Proceedings of the 10th International Conference on Software Paradigm Trends, pp. 95–102. SCITEPRESS, July 2015

---

[3] http://btn1x4.inf.uni-bayreuth.de/famile/update/.
[4] http://btn1x4.inf.uni-bayreuth.de/famile/screencasts/.

9. Buchmann, T., Schwägerl, F.: Breaking the boundaries of meta models and preventing information loss in model-driven software product lines. In: Maciaszek, L., Filipe, J. (eds.) Proceedings of the 11th International Conference on the Evaluation of Novel Approaches to Software Engineering (ENASE 2016), pp. 73–83. SCITEPRESS, Rome, Italy, April 2016

10. Buchmann, T., Westfechtel, B.: Mapping feature models onto domain models: ensuring consistency of configured domain models. Softw. Syst. Model. **13**(4), 1495–1527 (2014). http://dx.doi.org/10.1007/s10270-012-0305-5

11. Clements, P., Northrop, L.: Software Product Lines: Practices and Patterns, Boston, MA (2001)

12. Czarnecki, K., Helsen, S., Eisenecker, U.W.: Formalizing cardinality-based feature models and their specialization. Softw. Process Improv. Pract. **10**(1), 7–29 (2005)

13. Frankel, D.S.: Model Driven Architecture: Applying MDA to Enterprise Computing. Wiley Publishing, Indianapolis (2003)

14. Gamma, E., Helm, R., Johnson, R., Vlissides, J.: Design Patterns - Elements of Reusable Object-Oriented Software (1994)

15. Gomaa, H.: Designing Software Product Lines with UML: From Use Cases to Pattern-Based Software Architectures. Addison-Wesley, Boston (2004)

16. Heidenreich, F., Kopcsek, J., Wende, C.: FeatureMapper: mapping features to models. In: Companion Proceedings of the 30th International Conference on Software Engineering (ICSE 2008), Leipzig, Germany, pp. 943–944, May 2008

17. Kang, K.C., Cohen, S.G., Hess, J.A., Novak, W.E., Peterson, A.S.: Feature-oriented domain analysis (FODA) feasibility study. Technical report CMU/SEI-90-TR-21, Carnegie-Mellon University, Software Engineering Institute, November 1990

18. Kang, K.C., Kim, S., Lee, J., Kim, K., Kim, G.J., Shin, E.: Form: a feature-oriented reuse method with domain-specific reference architectures. Ann. Softw. Eng. **5**, 143–168 (1998)

19. Kästner, C., Apel, S., Trujillo, S., Kuhlemann, M., Batory, D.: Guaranteeing syntactic correctness for all product line variants: a language-independent approach. In: Oriol, M., Meyer, B. (eds.) TOOLS EUROPE 2009. LNBIP, vol. 33, pp. 175–194. Springer, Heidelberg (2009). doi:10.1007/978-3-642-02571-6_11

20. Lopez-Herrejon, R.E., Batory, D.: A standard problem for evaluating product-line methodologies. In: Bosch, J. (ed.) GCSE 2001. LNCS, vol. 2186, pp. 10–24. Springer, Heidelberg (2001). doi:10.1007/3-540-44800-4_2

21. OMG: Object Constraint Language, Version 2.2. OMG, Needham, MA, formal/2010-02-02 edn., February 2010

22. OMG: Meta Object Facility (MOF) Core. Object Management Group, Needham, MA, formal/2011-08-07 edn., August 2011

23. OMG: Concrete Syntax For A UML Action Language: Action Language For Foundational UML (ALF). Object Management Group, Needham, MA, formal/2013-09-01 edn., October 2013

24. OMG: Unified Modeling Language (UML). Object Management Group, Needham, MA, formal/15-03-01 edn., March 2015

25. Pohl, K., Böckle, G., van der Linden, F.: Software Product Line Engineering: Foundations, Principles and Techniques. Springer, Heidelberg (2005)

26. Schwägerl, F., Buchmann, T., Westfechtel, B.: SuperMod - a model-driven tool that combines version control and software product line engineering. In: ICSOFT-PT 2015 - Proceedings of the 10th International Conference on Software Paradigm Trends, pp. 5–18. SCITEPRESS, Colmar (2015)

27. Steinberg, D., Budinsky, F., Paternostro, M., Merks, E.: EMF Eclipse Modeling Framework. The Eclipse Series, 2nd edn. Addison-Wesley, Boston (2009)

28. Taentzer, G.: AGG: a graph transformation environment for modeling and validation of software. In: Pfaltz, J.L., Nagl, M., Böhlen, B. (eds.) AGTIVE 2003. LNCS, vol. 3062, pp. 446–453. Springer, Heidelberg (2004). doi:10.1007/978-3-540-25959-6_35

29. Völter, M., Stahl, T., Bettin, J., Haase, A., Helsen, S.: Model-Driven Software Development: Technology, Engineering, Management. Wiley, Chichester (2006)

30. Weiss, D.M., Lai, C.T.R.: Software Product Line Engineering: A Family-Based Software Development Process, Boston, MA (1999)

31. Whittle, J., Jayaraman, P., Elkhodary, A., Moreira, A., Araújo, J.: MATA: a unified approach for composing UML aspect models based on graph transformation. In: Katz, S., Ossher, H., France, R., Jézéquel, J.-M. (eds.) Transactions on Aspect-Oriented Software Development VI. LNCS, vol. 5560, pp. 191–237. Springer, Heidelberg (2009). doi:10.1007/978-3-642-03764-1_6

32. Ziadi, T., Jézéquel, J.M.: Software product line engineering with the UML: deriving products. In: Käköla, T., Duenas, J.C. (eds.) Software Product Lines, pp. 557–588. Springer, Heidelberg (2006)

33. Zschaler, S., Sánchez, P., Santos, J., Alférez, M., Rashid, A., Fuentes, L., Moreira, A., Araújo, J., Kulesza, U.: VML* – a family of languages for variability management in software product lines. In: Brand, M., Gašević, D., Gray, J. (eds.) SLE 2009. LNCS, vol. 5969, pp. 82–102. Springer, Heidelberg (2010). doi:10.1007/978-3-642-12107-4_7

A New MARTE Extension to Address Adaptation Mechanisms in Scheduling View

Mohamed Naija$^{(\boxtimes)}$ and Samir Ben Ahmed$^{(\boxtimes)}$

Laboratory of Computer for Industrial Systems, INSAT, Tunis, Tunisia
naija.mohamed@gmail.com, samir.benahmed@fst.rnu.tn

Abstract. The modeling of Real-Time Embedded Systems (RTES) is one of the biggest challenges facing designers of such systems. These systems are considered high-assurance since errors during execution could result in injury, loss of life, environmental impact, and financial loss. The addition of adaptability to RTES further hardens and delays their modeling and validating especially with the current lack of design models and tools for adaptive RTES. The profile for Modeling and Analysis of Real-Time and Embedded systems (MARTE) defines a framework for annotating non-functional properties of embedded systems. In particular, the SAM (Schedulability Analysis Model) sub-profile offers stereotypes for annotating UML models with the needed information which will be extracted to fulfil a scheduling phase. However, SAM does not allow designers to specify data to be used in the context of adaptive systems development. It is in this context that we propose an extension for the MARTE profile, and especially the sub-profile Schedulability Analysis Modeling, to include adaptation mechanisms in scheduling view.

Keywords: Adaptability · Real-Time & Embedded Systems · MDE · MARTE · Scheduling analysis

1 Introduction

The modeling of Real-time & Embedded Systems (RTES) may be stated as a crucial problem in the software engineering domain. RTES are subject to a multitude of constraints (e.g., battery, temperature …) and real-time requirements. Thus, designers are encountering the challenge of resource limitations, time, highly variable environment, etc. The addition of adaptivity to such systems further hardens and delays their modelling and scheduling analysis especially with the current lack of design models and tools for adaptive RTES. Lightening the task of adaptive systems designers and reducing the development cost and time to market represent a major challenge in the field [1], which requires the use of high-level approaches such as MDE and MARTE [2].

MDE is a way to beat the growing complexity of real time systems and verifying their correctness. In particular, Unified Modeling Language (UML) profiles promote an adequate solution to support the whole lifecycle co-design of complex systems. In RTES domain, its adoption is seen promising for several purposes: requirements specification, behavioral and architectural modeling with their real time constraints and performance

© Springer International Publishing AG 2016
L.A. Maciaszek and J. Filipe (Eds.): ENASE 2016, CCIS 703, pp. 27–43, 2016.
DOI: 10.1007/978-3-319-56390-9_2

issues. In this context, the profile for Modeling and Analysis of Real-Time and Embedded systems (MARTE) fosters the building of models that support the specification of scheduling analysis problem. This profile has the capacity to model tasks, dependencies between them and events under shape a Workload Behavior of system. Subsequently, it promotes the validation of the system temporal accuracy. Unfortunately, MARTE does not define a clear semantics for modeling and analysis of the adaptation in RTES.

Thus, we propose in this paper the main changes to be made on MARTE profile for supporting adaptation mechanisms. These amendments affect mainly the stereotypes of MARTE/SAM (Scheduling Analysis Modeling) since it is the sub-profile intended to model the schedulability analysis.

Our contribution is to improve the meta-models of the existing annotations. We try to modify in the structure of existing annotations, by referring to their cardinality and by adding a new concept. This work is the result of previous investigations and published work. Starting from [3] a MARTE-based approach was proposed to concurrency model construction at early design stages. Moreover, we identify using Petri Nets formalism a new threading strategy in complex RTES. Particularly, we identified that operation (*saStep*) can be mapped in multiple Schedulable Resources. In [4], we have presented three technical reconfigurations of RTES to meet performance constraints. These software and hardware solutions are able to reduce the utilization factor of the processor by changing periods and deadlines of tasks, adjustment the frequency of the processors and software/hardware migration tasks. Notably, we perceive a MARTE semantics limitation in modeling level. Accordingly, we have identified the needed of the new version of the MARTE profile supporting adaptation mechanisms. In [1], we have proposed a new extension of MARTE to address adaptation in the scheduling view.

This work is to be integrated in a model-based approach to guide RTES designers for building and analysing adaptive RTES models. It facilitates complex systems modeling, reduces the development time and cost and improves software process quality. The above benefits have been illustrated through the application of our extensions to different examples of adaptive RTES [1].

The present paper is organized as follows. Section 2, introduces the concept of the adaptation. Section 3 surveys relevant related works in the adaptive RTES field. While a brief definition of the MDE paradigm, its MARTE profile and the SAM sub-profile is described in Sects. 4 and 5 present our research scope. Section 6 specifies our proposal. To better explain our contribution which is highlighted in Sect. 7, we rely on a case study. Finally, Sect. 8 concludes the paper and sketches some future work.

2   The Adaptability Concept

2.1   Definition

There are several definitions of adaptation in the literature. In [5], a software adaptation is defined as any software modification that changes the reliability or timeliness of the software without affecting other aspects of its functionality. Software adaptation encompasses many common software-tuning techniques. These include:

- resource reallocation, such as moving a software component from one processor to another,
- adjustments to processor schedules,
- modification of replication factors for N-modular-redundant software components,
- modification of retry limits or time-out periods for delivery of a service by a software component.

In [6, 7] adaptation means change in the system to accommodate change in its environment. More specifically, the adaptation of a software system (S) is caused by a change (Che) from an old environment (E) to a new environment (E'), and results in a new system (S') that ideally meets the needs of its new environment (E'). Formally, adaptation can be viewed as a function:

Adaptation: $E \times E' \times S \rightarrow S'$, where meet $(S', \text{need } (E'))$.

In [8] adaptive system is defined as a system that is able to change its structure or behavior at run-time in response to the execution context variations and according to adaptation engine decisions.

In our previous work [9], we define adaptation as any modification in the structure, behavior or architecture of the system to accommodate external or internal change of their operating environment or context and according to predefined adaptation plan and rules.

2.2 Axes of Adaptation

Several adaptation techniques are defined to manage reconfiguration in the software development lifecycle. In model-based approaches for RTES, these adaptation techniques can affect [9]: (i) the functional model in the case of a change in the behavior of the system, (ii) the platform model if there is an adjustment in performance of material resources or unavailability of a resource for a certain period at run-time, and (iii) the implementation model when a task migration between resources is required.

Possible changes in the system can be caused by external variation, such as change in the operational environment (e.g., airplane mode in smart phone) or internal variation (e.g., new requirement) [9]. The adaptation can be either static or dynamic. Since static adaptation requires stopping the system and restarting it with a new configuration. The dynamic adaptation is based on a set of predefined adaptation behavior, statically designed and verified at design time. At runtime, the system can select an alternative from the available ones in accordance with adaptation rules and context. The change undergone by the system can be qualified as partial or full adaptation. Full adaptation completely changes the initial configuration of the system, while partial adaptation concerns only one level of the system configuration while the remaining portions continue their normal execution.

Thus any software system could be reconfigurable in one or more axes of adaptation [9].

3 Related Work

The design of adaptive RTES presents many challenges due to the complexity of the problem it handles [10]. In the present paper, we limit our study to research works particularly tackling adaptive RTES using the MARTE profile.

Many researchers have benefited from the MARTE profile for the design and verification of adaptive RTES from high-level models. In [11] authors have benefited from MARTE to model reconfigurable architectures such as FPGAs based Systems-on-Chip (SOC). They extended the MARTE profile with some semantics and Xilinx specific concepts, which limits their applicability for diverse systems, to support Dynamic and Partial Reconfiguration (DPR) of FPGA. Unlike this contribution, we aim to propose a new extension to support adaptation which is independent from any specific platform.

In [12] the authors give a classification of 13 publications that have dealt with the subject of adaptation in the design approach. Following this classification, the authors illustrate using an avionic example the need for the validation of adaptation rules at design-time according to the real-time features of the system. In this context of verification approaches, they have proposed in [13] an MDE approach for modeling and offline validation of application timing constraints. In fact, this article uses state machine to represent the application configurations and transitions between them to represent adaptation rules. This work is based on the generation of all possible configurations of a system before running, in order to validate timing constraints. The number of configurations varies from one system to another and it can be very large, this combinatorial explosion makes the timing analysis inapplicable. Furthermore the proposed approach considers only periodic tasks and cannot be applicable to aperiodic and sporadic tasks.

Two major scheduling approaches are available in the literature: the partitioned and the global approaches. Originally, MARTE supports only the modeling of the systems to be scheduled according to the partitioned approach. In [14] the authors have proposed various updates for MARTE meta-models of specialization and generalization stereotype in order to support global scheduling approaches, allowing task migrations. Those changes allow a schedulable resource to be executed on different computing resources in the same period [15]. Unfortunately, extensions proposed in MARTE profile do not allow assessing the gain in time of an adaptation operation (task migration in this case).

In [10], five patterns have been proposed to model and evaluate adaptation. These design patterns are presented in a static form through class diagrams and stereotyped MARTE profile. In this work, adaptation is considered as a dynamic and partial change of the operating mode, without taking into account the platform adaptation which is essential in the verification of time constraints.

All the previously mentioned works are beneficial since they facilitate the design of adaptive real-time systems. However, they present some weaknesses. These research studies [10] are not sufficiently generic since they tackle a specific adaptation problem, which consequently compromises their reusability as well as their ability to adapt to new system requirements and constraints. Additionally, most of them only focus on the software side adaptation while ignoring the hardware and implementation adaptation which are essential in the design and analysis of complex systems.

Table 1 presents a classification of works around modeling and verification of adaptive real-time systems according to the level of adaptability considered and timing verification supported. As we can see in this classification, to the best of our knowledge, there is no work that deals with all axes of adaptability.

Table 1. State of the art classification.

Criteria	Related Work			
	[10]	[12]	[14]	[9]
MDE approach	+	+	+	+
Modeling software adaptability	–	+	–	+
Modeling hardware adaptability	+	–	–	–
Modeling implementation adaptability	–	–	+	–
Scheduling Analysis supported	–	+	–	–
Adaptation Type	Internal	Internal	Internal	External
	Dynamic	Static	Static	Dynamic
	Partial	Partial	Full	Full

4 MDE and RTES Development

The Model Driven Engineering (MDE) is a software development methodology aiming to increase the level of development and overcome the growing complexity challenge. It covers the entire systems lifecycle, simplifies the design process by using the concept of models and offers independency between different steps of development flow.

In the context of the schedulability analysis, MDE is mainly used in the modeling step and the transformation of scheduling analysis models to the models of the chosen scheduling analysis tool [15]. MDE uses the UML profile and especially MARTE.

4.1 MARTE Capabilities for RTES Modeling

MARTE is an extension of UML profile providing support for specification, modeling and verification step of real time and embedded systems. MARTE supports the modeling of software and hardware features at a high-level of abstraction. In addition, it offers a rich set of annotations for modeling schedulability analysis. This profile encompasses a lot of sub-profiles such as: SRM (Software Resource Modeling), HRM (Hardware Re-source Modeling), GQAM (Generic Quantitative Analysis Modeling), SAM (Schedulability

Analysis Modeling), PAM (Performance analysis Modeling), etc. In this paper, we will focus especially on the SAM sub-profile since it is the package affected by our proposal.

4.2 SAM

In order to establish an early validation of the system's temporal behavior a well-formed analyzable model, called SAM, is defined. It offers a variety of annotations related to temporal features. Thus this profile has the capacity to model tasks, dependencies between them and events. It has the capacity to predict if all tasks meet their time constraints by defining the workload behavior. This is a chain of operation activations representing executions scenarios for the application.

5 Scope of the Work in Relation to MARTE

Our research scope concerns mainly the usability of the UML/MARTE profile for modeling adaptive systems. In this section, we will discuss the need of a new version of MARTE on the three levels of modeling identified in Sect. 2.2: functional model, platform model and implementation model.

5.1 Adaptability in the Functional Model

To model the functional model of static systems, we use MARTE/SAM (Schedulability Analysis Model) capabilities which offer a variety of stereotypes for annotating models with real-time features. This profile has the capacity to model tasks, dependencies between them and events under shape a Workload Behavior of system. Subsequently, it promotes the validation of the system temporal accuracy by the construction of the end-to-end computation. The end-to-end computation represents the processing load of the system. It represents the different steps executed in the system and triggered by one or more external stimulus. *«saStep»* is a stereotype annotating an action/operation. A set of steps specify the so-called Schedulable Resources. This concurrency model is independent from any particular Real-Time Operating System (RTOS) in order to fulfill the MDA principals.

In adaptive system, additional information has to be modelled such as adaptation rules, transitional modes and conditions. Thus, we need to model all alternatives and possible variations of the system elements in order to validate the non-functional properties. Unfortunately, the designer is not able to specify all these properties with the actual version of MARTE.

5.2 Adaptability in the Platform Model

SAM platform is a package providing sufficient concepts to model a general platform, at a high-level of abstraction, for executing the functional model. It is a specialization of the sub-profile Generic Resource Modeling (GRM), which provides mechanisms to manage access to different execution resource. Originally it does not support modeling of unavailability of resource for a certain period at run-time. This uncertainty is a main factor that can influence the effectiveness of the configuration and affecting its performance considerably [9].

Moreover in literature a popular alternative to static power management in RTES is to allow the speed factor to adjust dynamically to the number of requests in the system. Using the MARTE/SAM, the designer is able to specify these properties. But, for each adjustment, he must repeat the modeling of the same resource to specify the new features this is due to the multiplicity of the concerned attributes [9].

5.3   Adaptability in the Implementation Model

To this end, at this level, functional model (event, end-to-end flow, shared resources) and platform model (execution resources) are specified. To be executed, a software resource must obviously be allocated on processors or busses. This allocation model, called implementation model, is needed to have an estimation of execution time for tasks. Consequently, a schedulability analysis test can be carried out on this model. The task migration is considered as an adaptive technique that allows improving application performance and achieves optimality. Currently, MARTE do not support this dynamic allocation technique. Thus, task that can be across multiple processors for different periods of time is not permitted in MARTE.

5.4   Example

In this section we illustrate the kind of problem we want to solve. The following Fig. 1 shows a description of a basic execution scenario. This is an example of adaptation mechanism that cannot be modeled using the actual version of the MARTE profile.

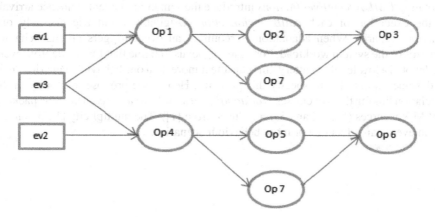

Fig. 1. Example of adaptation scenario.

The Workload Behavior of the system is activated by the both external events e1 and e2, initially. The event e1 (e.g., timers, internal event and external occurrences) triggers the first behavior scenario of a system and precedes all the operations (Op1, Op2 and Op3). The event e2 triggers the second behavior scenario of the system composed of the related operations (Op4, Op5 and Op6). Afterwards, the adaptive event e3 (e.g., new requirement) triggers the both execution scenarios of the system, which is impossible to modeled with MARTE. Additional, the operation Op7 appears in response to the need of an adaptation. When occurs, Op7 affects the both execution scenarios, this is also not possible to do with originally version of MARTE.

6   Our Proposal: Sam Extension

The scheduling analysis modeling is performed through the MARTE/SAM profile.

The idea of performing scheduling analysis based on MARTE models assumes that all the information that is needed for the analysis is already part of the MARTE model [3]. In fact, SAM meta-model supports the modeling of different systems as it models all the temporal features needed in the scheduling step except those used to model adaptation constraints. Consequently, we seek to improve SAM meta-model in order to support modeling and early analysis of adaptation process. The amendments to be done on the SAM sub-profile affects also the GQAM sub-profile since some classes of the sub-profile SAM inherit from GQAM sub-profile.

6.1   Amendments in the Functional Model

In this level, we propose to modify in the classes Event, Step and EndToEndFlow.

Changes to be Done for the Workload Event. The workload behavior of the system [2] is characterized by their workload events and behavior scenarios. Workload events annotating *UML AcceptEventActions* introduce the semantic of event sequence arrivals for the execution of each *callBehaviorAction*. Originally event triggers only one behavior scenario. When adaptation is required, an event triggers all the behavior scenarios of the system workload. For example, let us imagine that for an adaptive event that denoted a low level of battery, this can affect more than one behavior scenario. Thus, the designer is not able to specify this property. Hence, we propose to modify in the association linking the two classes *WorkloadEvent* and *BehaviorScenario* of the package GQAM Resources (Figs. 2 and 3, reproduced from [1]). The multiplicity [1..*] denotes that an event can affect one or more behaviour scenarios.

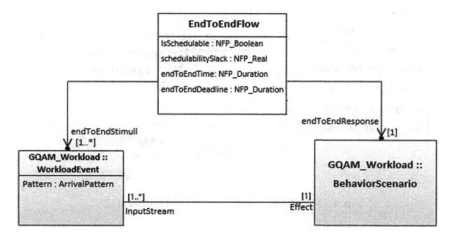

Fig. 2. The old meta-model of the GQAM package [1].

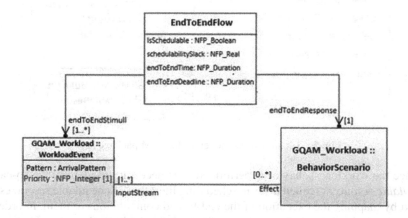

Fig. 3. The new meta-model of the GQAM package [1].

At run time, multiple events can occur simultaneously and must to be managed. Consequently, we propose to add the attribute «priority», which indicates the priority of the event. This additional real-time features, allows concurrency management. Indeed, GQAM is a generalization of the package SAM. So, this change will be inherited by SAM.

Changes to be Done for the Step. The class *Step* may represent a small segment of code execution [2]. It contains a lot of attributes specifying the temporal features of software resources. In UML MARTE model step can be part of only one behavior. Otherwise, in the case of adaptation process a new *Step* can appear in multiple behavior scenarios to manage adaptation. Thus, MARTE/SAM doesn't allow this specification. Thereby, we propose to change in the association linking the two classes *BehaviorScenario* and *Step* (Fig. 5).

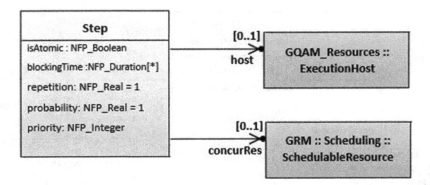

Fig. 4. The old meta-model of the SAM package [1].

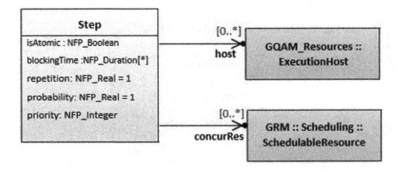

Fig. 5. The new meta-model of the SAM package [1].

Once the workload behavior is performed, it is necessary to identify the so-called *schedulable resources* (called tasks in scheduling literature). Schedulable resources are defined by mapping the execution of the end-to-end computations to them, in order to generate the task model. Different types of mapping exist in the literature [3, 16, 17]. As explained previously, a software resource can be mapped into more than one thread. Accordingly, the cardinality of the association between *Step* and *SchedulableResource* must be [0..*] (Fig. 4 reproduced from [1]).

Changes to be Done for the End-To-EndFlow. In adaptive systems, we model all alternatives and possible variations of the system elements. Moreover, the modeling step is based on the concept of mode (end-to-end Flow) which is a subset of system features: when the system is in a given mode, it provides this subset of features. We need to build a model for the source mode and a model for the target mode. The source and target models should not include information about each other, or about the adaptation. In addition, event signals are used between models of source and target to define transitional modes (Fig. 6).

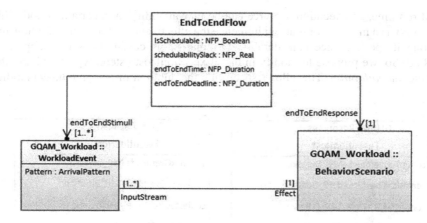

Fig. 6. The old meta-model of the GQAM package.

After identifying modes, it is necessary to specify adaptation rules. These are conditions that should be respected during and after adaptation step. In this context, we propose to extend the meta-model of SAM by the class *Rules*. This extension allows the modeling of the conditions that trigger modes and limit changes (Fig. 6).

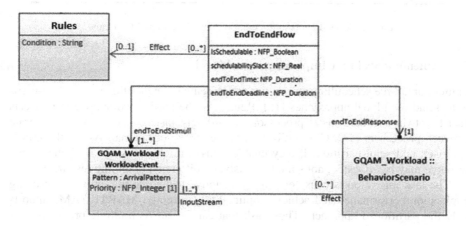

Fig. 7. The new meta-model of the GQAM package.

6.2   Amendments in the Platform Model

To this end an abstracted view of the execution platform resources is assumed to have execution time estimation for steps. Thus, the processor resources are represented as components with the «ExecutionHost» stereotype. To be executed, a software resource must obviously be mapped on processors or busses. Involved shared resources should also be described.

At run time, an execution resource can be unavailability for a certain period. This uncertainty is a main factor that can influence the effectiveness of the configuration and affecting its performance considerably. Originally this constraint is not support in MARTE. So, we propose to modify in the «ExecutionHost» stereotype by adding the attribute *unavailability*. This allows specifying the duration of resource unavailability (Fig. 8).

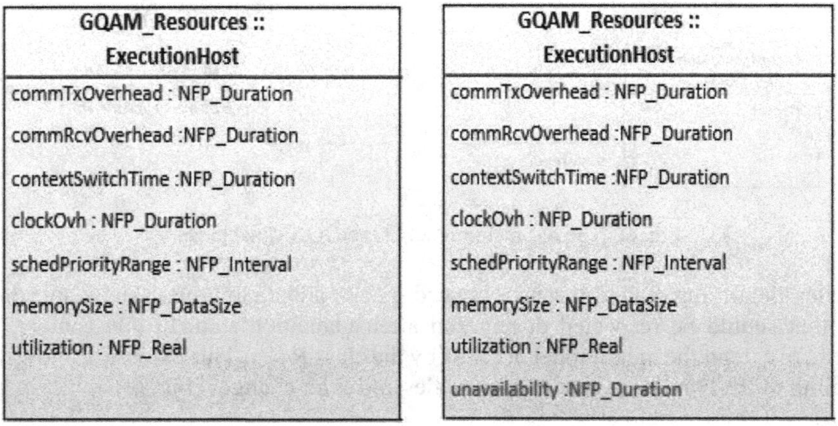

GQAM_Resources :: ExecutionHost
commTxOverhead : NFP_Duration
commRcvOverhead :NFP_Duration
contextSwitchTime :NFP_Duration
clockOvh : NFP_Duration
schedPriorityRange : NFP_Interval
memorySize : NFP_DataSize
utilization : NFP_Real

GQAM_Resources :: ExecutionHost
commTxOverhead : NFP_Duration
commRcvOverhead :NFP_Duration
contextSwitchTime :NFP_Duration
clockOvh : NFP_Duration
schedPriorityRange : NFP_Interval
memorySize : NFP_DataSize
utilization : NFP_Real
unavailability :NFP_Duration

Fig. 8. Amendments in the meta-model of the GQAM package.

6.3   Amendments in the Implementation Model

In literature, three scheduling approaches are presented: the partitioned, the semi-partitioned and the global approaches [18]. Regarding the partitioned approach, it affects each task to be executed on one processor. Accordingly, tasks are not allowed to migrate between processors [14]. CPU utilization is therefore not optimal. As for the global approach and semi-partitioned, they enable a tasks migration such that schedulable resource may be allocated, not simultaneously, on different computing resources.

The task migration is considered as an adaptive technique that allows improving application performance and achieves optimality. Currently, MARTE/SAM supports only the partitioned approach. Thus, task that can be across multiple processors for different periods of time is not permitted in SAM. Subsequently, the multiplicity of the attribute corresponding to the execution resource (ExecutionHost) on which a task (schedulableResource) is allocated must be [0..*] instead of [0..1] (Figs. 9 and 10). This extension is adopted from the research work [19].

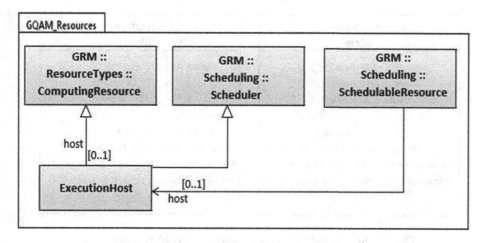

Fig. 9. Meta-model of the GQAM package [1].

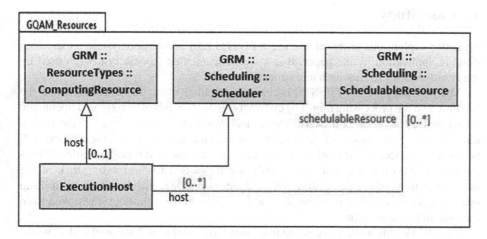

Fig. 10. Meta-model of the GQAM package with amendments [1].

While migrating from one processor to another, the execution time of a task is not the same, then the attribute «deadline» of the stereotype *SaStep* should have a multiplicity of [0..*]. In the same vein, a task can be interrupted several times during one period. Consequently the attribute «preemptT», which refers to the length of time that the step is preempted, must have a multiplicity [0..*] instead of [0..1]. Similarly for the attribute «readyT» which indicate length of time since the beginning of a period. Hence, this attribute must have a multiplicity of [0..*]. The set of values for the attributes «deadline», «preemptT» and «readyT» must be ordered (Fig. 11). This extension is adopted from the research work [15].

«Stereotype» SaStep
Deadline : NFP_Duration[0..1]
spareCap :NFP_Duration[0..1]
schSlack : NFP_Real[0..1]
preemptT :NFP_Duration[0..1]
readyT : NFP_Duration[0..1]
nonpreemptionBlocking : NFP_Duration[0..1]
selfSuspensionBlocking : NFP_Duration[0..1]
numberSelfSuspension : NFP_Duration[0..1]

«Stereotype» SaStep
Deadline : NFP_Duration [0..*]{ordered}
spareCap :NFP_Duration[0..1]
schSlack : NFP_Real[0..1]
preemptT :NFP_Duration[0..*]{ordered}
readyT : NFP_Duration[0..*]{ordered}
nonpreemptionBlocking : NFP_Duration[0..1]
selfSuspensionBlocking : NFP_Duration[0..1]
numberSelfSuspension : NFP_Duration[0..1]

Fig. 11. Amendments in the meta-model of the GQAM package [1].

7   Case Study

To better explain our proposal, we use a FESTO [20] production system as an intact running application in this paper. It is a well-documented laboratory system used by many universities for research and education purposes.

The working process of FESTO is composed of three units: the distribution unit, the test unit, and the processing unit. The distribution unit consists of two steps: a pneumatic feeder and a converter. It forwards cylindrical workpieces from a stack to the testing unit. The test unit consists of three steps: the detector, the tester, and the evacuator. It performs the checking of workpieces for their height, material type, and color. Workpieces that pass the test unit successfully are forwarded to the rotating disk of the processing unit, where the drilling of workpieces is done. The result of the drilling operation is next checked by a checker and finally the finished product is removed from the system by an evacuator.

Note that in this work two drilling machines Drill1 and Drill2 are used to drill workpieces. Drill1 is used in case of medium production. When high production is required, Drill2 is recommended. According to user requirements, the system FESTO is able to reconfigure automatically at run-time in response to any changed working environment caused by errors or new requirements to improve system performance without a halt. The workload behavior in Fig. 9, reproduced from [1], represents the processing load of the system, founded on our proposal.

After identifying the behavior model of the system, it is necessary to specify the so-called *schedulable Resources*. For sake of simplicity, we use in this paper the scenario-based mapping [16] which is also one of the most used. The idea is to regroup all the operations executed at the same rate and belonging to the same linear end-to-end computation to the same task. In our FESTO system, we obtain three different threads namely task1 (*pieceEjection*, *Convert*, *Test* and *Evacuate*), task2 (*pieceEjection*,

Convert, Test, Elevate, Rotate, Drill1, Checker and *Evacuate*) and task3 (*pieceEjection, Convert, Test, Elevate, Rotate, Drill2, Checker* and *Evacuate*) (Fig. 12).

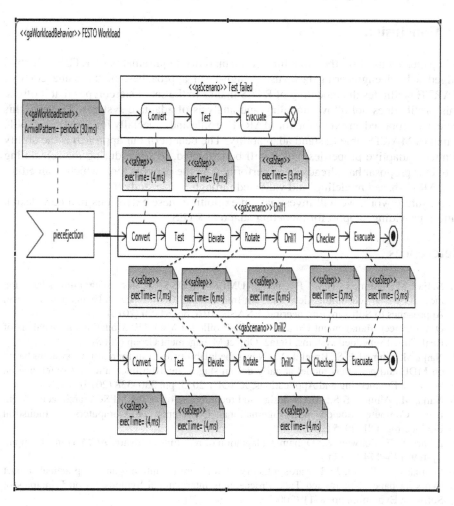

Fig. 12. The workload behavior of FESTO system.

Following this case study, founded on our proposal. We illustrate that an event (e.g., *epieceEjection*) triggers all tasks. The steps *Convert* and *Test* are part of three tasks. Similar for steps *Elevate, Rotate, Checker* and *Evacuate*, those participate for the execution of both schedulable resources Task2 and Task3. Compared to original version of MARTE, specifying these properties is not permitted. Note that, tasks can have dynamic properties (*readyT, preemptT* and *deadlines*) due to the concept of task migration, but we use the same corresponding values to facilitate our example. Anyway, we can add the different values and they will be ordered to perform scheduling analysis. After scheduling all tasks, we can specify in our SAM view the used allocations through the attributes *Host: GaExecHost* and the corresponding attribute *ExecT: NFP_Duration.*

8 Conclusion

This paper focused on the modeling of adaptability requirements of RTES, which is judged a hard engineering task, using high-level approaches. In the same context, MARTE facilitates the modeling of RTES thanks to the set of stereotypes that it offers. This profile does not allow modeling and analysis of adaptive systems. To solve this issue, we proposed an extension for MARTE profile and especially for SAM sub-profile to makes MARTE able to stand adaptability. The benefit of our approach is the ability to model adaptive properties which will be extracted, to serve during the scheduling step. Our proposal has already been performed on the papyrus tool, which is an editor of MARTE-based modeling, and validated through a case study.

As future work, we will investigate in exploiting these extensions in a new design pattern providing support for modeling adaptive RTES.

References

1. Naija, M., Ahmed, B.S.: Extending UML/MARTE-SAM for integrating adaptation mechanisms in scheduling view. In: 11th International Conference on Evaluation of Novel Approaches to Software Engineering, ENASE 2016, pp. 84–90 (2016)
2. OMG Object Management Group: A UML Profile for MARTE: Modeling and Anal sis of Real-Time Embedded systems, Beta2, Object Management Group (2008)
3. Naija, M., Ahmed, B.S., Bruel, J.-M.: New schedulability analysis for real-time systems based on MDE and petri nets model at early design stages. In: 10th International Conference on Software Engineering and Applications, ICSOFT 2015, pp. 330–338 (2015)
4. Naija, M., Ahmed, B.S.: Aid to design and reconfiguration of the MPSOC architectures. In: IEEE Computer Society 45th International Conference on Computers & Industrial Engineering, CIE 2015 (2015)
5. Bihari, T.-E., Schwan, K.: Dynamic adaptation of real-time software. ACM Trans. Comput. Syst. **9**, 143–174 (1991)
6. Lehman, M., Ramil, J.: Towards a theory of software evolution – and its practical impact (working paper). In: Invited Talk, Proceedings International Symposium on Principles of Software Evolution, pp. 2–11 (2000)
7. Subramanian, N., Chung, L.: Architecture – driven embedded systems adaptation for supporting vocabulary evolution. In: Proceedings of International Symposium Principles of Software Evolution International (2000)
8. Oreizy, P., Gorlick, M.M., Taylor, R.N., et al.: An architecture based approach to self-adaptive software. IEEE Intell. Syst. Appl. **14**(3), 54–62 (1999)
9. Naija, M., Bruel, J.-M., Ahmed, B.S.: Towards a MARTE extension to address adaptation mechanisms. In: 17th IEEE International Symposium on High Assurance Systems Engineering, HASE 2016, pp. 240–243 (2016)
10. Said, M., Kacem, Y.M., Kerboeuf, M., Amor, N.B., Abid, M.: Design patterns for self-adaptive RTE systems specification. Int. J. Reconfigurable Comput. **8** (2014)

11. Cherif, S., Quadri, I.R., Meftali, S., Dekeyser, J.-L.: Modeling reconfigurable Sytems-on-Chips with UML MARTE profile: an exploratory analysis. In: Proceedings of the 13th Euromicro Conference on Digital System Design, pp. 706–713 (2010)
12. Boukhanoufa, M.-L., Radermacher, A., Terrier, F.: Towards a model-driven engineering approach for developing adaptive real-time embedded systems. In: New Technologies of Distributed Systems, pp. 261–266 (2010)
13. Boukhanoufa, M.-L., Radermacher, A., Terrier, F.: Offline validation of real-time application constraints considering adaptation rules. In: International Conference on Trust, Security and Privacy in Computing and Communications, pp. 974–980 (2011)
14. Magdich, A., Kacem, Y.H., Kerboeuf, M.: A UML/MARTE-based design pattern for semi-partitioned scheduling analysis. In: International Workshops on Enabling Technologies: Infrastructures for Collaborative Enterprises, pp. 300–305 (2014)
15. Magdich, A., Kacem, Y.H., Mahfoudhi, A., Abid, M.: A MARTE extension for global scheduling analysis of multiprocessor systems. In: International Symposium on Software Reliability Engineering, pp. 371–379 (2012)
16. Masse, J., Kim, S., Hong, S.: Tool set implementation for scenario-based multithreading of UML-RT models and experimental validation. In: Proceedings of the 9th IEEE Real-Time and Embedded Technology and Applications Symposium, RTAS 2003. IEEE Computer Society (2003)
17. Mraidha, C., Tucci-Piergiovanni, S., Gerard, S.: Optimum: a marte-based methodology for schedulability analysis at early design stages. ACM SIGSOFT Softw. Eng. Notes 36(1), 1–8 (2011)
18. Muhammad, K.B., Cécile, B., Michel, A.: Two level hierarchical scheduling algorithm for real-time multiprocessor systems. J. Softw. 6(11), 2308–2320 (2011)
19. Magdich, A., Kacem, Y.H., Mahfoudhi, A.: Extending UML/MARTE-GRM for integrating tasks migrations in class diagrams. In: International Conference on Software Engineering Research, Management and Applications, pp. 73–84 (2013)
20. Khalgui, M., Hanisch, H.M.: Automatic NCES-based specification and SESA-based verification of feasible control components in benchmark production systems. Int. J. Model. Ident. Control 12(3), 223–243 (2011)

Model-Based Engineering and Spatiotemporal Analysis of Transport Systems

Simon Hordvik[1], Kristoffer Øseth[1], Henrik Heggelund Svendsen[1],
Jan Olaf Blech[2], and Peter Herrmann[1(✉)]

[1] NTNU, Trondheim, Norway
simon.hordvik@gmail.com, kristoffer.oseth@gmail.com, hsvendsen@gmail.com,
herrmann@item.ntnu.no
[2] RMIT University, Melbourne, Australia
janolaf.blech@rmit.edu.au

Abstract. To guarantee that modern transport systems carry their passengers in a safe and reliable way, their control software has to fulfill extreme safety and robustness demands. To achieve that, we propose the model-based engineering of the controllers using the tool-set Reactive Blocks. This leads to models in a precise formal semantics that can be formally analyzed. Thus, we can verify that a transport system prevents collisions and fulfills other spatiotemporal properties. In particular, we combine test runs of already existing devices to find out their physical constraints with the analysis of simulation runs using the verification tool BeSpaceD. So, we can discover potential safety hazards already during the development of the control software. A centerpiece of our work is a methodology for the engineering and safety analysis of transportation systems. We elaborate its practical usability by means of two control systems for a demonstrator based on Lego Mindstorms. This paper is an extension of [20].

Keywords: Software engineering · Spatial modeling · Cyber-physical systems

1 Introduction

In the development of control software for transport and other cyber-physical systems, safety is a major challenge to achieve [25]. Particularly, one has to analyze the software for compliance with spatiotemporal properties like guaranteeing a sufficient safety distance between devices at all times. This is mostly achieved by intensive and costly testing of the software for functional and quality of service attributes. To ease the analysis effort, we supplement traditional test-based development by applying a model-based software engineering technique. Its formal semantics facilitates the use of automatic model-checking and provers that can detect flaws in the control software. Since we perform the checks on the models and not on the later code, these flaws, which might be sources for

© Springer International Publishing AG 2016
L.A. Maciaszek and J. Filipe (Eds.): ENASE 2016, CCIS 703, pp. 44–65, 2016.
DOI: 10.1007/978-3-319-56390-9_3

violations of spatiotemporal properties, are discovered early making the overall development process more cost effective than plain system testing.

As a model-driven development tool, we chose Reactive Blocks [24]. It provides the ability to reuse and share building blocks. Further, Reactive Blocks enables us to simulate data and control flows, to model check the building blocks for functional correctness, and to create executable code automatically. Moreover, we use BeSpaceD [4], which enables the verification of spatiotemporal properties in safety-critical systems. It has been deployed in several applications implemented with Reactive Blocks and simulated in the Java software environment, e.g., [14,17].

A contribution of this paper is a methodology that defines the various engineering and analysis steps of the control software development process. It allows us to combine the analysis of kinematic behavior and other data obtained by gauging existing devices with the simulation and formal verification of the control software in order to guarantee that a device fulfills certain spatiotemporal properties. An example for measured data is the worst-case braking distance of a train that is observed by testing an actual unit. It is directly considered in a BeSpaced verification proving that the control software causes the train to brake sufficiently early such that collisions with other trains are prevented.

We apply the methodology by developing two different versions of the control software for a demonstrator which is built with Lego Mindstorms together with additional sensors and servers. Lego Mindstorms offers the necessary hardware components needed to build a physical autonomous rail-based system. It is an affordable way to create demonstrators such as robots, that can be used in hobby settings as well as research. Event-driven software can be run on the Lego Mindstorms components enabling the control entities to execute actions based on input received from the different types of sensors. In the original paper [20], we described an architecture in which the main control functionality is provided by fixed controllers each controlling a subset of the overall track layout (see also [19]). In this extension, we added a second architecture in which the functionality is autonomously handled by the controllers of the trains (see also [34]). Both solutions were developed following our methodology.

Reactive Blocks and BeSpaceD are introduced in Sect. 2 followed by the presentation of the methodology in Sect. 3. In Sect. 4, the two architectures for the demonstrator are discussed while Sect. 5 describes the development of the two control softwares based on the methodology. Section 6 refers to experience with the approach and in Sect. 7 we present related work. In Sect. 8, we conclude and name some ideas for future work.

2   Reactive Blocks and BeSpaceD

The model-driven engineering technique Reactive Blocks is a tool-set for the development of reactive software systems [24]. A system model consists of an arbitrary number of *building blocks*, i.e., models of subsystems or subfunctionalities, that are composed with each other. A major advantage of this modeling method is its reuse potential since a building block can comprise sub-functionality that is useful in many different applications. The building block is specified once, stored in a tool library, and, when needed, moved into a system model by simple drag and drop. The behavior of a building block is modeled by UML activities that may contain UML call behavior actions representing its inner building blocks. These inner blocks are also specified by UML activities such that the approach scales. The interface of a building block is specified by an *External State Machine* (ESM) that describes the abbreviated interface behavior of the block [21]. To make analysis of functional correctness by model checking possible, the activities and ESMs are supplemented with formal semantics [22]. Moreover, Reactive Blocks enables the automatic transformation of system models into well-performing Java code [23]. Some tool extensions allow us to analyze models also for safety [32] and probabilistic real-time [13,15] properties.

BeSpaceD is a constraint solving and non-classical model checking framework [3,4]. It emphasizes particularly on dealing with models of cyber-physical systems that usually comprise a large amount of time and space-based aspects. BeSpaceD provides a modeling language and a library to reason on models, using techniques such as state-space exploration, abstraction and reduction. It enables the creation of verification goals for SAT and SMT solvers and provides connections to these tools. Thus, these solvers can be used based on much more concrete models than their traditional inputs. On the other hand, BeSpaceD models are more abstract than typical use-case specific (meta-)models that are applied in case specific tools. From an expressiveness point of view, SAT and SMT offer the specification elements of propositional logic (+ Presburger arithmetic [31]). Semantically, using BeSpaceD the notions of time and space are added. Other semantic carrying elements are available: They are treated as predicate parameters and have to be resolved in programs building on the BeSpaceD frameworks or queries to BeSpaceD.

BeSpaceD is written in Scala and compatible with Eclipse/Java. The modeling language is based on abstract datatypes and integrates with the Scala language. It is possible to write one's own programs that construct BeSpaceD models and to write code using BeSpaceD functionality for checking it. In fact, as shown in [13,17], an extension of Reactive Blocks is able to transfer its models to BeSpaceD models such that they can be directly analyzed for spatiotemporal properties.

3   Methodology

The creation of control software for transport systems requires knowledge about central kinematic properties like braking distances or maximum accelerations. Since the systems and their environments are often too complex to gain such data exclusively by simulation, it has to be gathered by testing and observing prototypes. This feature is considered by our methodology (see Fig. 1). It consists of five major steps:

1. In parallel to the development of the physical device, an initial version of the control software is engineered with Reactive Blocks. This first model already contains several functions that will also be used later in the final version, e.g., the access to sensors and actuators. The functions guaranteeing safety, however, are either not implemented or based on initial data concluded from simulations resp. experience with previous versions.
2. Code is generated from the initial Reactive Blocks model and used in the prototypes which are tested in order to find out relevant kinematic properties.
3. When all relevant properties are observed, the control software is extended. For that, we amend the original Reactive Blocks model by adding building blocks and flows. In this way, existing sub-functionality will be preserved making the development process cheaper.
4. The extended Reactive Blocks model is analyzed by BeSpaceD for compliance with relevant spatiotemporal properties. Depending on the complexity of the verification runs, we may carry out the proofs in two different ways:
   (a) One extracts a descriptive formula of relevant system functionality from the Reactive Blocks model and transforms it into a format readable by BeSpaceD. Afterwards, BeSpaceD verifies that this specification keeps certain spatiotemporal properties. As shown in [17], the extraction of the descriptive formulas can be carried out automatically if the Reactive Blocks model was developed based on a certain course of action and a set of dedicated building blocks. Due to its completeness, this kind of analysis is preferred but according to the complexity of the problem might exceed the capabilities of the solvers used by BeSpaceD.
   (b) One composes the control software model with a simulator that is also created in Reactive Blocks [13]. Thus, several simulation runs can be performed and their logs are translated into input for BeSpaceD that analyzes the data for compliance with the spatiotemporal properties. The log data can be proved very efficiently (e.g., 10,000's of different spatiotemporal coordinates within a split second). But in contrast to the other solution, this one is not exhaustive such that it can only guarantee the preservation of the properties for the simulated cases.
5. When the developed control software fulfills all desired properties, the Reactive Blocks model is transformed into code that is installed in the transport devices and used for further certification steps.

Depending on the kind of system, these steps can also be iterated such that the control software is developed and analyzed in several cycles. Thanks to the fully automatic nature of the code generation in Reactive Blocks, the results of the engineering cycles can be easily transformed into executable code.

Due to the importance of system safety for life and limb of the later passengers, we do not see our methodology as a replacement for traditional certification but as a supplement. Yet, we expect that the model-based development and spatiotemporal analysis leads to a better quality of the produced software. In consequence, the certification process will have to deal with fewer software errors and therefore is getting smoother.

Fig. 1. Methodology overview (reproduced from [20]).

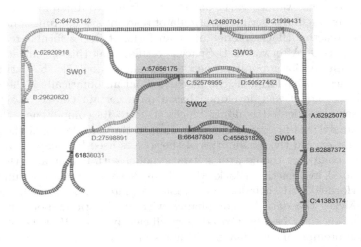

Fig. 2. Track with control zones. (Color figure online)

4 Demonstrator

As mentioned in the introduction, we use the Lego Mindstorms train-set to exemplify and evaluate our methodology. In the following, we will show two stages of expansion for the overall architecture of the system. The track layout is sketched in Fig. 2. It consists of five different stations that are connected by up to four trains. A train set comprises a motor, wheels and a train body (see Fig. 3). Further, we provide each train with a color sensor facing towards the tracks (in Fig. 3 on the right side of the train). It enables the train to count sleepers and to detect special sleepers that are furnished with colored Lego bricks. The coordination of the motor and the color sensor as well as the connection with a wireless communication device is provided by an EV3 controller, the standard

Fig. 3. Example Lego train.

control unit of Lego Mindstorms. This unit is transported in one of the cars. In the following, we will discuss both stages in greater detail.

4.1   Applying Zone Controllers

This system architecture was developed within a master's thesis [19]. It restricts the trains to purely counterclockwise operation albeit with possibly different speeds such that a train might catch up with another one. As shown by the colored backgrounds of Fig. 2, the tracks are partitioned into four *zones*. An EV3 unit, called *zone controller*, coordinates all trains in a particular zone in order to prevent collisions. This resembles the procedure used in the European Rail Traffic Management System (ERTMS), a novel train control system to be used in all European railway networks [10,37]. Moreover, the zone controller drives the switch points in its zone. The beginning of the zones are marked by colored sleepers such that the color sensors of a train can detect when a new zone is entered.

The train controllers are connected with the zone controllers by means of the Message Queuing Telemetry Transport Protocol (MQTT) [27]. This is a popular machine-to-machine connectivity protocol often used in the "Internet of Things" domain. Usually, both the routing of connections and the brokerage of users are done by a number of standard MQTT servers. Since tests, however, showed that the use of these servers lead to an unacceptably high transmission delay, we created our own MQTT server that is realized on a Raspberry Pi [38]. Figure 4 sketches the communication architecture used. A detailed technical evaluation of the demonstrator can be found in [19].

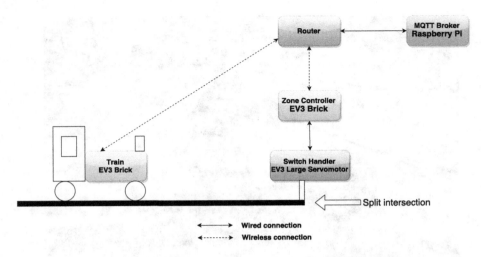

Fig. 4. Communication architecture (reproduced from [20]).

Figure 2 highlights that a station consists of two tracks. A stopping track is linked to a platform that allows passengers to enter and leave trains. A second track makes it possible that a train not stopping may pass the station while another one waits in it. Further, at some points we have alternate routes, e.g., for trains going from the station in the red zone to the one in the yellow one. Thus, the trains have to be routed which is done by the zone controllers. For that, the demonstrator is split into 23 different *tracks* that are each bordered by two switch points. The beginning of each track is marked by an unambiguously colored sleeper such that a train can always follow up on which track it is currently located. As shown in the message-sequence-chart in Fig. 5, a train provides the responsible zone controller with its destination. Based on that, the zone controller selects the tracks, the train has to pass in its zone, and sets the switch points accordingly. The routing algorithm is based on work described in [28].

The switching of zones by a train is realized by a sequence of colored sleepers as depicted in Fig. 6. First, the train passes a green sleeper indicating that a zone shift is coming up. Since a zone shift affords the time-consuming establishment of a new connection between the train and zone controller, we use overlapping segments in which the train is controlled by both involved zone controllers. The beginning of the overlapped segment is marked by a sleeper in the color of the new zone. When passing it, the train controller starts building up a MQTT connection with the new zone controller. The end of the overlapping segment is identified by a colored sleeper that signals the beginning of a new track in the newly entered zone. It may only be passed if the connection with the controller of the new zone is established and thereafter, the link with the controller of the old zone is released.

As mentioned above, the zone controllers are responsible for preventing collisions of trains in their zone. For that, they permanently need information about
the exact positions and speeds of the trains. Since color sensors are the only
sensing equipment used in our demonstrator and Lego trains have the nice feature that sleepers are always in the same distance from each other irrespectively
of the track shape, we use the sleepers as means to define exact train positions.
In particular, each train controller maintains a so-called *sleeper counter* that
totals how many regular, i.e., non-colored, sleepers of the track on which it currently moves, it already passed. Further, by using time-stamps and knowing the
distance between the sleepers, a train calculates its current speed. Whenever a
regular sleeper is passed, the train sends the value of its sleeper counter and
speed value to the responsible zone controller (resp. zone controllers if the train
is on an overlapping track), see Fig. 5.

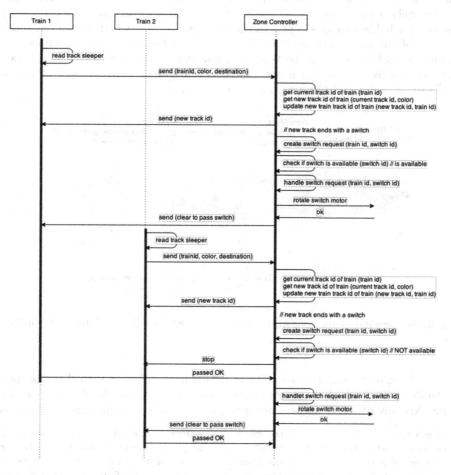

Fig. 5. Two trains interacting with a zone controller (reproduced from [20]).

From these data and its knowledge about the current track of the train, the zone controller establishes which sleeper the train just entered. It sets this sleeper and, with help of the information about the train's length, all other sleepers that are covered by the train into state *occupied*. Due to its knowledge about the system layout, the zone controller may also consider the sleepers of the previous track if the train just passes a track border. In addition, the sleepers vacated by the train since the last notification was received, are set to *free*.

The zone controller checks if the train is on a collision course with another one. Based on the current speed and position of the train, it calculates the distance needed for the train to come to a complete stop. This distance is converted into the number n of sleepers that are passed before the train stands after cutting power. Moreover, taking the communication delay between the zone and train controllers into consideration, we add a safety buffer b of sleepers[1] to n. If at least one of the $n + b$ buffers ahead of the train is occupied, the zone controller sends immediately a stop message to the train that initiates an emergency stop. Of course, this holds also for sleepers in the subsequent track when the train reaches the end of the previous one. If all the next $n + b$ buffers are not occupied, an all-clear signal is sent, and the train may continue with its current speed. Since the zone controller may have been broken, the train it also stopped when no signal at all arrives within a certain period of time.

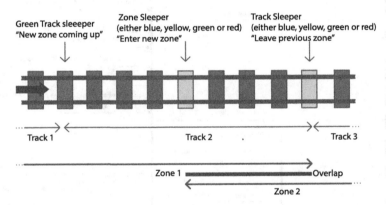

Fig. 6. Sleepers indicating zone switches (reproduced from [20]). (Color figure online)

The logic also includes the option of using an extra buffer such that the zone controller will check the state of sleepers that are even further in front of the train. Are any of these sleepers occupied, the controller commands the train to

---

[1] It is important to note that, the bigger the safety buffer b is, the more states of sleepers need to be checked, which means more processing time and again a bigger latency with regards to when the train receives a response. By testing the braking distances of the trains with various safety buffer values, we found out that $b = 10$ gives the best results.

slow down, instead of coming to a complete stop. If the blocking train in front continues to stand still, the emergency break is initiated a little closer to it due to the reduced speed, which leads to a smoother operation.

4.2   Autonomous Train Control

The second stage of extension was developed within a project thesis [34]. It comprises some significant changes to the system. Most prominently, the overall architecture was modified. While in the first stage, the main computational intelligence, in particular the routing and collision detection, was in the zone controllers, we moved them into the train controllers making the trains to truly autonomous units. In consequence, the zone controllers are now simple *switch point controllers* that just switch the points based on external commands received.

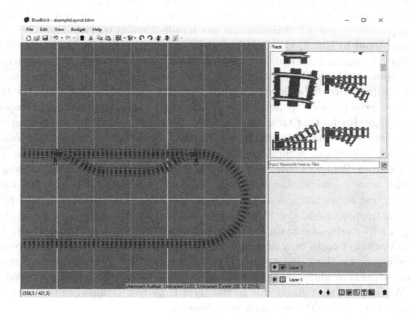

Fig. 7. The layout tool Bluebrick.

A second change is that the trains may now move in both directions. Further, we decided to make the adaptation to layout changes more flexible than in the first stage where the layout information was hardcoded. For that, we use the freely available Lego planning tool Bluebrick [26] (see Fig. 7) to model the track layout. Bluebrick allows us to draft a graphical model of a layout that is saved in form of an XML file from which the track structure can be automatically extracted and stored in the train controllers. To figure out the routing of a train, we realize a variant of Dijkstra's Shortest Path Algorithm [9]. For simplicity, a route to be performed is always chosen based on the shortest physical length but does not take possible waiting times at side tracks into account.

Allowing to operate trains in both directions affords to take measures in order to avoid front crashes. For that, we use *distributed interlocking*, a technique based on Gray's Two Phase Commit Protocol [12]. This protocol was originally developed to ensure that distributed transactions are carried out consistently. It uses an coordinator that first sends the relevant commands of a transaction to other stations involved. Thereafter, it triggers the Two Phase Commit Protocol that consists of a voting phase followed by a completion phase. In the voting phase, the coordinator queries from all other stations the confirmation that they are able to complete the transaction on their sites. After receiving positive confirmations from each station, the coordinator proceeds into the completion phase and sends a commit message to the other stations that thereupon make the transaction permanent. If at least one station answers with a negative confirmation, however, the coordinator sends an abort message leading all other stations to discard the transaction. Thus, as long as there are no data or station losses in the completion phase, all transactions are handled consistently.

As depicted in Fig. 8, the distributed interlocking algorithm is based on the Two Phase Commit Protocol. If a train wants to leave a station, it needs to lock the sub-route towards the next station on its path. For that, it checks whether the sub-route is already locked by another train. If that is not the case, the train starts to reserve the lock by asking the other trains in the layout using a *Request-Lock* message. Each other train may only confirm this request by answering with an *AllowLock* if it is neither on the sub-route nor has itself a request for locking it pending. Otherwise, it replies with a *DenyLock* message. Following the Two Phase Commit Protocol, the requesting train sends a *PerformLock* message if all replies were positive. Then it owns the lock and may enter the sub-route. If at least one other train denied the lock, the request is discarded by sending *AbortLock* messages and the train has to wait until getting the lock later. After leaving a sub-route, the train notifies the others about the release of the lock such that another train may acquire it. In principle, one can relax this algorithm by allowing more than one train to be on a sub-route as long as they run in the same direction and use the collision avoidance of the first stage to separate them. We omitted that since, due to the tight time restrictions of project theses, this modification would have been too complex.

The train controllers have to communicate with each other in order to exchange the distributed interlocking messages. They also need to call the switch point controllers to achieve the desired switch point settings. Further, we combined this project with another one making the remote monitoring of the system over large distances possible [18]. For that, relevant data like the position, length and speed of a train have to be send to a remote server. Due to decision within the scope of the other project, in this state the Advanced Message Queuing Protocol (AMQP) [1] is used. It allows the subscription of topics relevant for a party such that an AMQP Broker may forward received messages to all stations that subscribed them. Thus, it was possible to develop the architecture shown in Fig. 9

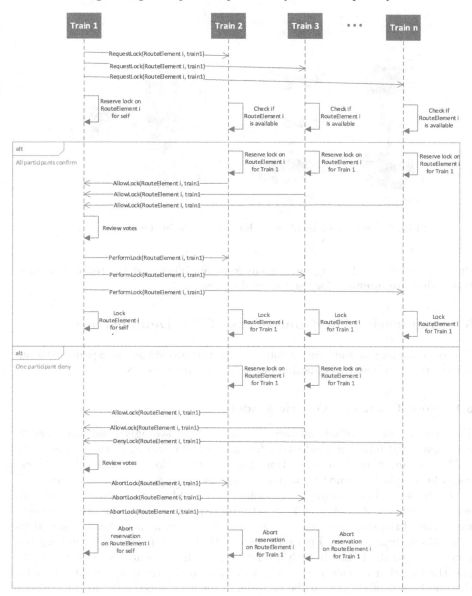

Fig. 8. Collision avoidance by distributed interlocking.

such that the train controllers, switch point controllers, and external servers are unburdened from receiving messages not relevant for them. For instance, a train controller can subscribe to the other ones in order to receive the messages of

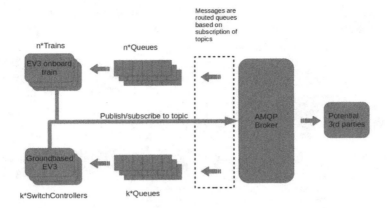

Fig. 9. The communication architecture used in the second stage.

the distributed interlocking but refrain from receiving position reports of other trains that are intended for the external servers.

5   Engineering the Controllers of the Demonstrator

The development of the control software for the two stages of expansion of our demonstrator followed the methodology presented in Sect. 3.

5.1   Zone Controller-Centric Model

The creation of an initial software version profited strongly from work by [28] who developed building blocks that facilitated the handling of the access to the EV3 train and zone controllers from the Reactive Blocks model. These blocks could be simply combined to achieve a first user-managed control system.

In the second step of our methodology, we could use the initial control software to find out the relevant kinematic properties of the trains. In particular, we analyzed the stopping distances for five of the seven speed levels[2] offered for Lego Mindstorms trains. Figure 10 depicts that, as expected, the braking distances are parabolic albeit with a relatively small gradient. Using these results and the fact that two sleepers are in a distance of 32.5 mm, we could determine the numbers n of sleepers to be considered for each speed level in the collision avoidance scheme discussed in Sect. 4.1.

Moreover, in this phase we examined the color sensors more closely to get good readings. With respect to using the sensors for speed calculation, we checked three alternatives, i.e., computing the speed after passing 16.25 mm, 32.5 mm resp. 65 mm. The tests revealed that the longest distance which corresponds to computing the speed only after every second sleeper, rendered by far

---

[2] The track layout contains many turns such that the two highest speed levels would often lead to derailments. Therefore, we did not consider them further.

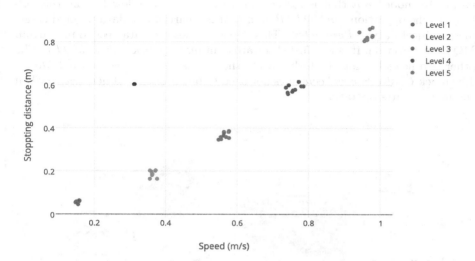

Fig. 10. Breaking distance for different speed levels (reproduced from [20]). (Color figure online)

the best measurements. Further, we detected quality issues for sensing different colors. We found out that we get better results if the color sensor is in a distance of 12 mm above the track than the 6 mm tried by [28]. We also discovered that the likelihood to detect the correct color is significantly improved when the thread handling color changes pauses between two checks for exactly 14 ms. When it runs without pausing, often white color is falsely read. In addition, we found out that, in general, blue and green render better results than red and yellow. We took these experiments into consideration when deciding which colors to be used at which points in the layout.

After getting sufficient knowledge about the kinematic behavior of the demonstrator as well as the correct treatment of the color sensors, we continued with the third step of the methodology, i.e., the creation of the final control logic using Reactive Blocks. As an example, Fig. 11 depicts the UML activity of the building block *TrainLogic* specifying the control logic of the train controllers. It contains four inner building blocks. Block *Robust MQTT* was taken from a Reactive Blocks library. It specifies the logic to handle connections with the MQTT server. Building block *ControlSensorLogic* models the access to the color sensor and the interpretation of the metered colors as described in Sect. 4. Block *Motor* is based on work in [28] and specifies the control of the train engine. Finally, building block *Communication* defines the cooperation with the responsible zone controller(s) via MQTT.

The semantics of UML activities resemble Petri Nets such that we can interpret a control or data flow as tokens running via the edges to the various vertices of the activity. The block *TrainLogic* is started by a flow through the incoming parameter node[3] *init* that is forked into three flows. One flow leaving the fork leads to the operation *initMQTTParam* that is a carrier of a Java method creating an object of type *Parameters*. This object carries the data needed to start an MQTT connection. It is forwarded towards pin *init* of block *Robust MQTT*. The other two flows leaving the fork initiate the blocks *Communication* and *Motor*. The block *ControlSensorLogic* does not need to be initialized. It gets active when the motor starts operating.

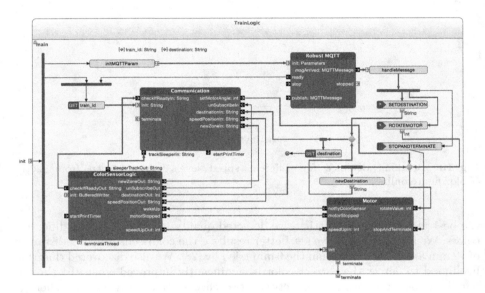

Fig. 11. Building block for the train control logic (reproduced from [20]).

The other flows of the activity are only sketched. There are several flows from *ControlSensorLogic* to *Communication* modeling the notification of the zone controller about the various findings of the color sensor. The control of the train speed by the zone controller is specified as a flow from pin *setMotorAngle* of building block *Communication* that defines the desired speed level as an integer value. This flow is forwarded to pin *rotateValue* of block *Motor* after which the engine speed is adjusted. Two flows from *Motor* to *ControlSensorLogic* realize that the color sensor is only operative if the motor turns. Finally, the activity contains three event receptions used to control the train directly from the central console. They can be used to set destinations for the train, to manage the motor directly from the console, and to terminate the train controller. In the latter case, an event of type *STOPANDTERMINATE* leads to block *Motor* in order to stop the train and to switch off the color sensor before the building block *TrainLogic* is terminated by a flow through parameter node *terminate*.

---

[3] The term *parameter node* refers to pins at the edge of a UML activity.

The model checker and animator of Reactive Blocks [24] proved helpful to check our controller models for functional correctness. The built-in model checker verified general functional properties, e.g., that all flows in a block are consistent to the interface descriptions of both, the ESM of this block and those of the inner blocks. The animation feature which allows to highlight flows of a block that can be executed in a certain state, was used to analyze our models for problem-specific properties. For instance, by inspecting all states of building block *TrainLogic* (see Fig. 11) we found out that a train controller does only unsubscribe the MQTT connection with a zone controller if it currently is connected with two of them. Thus, except for the system start, a train controller is always connected with at least one zone controller as long as no MQTT connection breaks.

```
BIGAND(
  List(
    IMPLIES(TimePoint(1429190484062),
      BIGAND(List(OccupyNode(288),
        OccupyNode(289), OccupyNode(290),
        OccupyNode(291), OccupyNode(292),
        OccupyNode(293), OccupyNode(294),
        OccupyNode(295), OccupyNode(296),
        OccupyNode(297)))),
    IMPLIES(TimePoint(1429190483864),
      BIGAND(List(OccupyNode(287),
        OccupyNode(288), OccupyNode(289),
        OccupyNode(290), OccupyNode(291),
        OccupyNode(292), OccupyNode(293),
        OccupyNode(294), OccupyNode(295),
        OccupyNode(296)))),
    ...
```

Fig. 12. Train data in BeSpaceD (reproduced from [20]).

In the forth step of the methodology, the completed system was analyzed with BeSpaceD for the presence of spatiotemporal properties. As stated above, the development of the Reactive Blocks model is in parts based on work from [28] which did not use the special building blocks needed to enable an automatic extraction of the control logic as described in step 4a of the methodology. Therefore, we decided to use alternative 4b instead, i.e., we applied BeSpaceD to check logs of runs observed by executing the control software. Since Lego trains are usually not damaged by crashes, we could not only get runs from pure simulation but also from running the real trains on the tracks. In Sect. 4.1, we explained that sleepers form the basis for describing the locations of trains as well as breaking distances. Therefore, it seemed natural to use them also in the BeSpaceD proofs. The simulation resp. operation of the train and zone controllers lead to formulas as sketched in Fig. 12. A formula comprises a long list of conjunctions marked by a BIGAND statement. Each conjuncted element features an IMPLIES statement describing that a time point implies that a train occupies a certain number of sleepers on the track.

We used BeSpaceD to check runs of various scenarios mostly to guarantee freedom of collisions. Here, the solvers were used to verify that no sleeper was occupied by more than one train[4] at any time. But we could also validate that the results observed in step 2 of the methodology are consistent with the observed runs. For instance, the higher complexity of the final control software did not impact the braking distances compared with the observed ones (see Fig. 10). The BeSpaceD proofs did not reveal any performance problems. The longest run comprised 1973 time points that correspond to more than 32 min of operation and afforded the check of 10,000's of sleepers. They were checked within 0.3 s each on a standard 2.8 GHz Intel Core i5 running MacOS.

After finishing the BeSpaceD test, we completed the engineering process with the fifth step of the methodology. Here, we automatically generated Java code from the Reactive Blocks models that was exported to the EV3 controllers as executable .jar files. This procedure could be performed for all controllers of our system within a few minutes.

5.2   Train Controller-Centric Model

Since we did not change the physical layout of the trains and only amended the track layout slightly, we could directly take over the results from the first two methodology steps carried out for the first stage. That holds particularly for the best handling of the color sensors and the determination of the braking distances as discussed in Sect. 5.1.

Due to the major architectural changes, i.e., the transfer of the routing and collision prevention from the zone controllers to the train controllers, the integration of Bluebrick, the use of the Shortest Path and distributed interlocking algorithms as well as the replacement of MQTT with AMQP, we had to develop a new model for the control software in the third step of the methodology. We could rely on the original building blocks for the access of the train motors resp. sensors and the control of the switch points but had to create novel ones for the various concepts mentioned above. As described in [34], altogether 12 building blocks were created for the train controller software and additionally four for the switch point controller. Moreover, a building block was integrated into the train software in order to handle the external monitoring of the trains (see [18]).

The amendment of the architecture and, in particular, the change of the collision prevention handling demands for a full replication of the BeSpaceD analysis in the forth step of the methodology. Mainly due to the strict time restrictions mentioned above, however, we decided to refrain from that in this stage. Another reason was that the distributed interlocking algorithm is a quite

---

[4] The inaccuracy of using sleepers for measurement was compensated by overapproximating the length of the trains, i.e., we declared a crash even when only one sleeper lay between those occupied by two trains.

conservative collision prevention technique precluding approximations of trains from the outset. Thus, the expected performance impact should be even less than the one experience for the first stage. Nevertheless, as soon as the distributed interlocking is combined with the approach mechanisms of the first stage such that several trains may be in the same sub-route as long as they operate in the same direction (see Sect. 4.2), there will be significant spatiotemporal issues. Thus, we plan to make leeway on the spatiotemporal analysis for this extension.

The fifth step of the methodology is identical with the first stage of expansion. We automatically generated the Java code for both, the train and switch point controllers as executable .jar files that can be directly executed in the various EV3 controllers.

6   Experience from Building the Demonstrator

Together with general library blocks like timers or buffers and, in particular, the blocks to handle MQTT [27], around 55% of the zone controller-centric model had not to be created from scratch but could be reused. For the train controller-centric model, this number is with 52% nearly identical. Albeit we have used Reactive Blocks to build transport system controllers only for a relatively short time, these numbers are not too far from the reuse rate of 70% that is usually achieved when creating models in already well-supported application domains [21].

We were also pleased that the input formulas for BeSpaceD could be easily generated and proved within very short time frames. We learned, however, that the necessity to use certain blocks in order to create descriptive formulas of the control software as used in alternative 4a of the methodology, might lead to practical problems. The engineer likes to be as free as possible when creating or selecting models in order to be able to address particular design problems flexibly. Thus, the rigid structure of the blocks needed to facilitate the creation of the BeSpaceD formulas [17] may be seen as cumbersome. We need to spend more work in solving this conflict between easy development and analysis.

Building control software in two different stages of expansion poses the question to which degree the iteration of the methodology steps alleviates the efforts in the second project. As discussed in Sect. 5.2, we did not need to repeat the first two steps of the methodology, i.e., the development of the initial control software and the prototype testing, which saved us a significant amount of time. Engineering the control software in the third step was less relaxed than originally expected which, however, results from the fact that the various changes afforded a complete new Reactive Blocks model. At least, the building blocks accessing the motors and sensors of the trains as well as the switch points could be reused. That was helpful since, according to our experience, the access functionality for external devices is often the most complicated part to develop (see [16]). For a more evolutionary development, we yet expect a much higher degree of reuse. Experience to compare the forth step of the methodology, i.e., the BeSpaceD-based analysis, will be investigated in the future.

7   Related Work

In the past, verification and analysis tools have been typically studied with respect to the underlying verification and analysis techniques rather than emphasizing the domain. PHAVer [11] is a tool that allows the analysis of spatial properties in hybrid-systems. Another application of formal verification techniques to train systems is described in [30]. Here, deduction-based verification techniques from the KeYmaera system [29] are applied. An application of the SPIN model checker for the verification of control software aspects of a railway system is described in [7]. A variety of other generic tools, recent work and approaches, e.g., [5,8,36] for model checking spatial properties of cyber physical systems exist. The combination of Reactive Blocks with BeSpaceD has been studied, e.g., in [14,17]. Here, the emphasize is on robots and either measured or simulated spatiotemporal values. Unlike in this paper, the combination of simulation and measured values was not considered.

The European Rail Traffic Management System (ERTMS) is a major industrial project undertaken by the Association of the European Rail Industry members. Its main focus is on creating a seamless integrated railway system in Europe to increase European railways competitiveness, capacity, reliability rates and safety [10,37]. A relevant focus is the automatic train protection system named European Train Control System (ETCS), and the Global System for Mobile Communications – Railway (GSM-R). GSM-R is based on the GSM standard and provides voice and data communication between the track controllers and the train. It uses frequencies specifically reserved for railroad applications. A variety of other large scale European funded projects exists in the domain of safety-critical cyber-physical system. For example, the ARTEMIS Chess [6] project includes a focus on the rail domain. Among other results, it produced a modeling language.

The first stage of our work uses a similar lego infrastructure as [28] where new means for public transport have been studied based on Lego Mindstorms and Reactive Blocks. In contrast to Overskeid's work, however, ours is more centered on software quality, in particular, with respect to making systems safe. For that, the separation of the control functionality between train and zone software is performed in a novel way that disburdens the performance of the EV3 controllers better when a larger number of trains has to be coordinated. Further, the use of BeSpaceD enables us to verify relevant spatiotemporal properties formally. Finally, following the methodology presented in Sect. 3 facilitates carrying out a well-regulated software engineering process.

8   Conclusion

Above, we presented our approach to create control software for transport systems using the model-based engineering technique Reactive Blocks. The introduced methodology enables us to check safety properties on measured and simulated data collected from a transport system. We exemplified the use of the methodology and its evaluation by showing two realizations for our demonstrator that is based on Lego Mindstorms.

Currently, we continue our work by using the introduced methodology for other projects. In one, we have replaced the EV3 controller in a train by a Raspberry Pi [38] (see [35]). This allows us to use also other sensors like magnetometers, accelerometers, proximity sensors and readers for RFID chips positioned in the layout. The combination of these sensors will make more precise position and speed readings of the trains possible. In another approach, we use the methodology to create control software for transport robots that are each controlled by a Raspberry Pi. Besides preventing collisions, the robots collaborate in order to, e.g., transport certain pieces together without letting them fall down. Moreover, we cooperate with Statens Vegvesen, the Norwegian Public Roads Administration, and Jernbaneverket, the Norwegian Government's Agency for Railway Services, in order to find out in which respect our approach can be used for the development and licensing process of real transport systems.

Another interesting application domain for our approach is industrial automation [2, 16]. We provide the BeSpaceD-based safety analysis as a cloud based service and work also on using analysis results to provide adequate views to operators and other stakeholders. As a first use-case, we realized the remote monitoring of the Lego Mindstorms demonstrator that is located in Trondheim, Norway, from the monitoring platform VxLab in Melbourne, Australia [18, 33].

References

1. AMQP.org: Advanced message queuing protocol (AMQP) (2016). www.amqp.org/. Accessed 01 Feb 2016
2. Blech, J.O., Peake, I., Schmidt, H., Kande, M., Ramaswamy, S., Sudarsan, S.D., Narayanan, V.: Collaborative engineering through integration of architectural, social and spatial models. In: Proceedings of Emerging Technologies and Factory Automation (ETFA). IEEE Computer (2014)
3. Blech, J.O., Schmidt, H.: Towards modeling and checking the spatial and interaction behavior of widely distributed systems. In: Improving Systems and Software Engineering Conference (2013)
4. Blech, J.O., Schmidt, H.: BeSpaceD: towards a tool framework and methodology for the specification and verification of spatial behavior of distributed software component systems. Technical report. arXiv:1404.3537 (2014)
5. Caires, L., Vieira, H.T.: SLMC: a tool for model checking concurrent systems against dynamical spatial logic specifications. In: Flanagan, C., König, B. (eds.) TACAS 2012. LNCS, vol. 7214, pp. 485–491. Springer, Heidelberg (2012). doi:10.1007/978-3-642-28756-5_35
6. CHESS-Consortium: Chess modeling language and editor v1. 0.2 (2010)
7. Cimatti, A., Giunchiglia, F., Mongardi, G., Romano, D., Torielli, F., Traverso, P.: Model checking safety critical software with SPIN: an application to a railway interlocking system. In: Ehrenberger, W. (ed.) SAFECOMP 1998. LNCS, vol. 1516, pp. 284–293. Springer, Heidelberg (1998). doi:10.1007/3-540-49646-7_22
8. Cimatti, A., Griggio, A., Mover, S., Tonetta, S.: HyComp: an SMT-based model checker for hybrid systems. In: Baier, C., Tinelli, C. (eds.) TACAS 2015. LNCS, vol. 9035, pp. 52–67. Springer, Heidelberg (2015). doi:10.1007/978-3-662-46681-0_4

9. Dijkstra, E.W.: A note on two problems in connexion with graphs. Numer. Math. **1**, 269–271 (1959)
10. ERTMS Project: ERTMS in brief. http://www.ertms.net/?page_id=40. Accessed 14 Aug 2015
11. Frehse, G.: PHAVer: algorithmic verification of hybrid systems past HyTech. In: Morari, M., Thiele, L. (eds.) HSCC 2005. LNCS, vol. 3414, pp. 258–273. Springer, Heidelberg (2005). doi:10.1007/978-3-540-31954-2_17
12. Gray, J.N.: Notes on data base operating systems. In: Bayer, R., Graham, R.M., Seegmüller, G. (eds.) Operating Systems. LNCS, vol. 60, pp. 393–481. Springer, Heidelberg (1978). doi:10.1007/3-540-08755-9_9
13. Han, F., Blech, J.O., Herrmann, P., Schmidt, H.: Towards verifying safety properties of real-time probability systems. In: 11th International Workshop on Formal Engineering approaches to Software Components and Architectures (FESCA). EPTCS (2014)
14. Han, F., Blech, J.O., Herrmann, P., Schmidt, H.: Model-based engineering and analysis of space-aware systems communicating via IEEE 802.11. In: 39th Annual International Computers, Software & Applications Conference (COMPSAC), pp. 638–646. IEEE Computer (2015)
15. Han, F., Herrmann, P., Le, H.: Modeling and verifying real-time properties of reactive systems. In: 18th International Conference on Engineering of Complex Computer Systems (ICECCS), pp. 14–23. IEEE Computer (2013)
16. Herrmann, P., Blech, J.O.: Formal model-based development in industrial automation with reactive blocks. In: 3rd Workshop on Human-Oriented Formal Methods (2016, to appear)
17. Herrmann, P., Blech, J.O., Han, F., Schmidt, H.: A model-based tool chain to verify spatial behavior of cyber-physical systems. Int. J. Web Serv. Res. (IJWSR) **13**(1), 40–52 (2016)
18. Herrmann, P., Svae, A., Svendsen, H.H., Blech, J.O.: Collaborative model-based development of a remote train monitoring system. In: Proceedings of Evaluation of Novel Approaches to Software Engineering, COLAFORM Track (2016)
19. Hordvik, S.E., Øseth, K.: Control software for an autonomous cyber-physical train system. Master's thesis, Norwegian University of Science and Technology (NTNU) (2015)
20. Hordvik, S., Øseth, K., Blech, J.O., Herrmann, P.: A methodology for model-based development and safety analysis of transport systems. In: 11th International Conference on Evaluation of Novel Approaches to Software Engineering (ENASE) (2016)
21. Kraemer, F.A., Herrmann, P.: Automated encapsulation of UML activities for incremental development and verification. In: Schürr, A., Selic, B. (eds.) MODELS 2009. LNCS, vol. 5795, pp. 571–585. Springer, Heidelberg (2009). doi:10.1007/978-3-642-04425-0_44
22. Kraemer, F.A., Herrmann, P.: Reactive semantics for distributed UML activities. In: Hatcliff, J., Zucca, E. (eds.) FMOODS/FORTE -2010. LNCS, vol. 6117, pp. 17–31. Springer, Heidelberg (2010). doi:10.1007/978-3-642-13464-7_3
23. Kraemer, F.A., Herrmann, P., Bræk, R.: Aligning UML 2.0 state machines and temporal logic for the efficient execution of services. In: Meersman, R., Tari, Z. (eds.) OTM 2006. LNCS, vol. 4276, pp. 1613–1632. Springer, Heidelberg (2006). doi:10.1007/11914952_41
24. Kraemer, F.A., Slåtten, V., Herrmann, P.: Tool support for the rapid composition, analysis and implementation of reactive services. J. Syst. Softw. **82**(12), 2068–2080 (2009)

25. Lee, E.: Cyber physical systems: design challenges. In: 11th IEEE International Symposium on Object Oriented Real-Time Distributed Computing (ISORC), pp. 363–369. IEEE Computer (2008)
26. McKenna, A., Nanty, A.: BlueBrick – Version 1.8.0. (2015). www.bluebrick. lswproject.com/help_en.html. Accessed 02 Feb 2016
27. MQTT.org: Message queuing telemetry transport (MQTT). www.mqtt.org/. Accessed 14 Aug 2015
28. Overskeid, K.M.: Personal rapid transit (PRT) system using lego mindstorms. Master's thesis, Norwegian University of Science and Technology (NTNU) (2015)
29. Platzer, A., Quesel, J.-D.: KeYmaera: a hybrid theorem prover for hybrid systems (system description). In: Armando, A., Baumgartner, P., Dowek, G. (eds.) IJCAR 2008. LNCS (LNAI), vol. 5195, pp. 171–178. Springer, Heidelberg (2008). doi:10. 1007/978-3-540-71070-7_15
30. Platzer, A., Quesel, J.-D.: European train control system: a case study in formal verification. In: Breitman, K., Cavalcanti, A. (eds.) ICFEM 2009. LNCS, vol. 5885, pp. 246–265. Springer, Heidelberg (2009). doi:10.1007/978-3-642-10373-5_13
31. Presburger, M.: Über die Vollständigkeit eines gewissen Systems der Arithmetik ganzer Zahlen, in welchem die Addition als einzige Operation hervortritt. In: Comptes rendues du ler Congres des Math. des Pays Slaves, Warsaw, pp. 192–201 (1929). 395
32. Slåtten, V., Kraemer, F., Herrmann, P.: Towards automatic generation of formal specifications to validate and verify reliable distributed system: a method exemplified by an industrial case study. In: 10th International Conference on Generative Programming and Component Engineering (GPCE 2011), pp. 147–156. ACM (2011)
33. Svae, A.: Remote monitoring of lego-mindstorm trains. Project thesis, Norwegian University of Science and Technology, Trondheim (2016)
34. Svendsen, H.H.: Model-based engineering of a distributed, autonomous control system for interacting trains, deployed on a lego mindstorms platform. Project thesis, Norwegian University of Science and Technology, Trondheim (2016)
35. Svendsen, H.H.: Self-localization of lego trains in a modular framework. Master's thesis, Norwegian University of Science and Technology, Trondheim (2016)
36. Tiwari, A.: Time-aware abstractions in HybridSal. In: Kroening, D., Păsăreanu, C.S. (eds.) CAV 2015. LNCS, vol. 9206, pp. 504–510. Springer, Cham (2015). doi:10.1007/978-3-319-21690-4_34
37. UNIFE Project: UNIFE. http://www.unife.org/. Accessed 14 Aug 2015
38. Upton, E., Halfacree, G.: Raspberry Pi User Guide. Wiley, Hoboken (2014)

Quantitative and Qualitative Empirical Analysis of Three Feature Modeling Tools

Juliana Alves Pereira[1](✉), Kattiana Constantino[2], Eduardo Figueiredo[2], and Gunter Saake[1]

[1] Otto-von-Guericke-University Magdeburg (OvGU), Magdeburg, Germany
{juliana.alves-pereira,gunter.saake}@ovgu.de
[2] Federal University of Minas Gerais (UFMG), Belo Horizonte, Brazil
{kattiana,figueiredo}@dcc.ufmg.br

Abstract. During the last couple of decades, feature modeling tools have played a significant role in the improvement of software productivity and quality by assisting tasks in software product line (SPL). SPL decomposes a large-scale software system in terms of their functionalities. The goal of the decomposition is to create well-structured individual software systems that can meet different users' requirements. Thus, feature modeling tools provides means to manage the inter-dependencies among reusable common and variable functionalities, called features. There are several tools to support variability management by modeling features in SPL. The variety of tools in the current literature makes it difficult to understand what kinds of tasks are supported and how much effort can be reduced by using these tools. In this paper, we present the results of an empirical study aiming to support SPL engineers choosing the feature modeling tool that best fits their needs. This empirical study compares and analyzes three tools, namely SPLOT, FeatureIDE, and pure::variants. These tools are analyzed based on data from 119 participants. Each participant used one tool for typical feature modeling tasks, such as create a model, update a model, automated analysis of the model, and product configuration. Finally, analysis concerning the perceived ease of use, usefulness, effectiveness, and efficiency are presented.

Keywords: Software product lines · Variability management · Feature models · SPLOT · Featureide · Pure::variants

1 Introduction

The growing need for variability management in larger and complex software applications demands better support in benefiting from reusable software artifacts. *Software Product Line* (SPL) has proven to be an efficient software development practice by exploiting large-scale reuse and dealing with many challenges of today's software development, such as variability [26]. Experience already shows that SPL can allow companies to realize order-of-magnitude improvements in time to market, cost, productivity, quality, and flexibility [9]. Large industries, such as Hewlett-Packard, Nokia,

L.A. Maciaszek and J. Filipe (Eds.): ENASE 2016, CCIS 703, pp. 66–88, 2016.
DOI: 10.1007/978-3-319-56390-9_4

Motorola, and Dell have been investing significant effort incorporating software variability into their product line approaches [8, 28].

Variability is one of the key concepts in SPL. It allows the development of similar
applications from a shared and interdependent set of software functionalities, called
features [2]. Feature modeling is a way for representing variability in SPL [20]. A *feature
model* provides a formal notation to represent and manage the interdependencies among
reusable common and variable features. Interdependencies are employed to delimit the
variability's space and to define the incompatibilities of infeasible combinations of
features. The term feature model was proposed by Kang et al. [19] in 1990 as a part of
the *Feature-Oriented Domain Analysis* (FODA) method. Since then, features models
have been applied in a number of domains, including mobile phones [14, 16], telecom
systems [17, 22], automotive industry [5, 13], template libraries [11], network protocols
[3], and others.

Due the complex interdependencies among features, the adoption of SPL practices
by industry depends on adequate tooling support. However, in the current literature there
are several available tools to support variability management by modeling features in
SPL [25]. The variety of tools makes it difficult to choose one that best meets the SPL
development goals. Hence, most software development teams adopt new tools without
establishing a formal evaluation. Thus, in order to contribute with relevant information
to support software development teams choosing a feature modeling tool that best fits
their needs, this paper presents a detailed empirical analysis of three tools, namely
SPLOT [23], FeatureIDE [29], and pure::variants [7]. We choose to focus our
analysis on these tools because they provide the key functionality of typical feature
modeling tools, such as to edit (create and update) a feature model, to automatically
analyze the feature model, and to configure a product from a model.

The empirical study presented in this paper involves 119 participants enrolled in
Software Engineering courses. Each participant used only one tool: SPLOT, FeatureIDE, or pure::variants. We relied on a background questionnaire and a 1.5-hour
training session to balance knowledge of the participants. The experimental tasks exercise different aspects of feature modeling. All participants answered a questionnaire
about the functionalities they used in each tool. We focus on quantitative and qualitative
analyses of four typical functionalities of feature modeling tools: *Feature Model
Edition*, *Automated Feature Model Analysis*, *Product Configuration*, and *Feature Model
Import & Export*. Based on this analysis, we uncover several interesting findings of the
analyzed tools. For instance, we observed that SPLOT presented the best results for
Automated Feature Model Analysis with twenty-five different operation of analysis
mechanisms. The *Feature Model Editor* of FeatureIDE was considered the easiest
and most intuitive one with many mechanisms available. Moreover, FeatureIDE also
achieved the best results for the *Feature Model Import & Export* functionalities with a
total of eight different possible either import or export formats. In general, the main
issues we observed in the three analyzed tools are the lack of adequate mechanisms for
managing the variability, such as visualization mechanisms to support the *Product
Configuration* functionality.

The remainder of this paper is organized as follows. Section 2 describes the empirical
study settings. Section 3 reports and analyzes the results. Section 4 points out the main

issues to be addressed in the future. Section 5 discusses some threats to the study validity. In Sect. 6, some related works are discussed. Finally, Sect. 7 concludes this paper by summarizing its main contributions and directions for future work.

2   Study Settings

In this section, we present the study configuration aiming to evaluate and compare three alternative feature modeling tools, namely SPLOT, FeatureIDE, and pure::variants. Section 2.1 defines the study research questions. Section 2.2 introduces the three analyzed tools and explains the reasons for selecting them. Section 2.3 summarizes the background information of participants that took part in this study. Finally, Sect. 2.4 explains the training session, describes the target feature model used in the experiment, and the tasks assigned to each participant.

2.1   Research Questions

The goal of this study is to investigate how feature modeling tools are supporting variability management in SPL. We formulate three *Research Questions* (*RQ*) focusing on specific aspects of the evaluation. The answer to these questions may support researchers and practitioners, for instance, in selecting or developing new feature modeling tools. The research questions investigated in this study are as follows.

RQ1.   What functionalities of feature modeling tools are hard and easy to use?
RQ2.   Does the developer background impact on the use of feature modeling tools?
RQ3.   What are the strengths and weaknesses of these feature modeling tools?

To address *RQ1*, we list a four-level ranking in relation to the degree of difficulty for each of the analyzed functionalities (see Sect. 3.1). With respect to *RQ2*, we are willing to investigate whether the developers background can impact on the results of this study (see Sect. 3.2). Finally, with respect to *RQ3*, we aim at highlighting the strengths of the analyzed tools and identifying weaknesses and missing mechanisms to be addressed by researchers and practitioners in the future (see Sect. 3.3).

2.2   Feature Modeling Tools

A previous systematic literature review [25] identified 41 tools for SPL development and feature modeling. Based on this review, we used the following three *Exclusion Criteria* (*EC*) in order to filter tools to be analyzed in this study.

EC1.   (Functionalities) We excluded all tools that do not include the main functionalities required for variability management in SPL [12].
EC2.   (Prototype tools) We excluded all prototype tools from our study because they are not applicable to industry, as they do not cover all relevant functionalities that we aim to evaluate, hindering some sorts of analysis.

EC3. (*Material available*) We excluded all tools without enough examples available, tutorials, or user guides. This criterion was required in order to prepare the experimental material and training session.

EC4. (*Unavailable tools*) We excluded all tools unavailable for download and the commercial tool without an evaluation version.

After applying the exclusion criteria (*EC1–EC3*), we filter six feature modeling tools that might be used in our empirical study: SPLOT, FeatureIDE, pure::variants, FAMA, VariAmos, and Odyssey. From the six candidate tools, we used the following *Inclusion Criteria (IC)* in order to choose a set of three tools and make possible to conduct a deeper study.

IC1. (*Mature tools*) We include the three most mature tools, as the maturity has a great effect on software quality and productivity (e.g., less errors are likely to be introduced during the development and consequently less effort is required to correct errors). However, in order to verify how mature a feature modeling tool is for variability management, we analyze the most cited tools in the SPL literature. For that, we identify primary studies from three scientific database libraries, namely ACM Digital Library[1], IEEE Xplore[2], and ScienceDirect[3]. *IC1* relies on the following search string: (*"splot" OR "featureide" OR "pure:variants" OR "fama" OR "variamos" OR "odyssey"*). The search was performed using the specific syntax of each specific database and considering only the title, abstract, and keywords. The search strings and results of each scientific database engine are provided in the Web supplementary material [1].

We found 256 primary studies for Pure::Variants, 251 for SPLOT, 96 for FeatureIDE, 74 for Odissey, 35 for VariAmos, and 3 for FAMA. Thus, we choose pure::variants[4], SPLOT[5], and FeatureIDE[6] as representative tools. These tools are actively used (by industry or academic researchers), and accessible tools in order to evaluate the state-of-the-art of feature modeling tools. Next, we present a brief overview of the selected tools.

SPLOT. SPLOT (Software Product Lines Online Tools) is an open source Web-based tool. It does not provide means for code generation or integration [23]. However, at the tool website, we can find a repository with more than four hundred feature models created by tool users for over 5 years. You can download the tool's code and also a Java library (SPLAR) created by the authors to perform the analysis of feature models. It also provides a standalone tool version that can be installed on a private machine. We used the online version of SPLOT for this empirical study.

---

[1] http://dl.acm.org/.

[2] http://ieeexplore.ieee.org/.

[3] http://link.springer.com/.

[4] http://www.pure-systems.com/pure_variants.49.0.html.

[5] http://www.splot-research.org.

[6] http://featureide.cs.ovgu.de.

FeatureIDE. FeatureIDE is an open-source Eclipse-based tool which widely covers the SPL development process [29]. Besides having feature model editor and product configurator, it is integrated with several programming and composition languages with a focus on development for reuse [4, 21]. FeatureIDE can be downloaded separately or in a package with all dependencies needed for implementation.

pure::variants. pure::variants is a commercial Eclipse-based tool developed by the Pure-Systems GmbH to support the development and deployment of SPL [7]. It supports all phases of SPL development from requirements specification to test cases and maintenance. Although it is a commercial tool, there is an evaluation version available in its web site (http://www.pure-systems.com/pure_variants. 49.0.html). We used the evaluation version of pure::variants in this study.

2.3 Background of the Participants

Participants involved in this study are 119 young developers taking a Software Engineering course. They were organized as follows: 41 participants worked with SPLOT, 42 participants worked with FeatureIDE, and 36 participants worked with pure::variants. All participants are graduated or close to graduate since they are mostly post-graduated MSc and Ph.D students from four different Brazilian universities: UFLA[7], UFMG[8], UFJF[9], and PUC-Rio[10]. To avoid biasing the study results, each participant only took part in one study semester and only used one tool, either FeatureIDE or SPLOT or pure::variants. The participants were nicknamed as follows: (i) F1 to F42 worked with FeatureIDE, (ii) S1 to S41 worked with SPLOT and (iii) P1 to P36 worked with pure::variants. Our goal is to use these nicknames while keeping the anonymity of the participants separating them by the tool since we did not repeat participants in the experiments. Further details about the distribution of participants are available at the project website [1].

Before starting the experiment, we used a background questionnaire to acquire previous knowledge of each participant. Figure 1 summarizes knowledge that participants claimed to have in the background questionnaire with respect to *Object-Oriented Programming* (OOP), *Unified Modeling Language* (UML), and *Work Experience* (WE). The bars show the percentage of participants who claimed to have knowledge high, medium, low, or none in OOP and UML. For WE, the options were: more than 3 years, 1 to 3 years, up to 1 year, and never worked in software development industry. Answering the questionnaire is not compulsory, but only 2 participants did not answer the questionnaire about UML knowledge and 3 participants did not answer about WE. In summary, we observe that about 75% of participants have medium to high knowledge in OOP and 48% have medium to high knowledge in UML. In addition, about 52% have

---

[7] Federal University of Lavras.
[8] Federal University of Minas Gerais.
[9] Federal University of Juíz de Fora.
[10] Pontifical Catholic University of Rio de Janeiro.

more than 1 year of work experience in software development. Therefore, despite heterogeneous backgrounds, we can conclude that all participants have at least the basic knowledge in the technologies required to perform the experimental tasks.

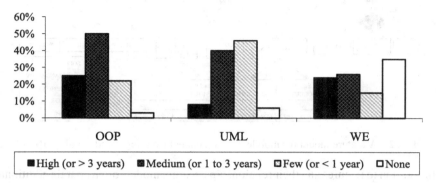

Fig. 1. Background of participants with respect to object-oriented programming (OOP), unified modeling Language (UML), and work experience (WE). Reproduced from [10].

2.4 Training Session and Tasks

In order to balance knowledge of participants, we conducted a 1.5-hour training session where we introduced participants to the basic concepts of SPL and the analyzed tools. The same training session by the same researcher to all participants was performed in all four institutions (Sect. 2.3). All material about the course was available for all participants. In addition, we have not restricted participants of accessing (e.g., via Web browsers) other information about the tools, such as tutorials and user guides.

After the training session, we asked the participants to perform some tasks using either `FeatureIDE` or `SPLOT` or `pure::variants`. These tasks were based on the target feature model of *Mobile Media* [16]. Mobile Media is an SPL for applications with about 3 KLOC that manipulate photo, music, and video on mobile devices, such as mobile phones [16]. Second Eduardo et al. [16], Mobile Media was developed for a family of 4 brands of devices, namely Nokia, Motorola, Siemens, and RIM. As an example, consider the simplified view of the Mobile Media feature model presented in Fig. 2. The features are represented by boxes, and the interdependencies between the features are represented by edges [11]. In feature models, there are common features found in all products of the product line, known as mandatory features, such as *Media Management*, and variable features that allow the distinction among products in the product line, referred to as optional and alternative features, such as *Copy Media* and the group *Screen Size*, respectively. The optional and alternative features are configurable on selected devices depending on the provided API support. Notice that a child feature can only appear in a product configuration if its parent feature does. Thus, each of the primitive features (i.e., atomic features) is a decision option related to the given parent feature, resulting in eleven decision options.

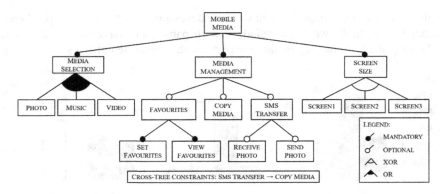

Fig. 2. A feature model for mobile media (adapted from Figueiredo et al. [16]).

In addition to features and their relationships, feature models often contain additional composition rules [11]. Composition rules refer to additional cross-tree constraints to restrict feature combinations that cannot be expressed by the feature tree. Cross-tree constraints are responsible for validating a combination of not directly connected features (i.e., they add new relations to the feature model not described in the feature tree). As an example, the cross-tree constraint *"SMS Transfer → Copy Media"* ensures that all product configurations containing the feature *SMS Transfer* must contain the feature *Copy Media*.

All tasks were based on the Mobile Media feature model to provide the same level of difficulty among the participants. We performed a four-dimension task analysis with respect to common functionalities provided by feature modeling tools as follows: *Feature Model Edition, Automated Feature Model Analysis, Product Configuration*, and *Feature Model Import & Export*. *Feature Model Edition* includes representing variability, such as creating, updating, and adding features and interdependencies in the feature model. Product' requirements are the main entry in this step. *Automated Feature Model Analysis* refers to extract information from the feature model. Based on Benavides et al. [6], we consider the following *Operations of Analysis* (OA):

OA1.   (*Void Feature Model*) A feature model is void if it represents no products.

OA2.   (*Valid Configuration*) A valid product configuration must not violate the feature model constraints (i.e., all features interdependencies must be considered).

OA3.   (*Valid Partial Configuration*) A partial configuration requires additional features to be a complete configuration. A complete configuration has a defined selection state for each feature from the feature model.

OA4.   (*Number of Configurations*) This operation returns the number of valid configurations represented by the feature model. As an example, the number of product configurations from the feature model presented in Fig. 2 is 252.

OA5.   (*Dead Features Detection*) A feature is dead if it cannot appear in any of the products of the SPL. In addition, a feature is conditionally dead if it becomes dead under certain circumstances, e.g. when selecting another feature(s).

OA6. (*False Optional Features*) A feature is false optional if it is included in all the products of the product line despite not being modeled as mandatory.

OA7. (*Redundancies*) A feature model contains redundancies when the interdependencies among features are modeled in multiple ways.

OA8. (*Core Features*) This operation returns the set of features that are part of all the product configurations in the product line.

OA9. (*Variant Features*) Variant features are those that do not appear in all the products of the product line.

OA10. (*Dependency Analysis*) This operation returns all the feature dependencies from a defined partial configuration as a result of the propagation of constraints in the feature model.

In the *Product Configuration* task, a mobile phone should be configured by (de)selecting a set of features from the product line that forms a valid and concrete resultant configuration. A concrete configuration defines a set of (de)selected features from a feature model that covers as much as possible the product' requirements. Finally, the feature model should be *exported* and *imported* (e.g., using the formats XML and CSV) to a new project.

We ran seven rounds of this experiment, three of them for SPLOT, two for FeaturEIDE and two for pure::variants. Each round of the experiment was performed in a computer laboratory with configured machines satisfying the minimum configuration required for each tool. While performing the tasks, all participants answered a questionnaire with open and closed questions. All answers are available in the project website [1].

3   Results and Discussion

This section reports and discusses data of this empirical study. Section 3.1 reports the degree of difficulty encountered by participants when performing the requested tasks. Section 3.2 focuses the discussion on whether the background of participants can impact on the use of each tool. Finally, Sect. 3.3 discusses the strengths and weaknesses of the analyzed tools.

3.1   Problems Faced by Developers

This section analyzes the level of problems that developers may have to carry out tasks in each analyzed tool. In other words, we aim to answer the following research question.

RQ1:   What functionalities of feature modeling tools are hard and easy to use?

For this evaluation, we have identified interesting results extracted from the analysis of quantitative and qualitative data from the questionnaires answered by the participants after performing each task (see Sect. 2.4). The questionnaires are composed with open and closed questions. For closed questions, participants had the following options to answer (i) *I was unable to perform the task*, (ii) *I performed the task with a major problem*, (iii) *I performed the task with a minor problem*, and (iv) *I had no problem performing the task*. Note, in order to validate the closed questions, we look up for the opened questions to know whether the participants finished the task properly (i.e., for options (ii), (iii), or (iv)).

3.1.1   Hard and Easy Functionalities

In order to answer the research question *RQ1*, we first rely on data presented in Fig. 3. This figure summarizes the results grouped by functionality and tool. We defined a Y-axis to quantify the cumulated results, where the negative values mean *hard to use* and positive values mean *easy to use* the respective functionality.

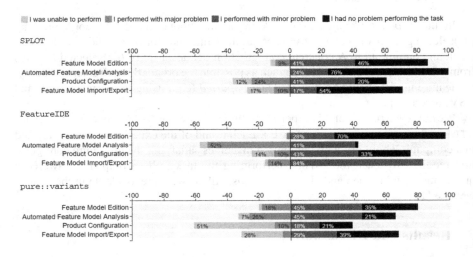

Fig. 3. Problems reported by participants to complete their tasks (reproduced from [10]).

We first investigated the SPLOT tool. On the one hand, *Product Configuration* seems the most challenge functionality to use by the SPLOT participants. About 12% of them were unable, and 24% had major problems to perform the *Product Configuration* task. On the other hand, 24% participants of SPLOT had minor problems and 76% performed without problems the *Automated Feature Model Analysis* task. These results endorse one major goal of this tool, which is to support developers with automatic operations of analysis [23], such as depth of the feature tree and number of possible configurations. Moreover, SPLOT also focuses on critical debugging tasks, such as checking the consistency of feature models, and detecting the presence of dead and common features.

Unlike SPLOT, about 57% of the participants using FeatureIDE indicated that they failed and had major problems to perform the *Automated Feature Model Analysis* task. That is, 52% of participants had major problems and 5% were unable to perform this task. Thus, this functionality was considered the hardest one to be used by participants using FeatureIDE (see Fig. 3). The most of the participants concerned about the limited support to guide them into the functionality. Regarding *Feature Model Edition*, about 28% had minor problems and 70% had no problem to perform this task.

This seems a positive result for `FeatureIDE` because only 2% (1 participant of 42) reported a major problem to edit a feature model.

Finally, we investigated the `pure::variants` tool. On the one hand, the *Product Configuration* functionality presented the worst result for this tool with a total of 61% of participants unable and with major problems to perform this task. On the other hand, the tool succeeds for the *Feature Model Edition* functionality where 80% of the participants had minor or no problems performing the task. As both `pure::variants` and `FeatureIDE` are Eclipse plug-in, this fact could be the reason why participants had minor or no problems with this task.

The general observation is that participants had more difficulties to perform the *Product Configuration* task in `pure::variants`. We believe that this task was a challenge in `pure::variants` because the tool still lacks powerful-enough solutions for managing the variability, such as the resolution of valid feature models applying decision propagation mechanisms dynamically. Next, we have identified the ranking of negative and positive functionalities for each tool.

3.1.2 Ranking of Negative Functionalities

Table 1 summarizes the rank of the three analyzed tools with respect to two negative answers "*I was unable to perform the task*" and "*I performed the task with major problem*" given by all participants. The first column relates to the feature modeling tools and the other columns relate to the functionalities analyzed. The first (1st) in Table 1 means that the respective tool presented more negative answers compared to the other tools. For instance, `pure::variants` can be considered the worst tool with respect to *Feature Model Edition* and *Product Configuration*.

Table 1. The rank of the three tools by functionalities from problems faced by developers.

Tools	Functionalities			
	Feature model edition	Automated feature model analysis	Product configuration	Feature model import & export
SPLOT	2nd	3rd	2nd	1st
FeatureIDE	3rd	1st	3rd	3rd
pure::variants	1st	2nd	1st	2nd

According to the `SPLOT` users, the main issues in this tool are related to its interface. For instance, participants reported they had trouble in the task of renaming features in the model. They also complained about the lack of examples. Other problems mentioned freely by its participants were that the tool does not work in some browsers. Furthermore, they mentioned that some terms such as "CTRC" and "CTC" were confused and, so, they did not understand the terms used by this tool when they were trying to configure a product.

For `FeatureIDE` participants, although they manage to edit the feature model, the tool interface still was the target of complaints. Besides, the participants also claimed concerns about the confusing terms used by the tool, such as "primitive features", "compound feature", "abstract features", and "feature hidden". Another complaint was regarding the navigation to find the related menu for the *Automatic Feature Model Analysis* and *Product Configuration*. Thus, they consider that the tool is not intuitive.

With respect to `pure::variants`, the main issues pointed out by participants were difficult to add cross-tree constraints in the feature model and many problems to perform the tasks about *Product Configuration*. Moreover, some participants also had trouble with the *Automatic Feature Model Analysis*, such as finding the activity menu for this task and the dead features. Furthermore, like in `FeatureIDE`, they claimed about terms used. Lastly, they also had interpreting problems in the results analyzed.

As a general observation, we encourage researchers and developers of feature modeling tools to unify vocabulary or notation in order to work in better way. In our study, we are convinced that the current examples available, technical report, tutorial, and users' guide are not clear enough to help the software developers using the tools and, consequently, adopting SPL. In addition, our results indicate that the developers of SPL tools need to focus more on usability and in human-computer interaction to provide the better user experience for their users.

3.1.3   Ranking of Positive Functionalities

Tables 2 and 3 summarize the ranking of the three analyzed tools considering the answers *"I performed with minor problem"* and *"I had no problem performing the task"*, given by participants with strong and weak backgrounds, respectively. The first column in these tables is the feature modeling tools and the second column relates the functionalities analyzed. The first (1st) means that the respective tool presented more positive answers compared to the other tools. For instance, `SPLOT` was considered the best tool with respect to the *Automated Feature Model Analysis* functionality by participants with strong and weak backgrounds.

Table 2. The rank of the three tools by functionalities from strong background participants.

Tools	Functionalities			
	Feature model edition	Automated feature model analysis	Product configuration	Feature model import & export
SPLOT	3rd	1st	2nd	3rd
FeatureIDE	1st	3rd	1st	1st
pure::variants	2nd	2nd	3rd	2nd

Table 3. The rank of the three tools by functionalities from weak background participants.

Tools	Functionalities			
	Feature model edition	Automated feature model analysis	Product configuration	Feature model import & export
SPLOT	2nd	1st	2nd	3rd
FeatureIDE	1st	2nd	1st	1st
pure::variants	3rd	3rd	3rd	2nd

It is interesting to note that developers with weak and strong backgrounds have different viewpoints about the analyzed tools. For instance, on the one hand, `pure::variants` can be considered the worst tool for developers with weak background regards to three functionalities (i.e., *Feature Model Edition, Automated Analysis*, and *Product Configuration*). On the other hand, this tool is only considered the worst option by highly skilled participants for *Product Configuration*. Therefore, this result suggests that `pure::variants` is more suitable for experienced developers than for novice ones.

3.2   Background Influence

This section analyzes whether the background of developers can impact on the use of the analyzed tools. In other words, we aim to answer the following research question.

RQ2.   Does developer background impact on the use of the feature modeling tools?

In order to answer *RQ2*, we first classified the participants by their level of knowledge and work experience into two groups. Group 1 (Strong Experience) includes participants that claimed to have high and medium knowledge in OOP, UML, and more than 1 year of work experience. Group 2 (Weak Experience) includes participants that answered few and no knowledge in OOP, UML, and less than 1 year of work experience. In this analysis, we excluded participants that did not answer the experience questionnaire and participants with mixed experiences. For instance, a participant with good knowledge in OPP, but less than one year of work experience.

3.2.1   Data Summary

Figure 4 shows pie charts summarizing the results. Similarly to Fig. 3, this figure depicts the percentage of participants who (i) *were unable to perform the task*, (ii) *performed the task with major problem*, (iii) *performed the task with minor problem*, and (iv) *had no problem to perform the tasks*. Charts on top indicate results for participants in the highly skilled group and charts on the bottom indicate participants with weak background. Besides, each pie chart summarizes the result of one task in one specific tool. The legend in the center of each pie is to identify the matching tool. That is, S means SPLOT, F means FeatureIDE and P means `pure::variants`. Each set of three pie charts relates to one of the four functionalities analyzed in this empirical study.

Based on the results of Fig. 4, we compared these two groups for each dimension. For *Feature Model Edition*, for instance, we realized that SPLOT (S) and `pure::variants` (P) showed some differences between these two groups. In the case of SPLOT, about 10% of participants with the weak background (Group 2) reported they were unable to conclude their task, while 99% of the participants with the highly skilled background (Group 1) completed their tasks. In addition, the total percentage of participants who had minor problems and had no problem did not change from Group 1 to Group 2. The reason for this result may be due to the Web interface of SPLOT and participants seem familiar with it. For `pure::variants`, the difference between Group 1 and Group 2 was even clearer. Approximately 92% of participants in Group 1 performed the *Feature Model Edition* task with minor or no problem. In Group 2, this percentage decreased to 60%. Therefore, we noticed the percentage of success is related to the skill level of participants in these cases. Good knowledge in OOP and UML may have contributed positively to the success of participants in this task because the task of editing a feature model involves creating an abstract representation and relationships, similarly to UML software modeling.

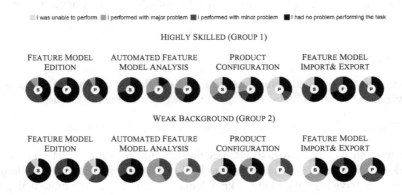

Fig. 4. Comparative results of participants with high skilled and with weak background.

For the *Automated Feature Model Analysis* functionality, the main difference between the groups occurred using the FeatureIDE and pure::variants tools. While 14% and 56% of the FeatureIDE and pure::variants participants in Group 1 had no problem performing the tasks, all participants in Group 2 failed or had some problem performing the tasks.

With respect to *Product Configuration*, while in SPLOT the Group 2 had 33% failures and the Group 1 only 13%, in FeatureIDE the Group 2 had no failures and the Group 1 had 13% failures. It shows that for FeatureIDE participants, the background did not influence the task performance. For pure::variants tool, both groups had a high percentage of failures. Although this seems a simple task, through (de)selecting features based on product requirements, pure::variants does not support the dynamic resolution of valid configurations. Thus, further knowledge about the feature model is also important, such as comprehension of the notations, and the relationships between features and constraints. Therefore, we realized that in this tool, this task is not trivial for either beginners or experienced SPL developers.

For the *Feature Model Import & Export* functionality, participants who used SPLOT presented a big difference in the results when comparing both groups, while for the other tools both groups had similar performance. For SPLOT, the percentage of failures increased from 17% in Group 1 to 33% in Group 2. Although the repository of the model is an interesting functionality of this tool, the participants of this study seem not familiar with it. Thus, it was difficult for participants with the weak background to perform this task in SPLOT. However, this task is easier for experienced software developers in Group 1.

Finally, based on the discussions described earlier, our analysis suggests that, in general, participants who have knowledge in OOP, UML, and high work experience have less trouble using the tools analyzed in this study. Therefore, as expected, the background of the participants has an impact on the use of the analyzed tools.

3.2.2 Statistical Analysis

To prove statistically the preliminary analysis, we apply a 2k full factorial design [18]. For this experiment, we have considered two factors (k = 2), namely the participants experience and the tool used. To quantify the relative impact of each factor on the participant effectiveness, we compute the percentage of variation in the measured effectiveness to each factor in isolation, as well as to the interaction of both factors. The higher the percentage of variation explained by a factor, the more important it is to the response variable [18].

In general, results show that the type of tool tends to have a higher influence on the effectiveness. Figure 5 outlines that for three out of the four functionalities (i.e., *Feature Model Edition*, *Product Configuration*, and *Feature Model Import & Export*), the type of tool used by the participants has the highest influence on the effectiveness. For the *Feature Model Edition* task, 96% of the total variation can be attributed to the type of used tool, whereas only 5% is due to participants' experience and 2% can be attributed to the interaction of these two factors. For *Product Configuration*, 57% is attributed to the type of tool, and 43% is due to participants' experience. Finally, for *Feature Model Import & Export*, 95% is attributed to the type of tool, whereas only 1% is due to participants' experience and 4% is attributed to the interaction of these two factors.

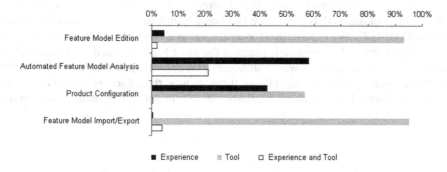

Fig. 5. Background Influence reported by factorial design test (reproduced from [10]).

Therefore, for the *Feature Model Edition* and *Feature Model Import & Export* tasks, both the participants experience factor and the interaction seem of little importance to the results. Indeed, the results clearly show that the participants who used the SPLOT and FeatureIDE tools achieved the better results for these tasks. One possible explanation is the complexity of pure::variants. Additionally, even participants who have no experience tend to obtain a higher effectiveness when they use SPLOT and FeatureIDE in these two tasks.

For *Automated Feature Model Analysis*, the participants experience factor was more significant. 58% of the total variation is attributed to the participants' experience factor, and whereas only 21% is due to the type of tool used and to the interaction of these two factors. Therefore, the results for this task clearly show that the participants with strong experience achieved the better results. One possible explanation is the complexity of the terms used during the analysis task, which requires more knowledge from participants.

3.3 Strengths and Weaknesses in Feature Modeling Tools

This section investigates some of the strengths and weaknesses of SPLOT, FeatureIDE, and pure::variants tools. We aim to answer the following research question.

RQ3. What are the strengths and weaknesses of the feature modeling tools?

Figures 6, 7, and 8 show diverging stacked bar chart of the strengths and weaknesses of SPLOT, FeatureIDE and pure::variants, respectively. In particular, we ask the participants about the following terms (i) tool interface, (ii) feature model editor, (iii) cross-tree constraints, (iv) automatic analysis, (v) product configuration, (vi) integration with code, (vii) hotkey mechanisms, (viii) online tool, (ix) feature model repository, (x) eclipse plug-in, and (xi) examples and user guides. The percentages of participants who considered the items as strengths are shown to the right of the zero line. The percentages who considered the items as weaknesses are shown to the left of the zero line. These items are sorted in alphabetical order in all figures. Participants could also freely express about other strengths or weaknesses they encountered during the tasks.

For SPLOT participants (see Fig. 6), the three most voted strengths were: the automatic analysis of the models (76%), the fact being an online tool (63%), and the feature model editor (41%). We believe that the automatic analysis of SPLOT was pointed out as the biggest strengths, because it presents the most basic required operations while compared with other tools. However, although 41% of participants have considered the editor as a strength of this tool, 44% of them pointed the editor as a weakness. The participants claimed mainly about the shape size. Second the participants, each feature

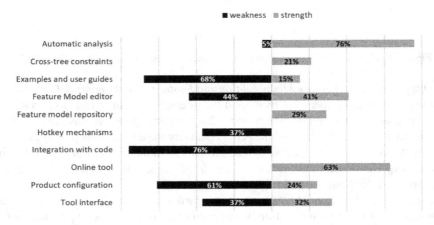

Fig. 6. Strengths and weaknesses reported by participants using SPLOT.

should be presented with sufficient size to be readable. Moreover, 68% of them pointed out the lack of examples available as a problem to understand the tool, and 76% indicated integration with source code as a missing mechanism. Lastly, the product configuration was one of the main concerns with 61% of votes. The participants claimed mainly regards the missing functionalities, such as to set multiple configurations and to save them. SPLOT does not allow users to create multiple configurations and keep the specified ones. In this tool, only the feature model can be exported or (and) kept in the repository.

Analyzing the FeatureIDE tool (see Fig. 7), the three most voted strengths were: the fact being an Eclipse plug-in (64%), and the feature model (62%) and cross-tree constraints (57%) editors. Although, the feature model editor is similar mechanisms in all tools, FeatureIDE editor presents many additional functionalities when compared with the other tools (e.g., zoom, filter, hotkey, and layout organization mechanisms). Moreover, when creating cross-tree constraints, it is possible to have immediate feedback regards dead features, redundant constraints, and false-optional features. As a main weakness, 64% of FeatureIDE users voted in the interface. In accordance with the qualitative data, the main problem is regards to the navigation to find the related menu for automatic analysis of the model and product configuration. Moreover, as in SPLOT, the product configuration for large feature models is challenging. For both tools, when the automatic validation is applied the immediate changes in the visual representation generate unnecessary surprises and confusion to the users. In this context, interactive mechanisms (e.g., animations, color hue, and highlighting) can be used to support users navigate in the tree, (de)select the features, and understand the interdependencies among them.

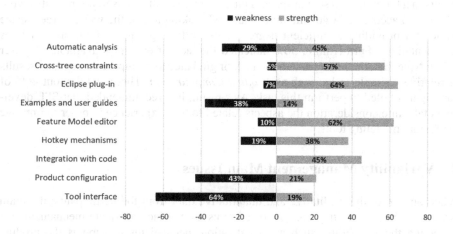

Fig. 7. Strengths and weaknesses reported by participants using FeatureIDE.

Finally, the pure::variants tool was analyzed (see Fig. 8). the three most voted strengths were: the fact being an Eclipse plug-in (78%), automatic analysis of the models (58%) and the feature model editor (56%). As weakness, 67% of its users voted in the product configuration functionality. The pure::variants tool configurator does not support the automatic validation of cross-tree constraints. Moreover, as in the other tools, it represents them only textually in the feature model editor screen. Thus, no cross-tree constraints visualizations are provided to the users in the configurator screen.

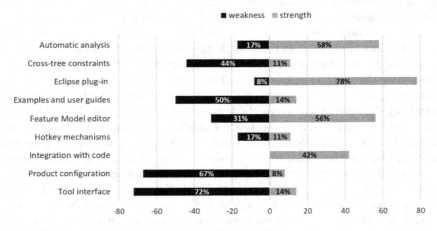

Fig. 8. Strengths and weaknesses reported by participants using pure::variants.

As in pure::variants, when considering all participants and tools, the most voted weaknesses were the tool interface (64%) and the product configuration mechanism (61%). The main drawback pointed out by participants is regards the information visualization when configuring a product. The product configuration layout in those tools results in a lot of unused screen space. Thus, the main challenge is to improve its layout taking into account a large amount of data and making use of the whole screen space while still providing a sufficient degree of usability (e.g., using multi-product lines representation). Furthermore, 50% indicated the lack of examples available and user guide. Note that, the interface and the lack of guidance may impact on negative results of relatively simple tasks, such as *Product Configuration*. That is why about 46% of participants failed to perform this task. As a result, it is recommended that SPL developers take into consideration the aspects related to user experience in order to improve the feature modeling tools.

4 Variability Management Main Issues

When analyzing the qualitative and quantitative data from the participants, the main issues we observed in the three analyzed tools are the lack adequate mechanisms for managing the variability, such as visualization mechanisms to support the product configuration task. Based on the expert knowledge from authors of this paper, we extract three main issues to be addressed in the future.

Issue 1: Current tools offer limited support for advanced visualization mechanisms (i.e., fish-eye views, filters, zooming, focus and context, cross-tree constraints, and others) making variability harder to manage.

Issue 2: When the products to be configured are highly customized, the users are usually unable to find satisfactory configurations. This happen because the amount and complexity of options presented by the configurator lead users to get lost with so much information and make poor decisions due complex and hard to reasoning dependencies. Moreover, the feature model may present many subjective features that cannot be matched with the product' requirements. In this context, none of the analyzed tools present additional information about features and variability to guide users in an easier configuration process.

Issue 3: Cross-tree constraints often create a nightmare for users because they crosscut feature models, and the resolution of valid product configuration becomes computationally complex. In SPLOT and FeatureIDE, the cross-tree constraints used to delimit the scope of allowed products are managed by SAT solvers that can automatically resolve the variability model's consistency and validity during the product configuration. Each time the user (de)selects a particular feature decision propagation strategies are applied to automatically validate feature models, which result in a non-conflicting configuration. However, such views add confusion to the users. Thus, they need additional visualization mechanisms to show which feature implied in a (de)selection of other feature(s). Moreover, the decision propagation mechanisms by themselves are not enough to support users getting a valid configuration (i.e., decision propagation can only benefit to configure partial configurations). In this case, when the user has selected all features of their choice, their configuration might still be invalid due to unsatisfied feature dependencies. Consequently, it may be very difficult to the users specifying a valid configuration since features of no interest to them also need to be (de)selected in order to fulfill the feature model's interdependencies. In this context, the analyzed tools lack appropriated mechanisms to show the users which features should be (de)selected to guide them into a valid final configuration.

In summary, the product configuration process can be challenging, as users regularly do not know every feature and their interdependencies, particularly for large product lines. Thus, in order to ease the configuration process, we believe that a successful product configuration functionality would need to be able to present the following characteristics:

- Guide the users over each step of the product configuration process through a restricted and detailed view of the configuration space and features.
- Guide the product configuration process by delivering capabilities to effectively communicate with the users and understand their needs and preferences.

5 Threats to Validity

A key issue when performing this kind of experiment is the validity of the results. The results should be valid for the population of which the set of participants were involved. It is also interesting to generalize the results to a broader population. The results have adequate validity if they are valid for the population, which they intend to be generalized. In this section, threats to the validity are analyzed. We discuss the study validity with respect to the four categories of validity threats [31]: *constructs validity, internal validity, external validity,* and *conclusion validity.*

Construct validity reflects what extent the operational measures that are studied really represent, what the researcher has in mind, and what is investigated according to the research questions [31]. The most common threats to this type of validity are related to experiment design: in general, poor definition of the theoretical basis or the definition of the testing process. For example, participants can base their behavior on the research hypotheses or they may be involved in other experiments. This type of threat can occur in formulating the questionnaire in our experiment, although we have discussed several times the experiment design. To minimize social threats, we performed the experiment in four different institutions.

Internal validity of the experiment concerns the question whether the effect is caused by the independent variables (e.g. course period and level of knowledge) or by other factors [31]. In this sense, a limitation of this study concerns the absence of balancing the participants in groups according to their knowledge. It can be argued that the level of knowledge of some participants may not reflect the state of practice (e.g., most of the participants have only minor knowledge of SPL). To minimize this threat, we provide a 1.5-hour training session to introduce participants to the basic required knowledge and a questionnaire for help the better characterize the sample as a whole. However, 1.5-hour training session may not have been enough for the participants with the weak background.

External validity concerns the ability to generalize the results to other environments, such as to industry practices [31]. A major external validity can be the selected tools and participants. We choose three tools, among many available ones, and we cannot guarantee that our observations can be generalized to other tools. Moreover, in Brazil there are not many SPL developers, then this group may not reflect the state of the practice. We tried to minimize this threat by working with both new and experienced developers. These participants are graduated or close to graduate since the course targets post-graduated MSc and Ph.D. students.

Conclusion validity concerns the relation between the treatments and the outcome of the experiment [31]. This involves the correct analysis of the results of the experiment, and the measurement reliability of the implementation of the treatments. Then, the conclusion of the analyzed made by us could be another if it were done by other researchers. To minimize this threat, we discuss the results data with experienced researchers to make a more reliable conclusion.

6   Related Work

This section presents some previous studies about tools for feature modeling and variability management in SPL. Djebbi et al. [15] perform an evaluate study of three SPL management tools (i.e., `XFeature`, `pure::variants`, and `RequiLine`) in collaboration with a group of industries. The purpose of this study was to understand the salient characteristics of SPL management tools and to evaluate the ability of those tools to satisfy industrial needs. In this evaluation, `pure::variants` and `RequiLine` were the tools that best satisfied the defined criteria.

Simmonds et al. [27] also investigated several tools (i.e., `Clafer`, `EPF Composer`, `FaMa-OVM`, `fmp`, `Hydra`, `SPLOT`, `VEdit`, and `XFeature`). The authors conduct an analysis based on the expressiveness of each notation for dealing with the required variability, as well as the understandability of the specification, adherence to standard formats, and the availability of tool support. Specifically, the tools were evaluated based on supported formats, underlying formalism, supported analyses, interface, availability, and usability. As in our study, the purpose of this study is to facilitate tool selection in the context of SPL.

In another study [30], ten variability modeling tools were compared (i.e., `AHEAD`, `FAMA`, `Feature Modeling Plug-in`, `Gears`, `Kumbang Tools`, `MetaEdit +`, `Product Modeler`, `Pure::Variants`, `RequiLine`, and `XFeature`). The authors categorize the comparisons into general information, technical infrastructure, operating systems support, rendering of modeling, format of input/output models support, modeling and configuration functionalities, and development functionalities. However, their results focus more on the implemented mechanisms than on the tool support, while our empirical study is based on experimental data.

In a previous preliminary work [24], we performed a preliminary and exploratory study that compares and analyzes two feature modeling tools, namely `FeatureIDE` and `SPLOT`, based on data from 56 participants that used these two tools. This empirical study involved other 84 new participants (i.e., none of the participant of this current empirical study was the same of the previous one). Therefore, this current study expanded and deepened the previous one in several ways. For instance, in addition to expanding the data set of participants, it includes one more tool, `pure::variants`, in the set of analyzed feature modeling tools. Moreover, the 84 new participants performed different tasks to exercise other aspects of SPL development. As a similarity, both studies aim to compare feature modeling tools and to support engineers in the hard task of choosing the tool that best fits their needs.

First, we extend the previous short paper with the empirical analysis of one more state-of-the-art SPL tool SPLOT. Second, we have significantly expanded the discussion of our results by analyzing the three state-of-the-art SPL tools and by presenting additional content, figures, and tables. Third, we extend our results pointing out a list of variability management issues faced by those tools to be addressed in future research. Finally, this empirical study presents a substantial extension of our preliminary short paper [10].

7   Conclusion and Future Work

SPL focuses on systematic reuse based on the composition of features and domain modeling. `SPLOT`, `FeatureIDE`, and `pure::variants` are tools used to support feature modeling in SPL. In this paper, these tools were quantitatively and qualitatively empirical analyzed and some interesting results were presented and discussed. The results reported in this paper aim to support software engineers to choose one of these tools for variability management. Additionally, this study can also be used by developers and maintainers of SPLOT, FeatureIDE, pure::variants - and other feature modeling tools - to improve them based on the issues reported. Besides, when choosing one of the tools, the needed and purpose of use is one of the main factors to be taken into consideration.

Our conclusions indicate that the main issues observed in the three feature modeling tools are related to the *Product Configuration* functionality. Our study does not aim to reveal "the best tool" in all functionality. On the contrary, the three analyzed tools have strength and weakness. For instance:

- SPLOT has as main strengths its *Automated Feature Model Analysis* functionality and the fact to be an online tool and as drawbacks, the interface and hotkeys.
- The main strength of FeatureIDE is the *Feature Model Editor* functionality. Its drawbacks include a limited user guide and no intuitive interface (e.g., no guide to support users finding the *Product Configuration* and *Automated Feature Model Analysis* functionalities).
- The main strengths of pure::variants are the *Feature Model Editor* and the *Automated Feature Model Analysis* functionalities. Its main drawbacks include the lack of examples and the *Product Configuration* functionality.

Today research on variability tools in academia and industry is attempting to solve the variability management problem. However, when hundreds of variants must be captured, visualized, and modified, the variability management still becomes challenging for companies. As future work, developers can provide a more adequate and advanced support in this context. Moreover, this study can be extended in further experiment replications. For instance, other tools can be analyzed and compared using similar experiment design in order to contribute to improving the body of knowledge about feature modeling tools. We hope that with the ongoing studies, as the one provided in this paper, feature modeling tools will become more mature and established, such that there will be more use of such tools in real practical scenarios.

Acknowledgements. This work was partially supported by CNPq (grant 202368/2014-9). We are grateful to the reviewers who contributed significantly to the improvement of the paper.

References

1. Data of the Experiment: http://homepages.dcc.ufmg.br/~kattiana/visplatform
2. Bachmann, F., Clements, P.C.: Variability in software product lines. Software Engineering Institute, CMU/SEI Report Number: CMU/SEI-2005-TR-012 (2005)
3. Barbeau, M., Bordeleau, F.: A protocol stack development tool using generative programming. In: Batory, D., Consel, C., Taha, W. (eds.) GPCE 2002. LNCS, vol. 2487, pp. 93–109. Springer, Heidelberg (2002). doi:10.1007/3-540-45821-2_6
4. Batory, D., Sarvela, J., Rauschmayer, A.: Scaling step-wise refinement. IEEE Trans. Softw. Eng. 30(6), 355–371 (2004)
5. Benavides, D., Ruiz–Cortés, A., Trinidad, P., Segura, S.: A survey on the automated analyses of feature models. In: JISBD, Barcelona (2006)

6. Benavides, D., Segura, S., Ruiz-Cortés, A.: Automated analysis of feature models 20 years later: a literature review. Inf. Syst. **35**(6), 615–636 (2010)
7. Beuche, D.: Modeling and building software product lines with pure::variants. In: International Software Product Line Conference (SPLC), p. 255 (2012)
8. Bosch, J., Capilla, R., Hilliard, R.: Trends in systems and software variability. IEEE Softw. **32**(3), 44–51 (2015)
9. Clements, P., Northrop, L.: Software Product Lines: Practices and Patterns. Addison-Wesley, Reading (2001)
10. Constantino, K., Pereira, J.A., Padilha, J., Vasconcelos, P., Figueiredo, E.: An empirical study of two software product line tools. In: International Conference on Evaluation of Novel Approaches to Software Engineering (ENASE), pp. 164–171 (2016)
11. Czarnecki, K., Eisenecker, U.W.: Generative Programming: Principles, Techniques and Tools. Addison-Wesley, Reading (2000)
12. Czarnecki, K., Helsen, S., Eisenecker, U.: Formalizing cardinality-based feature models and their specialization. In: Software Process: Improvement and Practice, pp. 7–29 (2005)
13. Czarnecki, K., Wasowski, A.: Feature models and logics: there and back again. In: International Software Product Line Conference (SPLC), pp. 23–34 (2007)
14. Czarnecki, K., Grünbacher, P., Rabiser, R., Schmid, K., Wąsowski, A.: Cool features and tough decisions: a comparison of variability modeling approaches. In: Workshop on Variability Modeling of Software-intensive System (VaMoS), pp. 173–182 (2012)
15. Djebbi, O., Salinesi, C., Fanmuy, G.: Industry survey of product lines management tools: requirements, qualities and open issues. In: IEEE International Requirements Engineering Conference (RE), pp. 301–306 (2007)
16. Figueiredo, E., Cacho, N., Sant'Anna, C., Monteiro, M., Kulesza, U., Garcia, A., Soares, S., Ferrari, F., Khan, S., Filho, F.C., Dantas, F.: Evolving software product lines with aspects: an empirical study. In: International Conference on Software Engineering (ICSE), pp. 261–270 (2008)
17. Griss, M., Favaroand, J., d'Alessandro, M.: Integrating Feature Modeling with the RSEB. In: International Conference on Software Reuse (ICSR), pp. 76–85 (1998)
18. Jain, R.: The Art of Computer Systems Performance Analysis: Techniques for Experimental Design, Measurement, Simulation, and Modeling. Wiley, New York (1990)
19. Kang, K.C., Cohen, S.G., Hess, J.A., Novak, W.E., Peterson, A.S.: Feature oriented domain analysis (FODA) feasibility study. Software Engineering Institute, CMU/SEI Report Number: CMU/SEI-90-TR-021 (1990)
20. Kang, K., Kim, S., Lee, J., Kim, K., Shin, E., Huh, M.: FORM: a feature-oriented reuse method with domain-specific reference architectures. Softw. Eng. **5**(1), 143–168 (1999)
21. Kiczales, G., Lamping, J., Mendhekar, A., Maeda, C., Lopes, C., Loingtier, J.-M., Irwin, J.: Aspect-oriented programming. In: Akşit, M., Matsuoka, S. (eds.) ECOOP 1997. LNCS, vol. 1241, pp. 220–242. Springer, Heidelberg (1997). doi:10.1007/BFb0053381
22. Lee, K., Kang, Kyo C., Lee, J.: Concepts and guidelines of feature modeling for product line software engineering. In: Gacek, C. (ed.) ICSR 2002. LNCS, vol. 2319, pp. 62–77. Springer, Heidelberg (2002). doi:10.1007/3-540-46020-9_5
23. Mendonça, M., Branco, M., Cowan, D.: SPLOT - software product lines online tools. In: Conference on Object Oriented Programming Systems Languages and Applications (OOPSLA), pp. 761–762 (2009)
24. Pereira, J.A., Souza, C., Figueiredo, E., Abilio, R., Vale, G., Costa, H.A.: Software variability management: an exploratory study with two feature modeling tools. In: Brazilian Symposium on Software Components, Architectures and Reuse (SBCARS), pp. 20–29 (2013)

25. Pereira, J.A., Constantino, K., Figueiredo, E.: A systematic literature review of software product line management tools. In: Schaefer, I., Stamelos, I. (eds.) ICSR 2015. LNCS, vol. 8919, pp. 73–89. Springer, Cham (2014). doi:10.1007/978-3-319-14130-5_6

26. Pohl, K., Metzger, A.: Variability management in software product line engineering. In International Conference on Software Engineering (ICSE), pp. 1049–1050 (2006)

27. Simmons, J., Bastarrica, M.C., Silvestre, L., Quispe, A.: Analyzing methodologies and tools for specifying variability in software processes. Computer Science Department, Universidad de Chile, Santiago. http://swp.dcc.uchile.cl/TR/2011/TR_DCC-20111104-012.pdf

28. Software product line hall of fame. http://www.splc.net/fame.html. Accessed 14 May 2015

29. Thüm, T., Kästner, C., Benduhn, F., Meinicke, J., Saake, G., Leich, T.: FeatureIDE: an extensible framework for feature-oriented software development. Sci. Comput. Program. **79**, 70–85 (2014)

30. Uphon, H.: A comparison of variability modeling and configuration tools for product line architecture. IT University of Copenhagen (2008)

31. Wohlin, C., Runeson, P., Höst, M., Ohlsson, M.C., Regnell, B., Wesslén, A.: Experimentation in Software Engineering. Springer, Heidelberg (2012)

Towards a Secure RA2DL Based Approach

Farid Adaili[1,2,3(✉)], Olfa Mosbahi[1], Mohamed Khalgui[1,4],
and Samia Bouzefrane[3]

[1] LISI Laboratory, INSAT Institute, University of Carthage, Tunis, Tunisia
olfamosbahi@gmail.com, khalgui.mohamed@gmail.com
[2] Tunisia Polytechnic School, University of Carthage, Tunis, Tunisia
[3] CEDRIC Laboratory, National Conservatory of Arts and Crafts, Paris, France
{farid.adaili,samia.bouzefrane}@cnam.fr
[4] Systems Control Laboratory, Xidian University, Xian, China

Abstract. This chapter deals with secured reconfigurable AADL based-control component of embedded system (to be named by RA2DL) that should be adapted their behaviours to environment execution according to user requirements. For various reasons, we propose a new method denoted by $RA2DL - Pool$ for guarantee and control the security of RA2DL component. $RA2DL - Pool$ is a container of sets of RA2DL components characterized by similar properties. Also, it holds well-defined methods for grouping RA2DL components together. To consolidate $RA2DL - Pool$ technology, we will put a set of security-mechanisms divided into two families: (i) Authentication Mechanism where all users must authenticate to access to the reserved services of $RA2DL - Pool$ or RA2DL components and (ii) Access Control Mechanism to control the access to the RA2DL components. We model and verify this solution and develop a tool for its simulation by taking a real-case study dealing with the Body-Monitoring System (BMS) as a running example.

Keywords: Pooling · Component-based approach · Dynamic reconfiguration · Security · Authentication · Access control · RA2DL · Implementation · Modelling · Evaluation

1 Introduction

Nowadays in the academy and manufacturing industry, many research works have been made to deal with real-time reconfiguration of embedded control systems. The new generation of these systems are addressing today a new criteria such as flexibility and agility. To reduce their cost, these systems have to be changed and adapted to their environment without any disturbance. We are interested in this chapter in the reconfigurable AADL technology. AADL component is a software unit to be encoded with a set of algorithms that implement its control functions. Each algorithm is activated by corresponding external event-data inputs, and generally produces the results of its execution on corresponding data-event outputs.

© Springer International Publishing AG 2016
L.A. Maciaszek and J. Filipe (Eds.): ENASE 2016, CCIS 703, pp. 89–110, 2016.
DOI: 10.1007/978-3-319-56390-9_5

The usability of the embedded and reconfiguration technologies in the information systems is not only a concern of major corporations and governments but also an interest of individual users. Due to this wide use, many of these systems manage and store information that is considered sensitive, such as personal or business data. The need to have secured components for each system that contains such information becomes a necessity rather than an option [16]. The embedded components [17] are getting increasingly connected and are more and more involved in networked communications. The users of these components are now able to execute almost all the network/internet applications. These components are also increasingly involved in the transfer of secured data through public networks that need protection from unauthorized access. Thus the security requirements in embedded systems have become critical.

Traditional security research has been focusing on how to provide assurance on confidentiality, integrity, and availability [8]. However, with the exception of mobile code protection mechanisms, the focus of past research is not how to develop secured software that is made of components from different sources. Previous research provides necessary infrastructures, but a higher level perspective on how to use them to describe and enforce security, especially for component-based systems, has not received sufficient attention from research communities so far.

We define in a previous paper [10] a new concept of components named RA2DL as a solution for reconfigurable AADL components composed of controller and controlled modules. The first one is a set of reconfiguration functions applied in RA2DL to adapt its execution to any evolution in the environment, described by three reconfiguration forms:

(i) **Form 1:** Architectural level: modifies the component architecture when particular conditions are met. This is made by adding new algorithms, events and data or removing existing operations in the internal behaviors of the component.

(ii) **Form 2:** Compositional level: modifies the composition of the internal components (algorithms) for a given architecture.

(iii) **Form 3:** Data level: changes the values of variables without changing the component algorithms, and the second one is a set of input/output events, algorithms, and data as represented by reconfiguration modules.

However, securing an RA2DL component is not an easy task. With rapidly advancing hardware/software technologies and ubiquitous use of computerized applications [19], modern software is facing challenges that it has not seen before. More and more software is built from existing components which come from different sources. This complicates analysis and composition, even if a dominant decomposition mechanism is available. Additionally more and more software/hardware components are running in a networked environment. These network connections open possibilities for malicious attacks that were not possible in the past. These situations raise new challenges on how to handle security so that to design a component-based architecture that is more resistant to attacks and less vulnerable.

Facing the new challenges for security of reconfigurable RA2DL-based systems, we propose new solutions allowing the required authentification for the access control to components under a set of constraints such as the limitation in memory. These solutions are supported by a new concept called pool which is a container that gathers networked RA2DL under security constraints. The container allows the control of any operation allowing the reconfiguration of RA2DL components as well as the access to local algorithms and data.

The chapter's contribution is applied to a case study of an Body-Monitoring System (BMS) that will be followed as a running example. A tool is developed in a collaboration between LISI Lab at University of Carthage in Tunisia and CEDRIC Lab at CNAM in France to implement and simulate the security in the case study.

The current chapter is organized as follows: We discuss in Sect. 2 the originality of the chapter by studying the state of the art. Section 3 describes the background of RA2DL. Section 4 defines the new extension for secured RA2DL components. We expose in Sect. 5 the case study: Body-Monitoring System (BMS) and how the implementation is performed to secure RA2DL. Section 6 concludes the chapter and gives some perspectives as a future work.

2   State of the Art of Secured Component-Based Design Approaches

In this section, we present a state of the art of secured component-based design approaches. In [6], the authors present a classification of component-based systems by describing software components as independent units that interact to form a functional system. A component does not need/have to be compiled before it is used. Each component offers services to the rest of the system and adopts a provided interface that specifies the services that other components can use.

The authors in [19] present a treatment of an important security aspect, access control, at the architecture level and modeling of security subject, resource, privilege, safeguard, and policy of architectural constituents. The modeling language, Secure xADL, is based on the existing modular and extensible architecture description language.

In [7], the authors propose a QA (Quality Assurance) model for component-based software which covers component requirement analysis, component development, component certification, component customization, and system architecture design, integration, testing and maintenance. An extension of the Component Object Model (COM), Distributed COM (DCOM), is a protocol that enables software components to communicate directly over a network in a reliable, secure, and efficient manner. DCOM is designed for use across multiple network transports, including internet protocols such as HTTP. When a client and its component reside on different machines, DCOM simply replaces the local interprocess communication with a network protocol. Neither the client nor the component is aware of the changes of the physical connections.

In [9], Rugina et al. present an iterative dependency-driven approach for dependability modeling using AADL. This approach is a part of a complete framework that allows the generation of dependability analysis and evaluation models from AADL models to support the analysis of software and system architectures in critical application domains.

AADL and OSATE tools can be used to validate the security of systems designed using MILS4 architecture [11]. The work in [13] uses two mechanisms to modularize or divide and conquer in secure systems: partitions, and separation into layers. The MILS architecture isolates processes in partitions that define a collection of data objects, code, and system resources and can be evaluated separately. Each partition is divided into the following three layers: Separation Kernel Layer, Middleware Service Layer and Application Layer each of which is responsible for its own security domain and nothing else.

In [14], the author presents the extension UMLsec of UML that allows to express security relevant information within the diagrams in a system specification. UMLsec is defined as an UML profile using the standard UML extension mechanisms. In particular, the associated constraints give criteria to evaluate the security aspects of a system design by referring to a formal semantic of a simplified fragment of UML.

In [4], Bernstein define a Docker (www.docker.com) is an open source project providing a systematic way to automate the faster deployment of Linux applications inside portable containers. Basically, Docker extends LXC with a kernel- and application-level API that together run processes in isolation: CPU, memory, I/O, network, and so on. Docker also uses namespaces to completely isolate an applications view of the underlying operating environment, including process trees, network, user IDs, and file systems.

Docker containers are created using base images. A Docker image can include just the OS fundamentals, or it can consist of a sophisticated prebuilt application stack ready for launch. When building images with Docker, each action taken (that is, command executed, such as apt-get install) forms a new layer on top of the previous one. Commands can be executed manually or automatically using Dockerfiles.

Note that, no one in all related works deals with secured reconfigurable components. We propose in this chapter a new concept of security of RA2DL components to be named *RA2DL − Pool* that allows: (i) Grouping of RA2DL components that have the same similar properties. (ii) Associating to each *RA2DLPool* a security mechanism like authentication and access control mechanisms.

3   RA2DL Background

We defined in a previous paper [10] the concept of RA2DL components as an extension of reconfigurable AADL [21] (Architecture Analysis and Design Language). RA2DL as depicted in Fig. 1 is composed of controller and controlled modules where the first one is a set of reconfiguration functions applied in AADL, and the second one is a set of input/output events, algorithms, and data. The controlled module is described by the following four modules:

IEM (Input Events Module): This module processes the reconfiguration of input events (IE) stored in the $IEDB$ database of input events. It defines and activates at a particular time a subset of events to execute the corresponding algorithms in RA2DL.

OEM (Output Events Module): This module processes the reconfiguration of output events (OE) stored in the $OEDB$ database of output events. It defines and activates at a particular time a subset of events to be sent once the corresponding algorithms finish their execution in RA2DL.

ALM (Algorithms Module): This module processes the reconfiguration of the active algorithms (addition or removal) at a particular time in order to be coherent with active input and output events of IEM and OEM. These algorithms are stored in the $ALDB$ database of algorithms.

DM (Data Module): This module processes the reconfigurations of *data* in RA2DL in coherence with the rest of modules. It is stored in the DDB database of data values.

We focus on three hierarchical reconfiguration levels in RA2DL:

(i) Form 1: Architectural level: Deals with the changes of the architecture of the RA2DL component when particular conditions are satisfied. In this case, it is possible to add, remove or also change the internal behavior of the component in IEM, OEM, ALM and DM. We denote by Ψ_{Cmp} the big set in $ALDB$ of all the possible algorithms involved in the different implementations of the component Cmp, which is implemented at any particular time t by a subset ξ_{Cmp} that represents the set of algorithms involved in a particular implementation $\xi_{Cmp} \subseteq \Psi_{Cmp}$. We model the architectural level AL by a finite state machine $\mathbf{S}_{AL}$ such that each state of $\mathbf{S}_{AL}$ corresponds to a particular implementation of IEM, OEM, ALM and DM.

$\mathbf{S}_{AL} = (\Psi_{Cmp}, \mathbf{O}, \delta)$, where:

$\mathbf{O}$ is a set of n states in $\mathbf{S}_{AL}(\mathbf{O} = \{\mathbf{S}_{AL}^i \mid i \in 1..n\})$,
δ is a state-transition function $\Psi_{Cmp} \times \mathbf{O} \rightarrow \Psi_{Cmp} \times \mathbf{O}$.

(ii) Form 2: Compositional level: This level keeps the same architecture in Cmp but just changes the composition of algorithms, input-output events in order to adapt the component to its environment. It is formalized by different Composition State Machines CSM, such that each one CSM corresponds to a particular state in the Architecture Level S_{AL}. For each state S_{AL}^i in S_{AL}, we define in the second hierarchical level (Composition Level CL) a particular state machine to be denoted by S_{CL}^i. Each state in $S_{CL}^{i,j}$ in S_{CL}^i defines a particular composition of the subset of algorithms and input-output events. This composition affects a priority to each algorithm in order to get a deterministic execution model of the AADL component Cmp. We denote by $\Gamma(\delta_{Cmp})$ the set of all possible execution models of algorithms of δ_{Cmp} at the composition Level.

$\mathbf{S}_{CL} = (\Gamma(\delta_{Cmp}), \mathbf{P}, \gamma)$, where:

$\mathbf{P}$ is a set of m composition states in $\mathbf{S}_{CL}(\mathbf{P} = \{ \mathbf{S}^i_{CL} \mid i \in 1..m\})$,
γ is a state-transition function $\Gamma(\delta_{Cmp}) \times \mathbf{P} \to \Gamma(\delta_{Cmp}) \times \mathbf{P}$.

(iii) Form 3: Data level: A reconfiguration scenario $R^{i,j}_{CL}$ at Composition Level CL, is a transition from a state S^i_{CL} to another state S^i_{CL} of S_{CL}. The reconfiguration of the AADL component Cmp at the third hierarchical level DL corresponds to the update of *data*. We define for each state S^i_{AL} of S_{AL} and for each state S^j_{CL} of S_{CL} a new state machine S_{DL} where each state corresponds to new values to be affected to *data* belonging to μ_{Cmp} under the composition S^i_{CL}. Let $\Gamma(\mu_{Cmp})$ be the set of all possible values of data under the composition S^j_{CL}.

This level deals with the light reconfiguration of data of the RA2DL component. It is formalized by a set of Data State Machines where each state of them corresponds to particular values of data. We define for each state $\mathbf{S}^i_{AL}$ of $\mathbf{S}_{AL}$ and for each state $\mathbf{S}^{i,j}_{CL}$ of $\mathbf{S}^i_{CL}$ a new state machine $\mathbf{S}^{i,j,k}_{DL}$ where each state corresponds to new values of data.

$\mathbf{S}_{DL} = (\Gamma(\mu_{Cmp}), \mathbf{Q}, \vartheta)$, where:

$\mathbf{Q}$ is a set of k composition states in $\mathbf{S}_{DL}(\mathbf{Q} = \{ \mathbf{S}^i_{DL} \mid i \in 1..k\})$,
ϑ is a state-transition function $\Gamma(\mu_{Cmp}) \times \mathbf{Q} \to \Gamma(\mu_{Cmp}) \times \mathbf{Q}$.

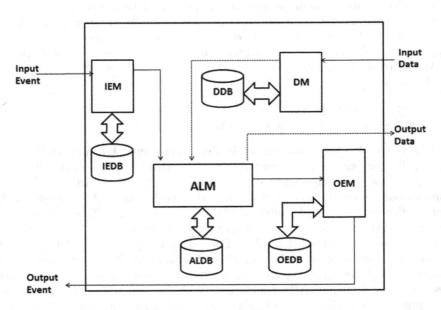

Fig. 1. Architecture of an RA2DL component.

In another extension in [1] for enhancing the execution of RA2DL components, a new execution model is proposed which is composed of three layers: **(i)
Middleware Reconfiguration level** that handles the input reconfiguration
flows, **(ii) Execution Controller level** to control the execution and reconfiguration of RA2DL and **(iii) Middleware Synchronization level** that controls
and manages the synchronization of the reconfiguration. Additionally, we proposed a new approach to coordinate several RA2DL components in a distributed
architecture based on a coordination matrix.

Because of the resource limitations in adaptive systems, satisfying a non-
functional requirement such as security requires careful balance and trade-off
with other properties and requirements of the system such as performance, memory usage and access rights of the RA2DL. This further emphasizes the fact that
security cannot be considered as a feature that is added later to the design of an
RA2DL component. It needs to be considered from early stages of development
and along with other requirements. In fact, the security by design approach as
defined by Ray and Cleaveland [18] in software engineering ensures that security is addressed at the point of conception to avoid the security vulnerabilities.
Considering the characteristics of RA2DL components, major impacts of security
features in these systems are based on performance, power consumption, flexibility, maintainability and cost [15]. Therefore in the design of RA2DL components,
implications of introducing security decisions should be taken into account and
analyzed. Several related works do not provide solutions to develop security of
RA2DL components of adaptive embedded systems. The current chapter proposes new extended solutions to secure an RA2DL component. However, in this
work we want to extend this study by considering a new architecture of secured
RA2DL-based pools.

4   New Extension for Secured RA2DL

In this section, we enrich RA2DL by security mechanisms that undergo such a
failure to enhance their execution and simulation.

4.1   Motivation: RA2DL-Pool

Security is an aspect that is often neglected in the design of adaptive systems. However, the use of these systems for critical applications such as controlling power plants, vehicular systems control, and medical devices [20] makes
security considerations even more important. Also because of the operational
environment of adaptive systems and the reconfiguration actions applied by an
RA2DL component. To allow the required security, we introduce the concept of
RA2DL − Pool as a container which is an abstract class that offers different services dealing with security, where each *RA2DL − Pool* has a level of sensitivity
of the information of its RA2DL components. *RA2DL − Pool* container serves

as a general purpose holder of other components. It holds well-defined methods for grouping RA2DL components together. $RA2DL - Pool$ is represented by the following elements:

- **Controller:** it is the crucial part of the pool that contains methods and represents firstly the interface between the user and the pool, and secondly between the pool and the RA2DL components,
- **Tables:** there are three kinds of tables: use table (UT), reconfiguration table (RT) and security table (ST),
- **Database:** is the database containing the sets of RA2DL components,
- **Reconfiguration Scenarios:** define the set of reconfiguration scenarios realized in pool or in its RA2DL components. Each scenario will be applied in relation with the three tables (UT, RT and ST),
- **RA2DL:** it is the RA2DL component with its algorithms and input/output ports.

Figure 2 reproduced from [2] presents the class diagram of $RA2DL - Pool$. An $RA2DL - Pool$ container holds a set of RA2DL components with a set of methods. This set of components has a set of methods that describe how to examine and add or delete components to the $RA2DL - Pool$. It contains the following methods described in Table 1 presented in [2].

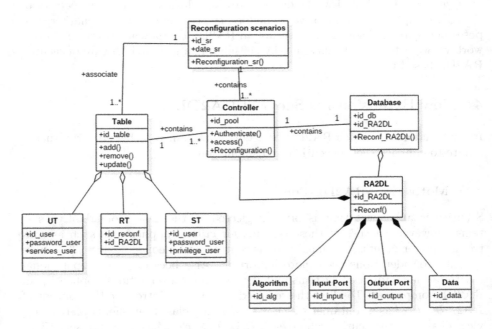

Fig. 2. Class diagram of RA2DL-Pool.

Table 1. RA2DL-pool methods.

Method	Description
getRA2DL ()	Number of components within the $RA2DL - Pool$
Component-getRA2DL(int position)	Component at the specific position
Component⌐ getRA2DL ()	Array of all the RA2DL components held within the container
RA2DL-add (Component RA2DL, int position)	Adds RA2DL component to $RA2DL - Pool$ at position
add (Component RA2DL, RA2DL constraints)	Layouts that require additional information
public void remove (int index)	Deletes the RA2DL at position index from the $RA2DL - Pool$
remove (RA2DL component)	Deletes the RA2DL from the $RA2DL - Pool$
removeAll ()	Removes all RA2DL from the $RA2DL - Pool$
boolean isAncestorOf (RA2DL)	Checks if the RA2DL is a parent of container
addContainerListener (pool)	Registers listener as a controller of RA2DL-Pool
removeContainerListener (pool)	Removes listener as an interested listener of RA2DL-Pool
processEvent (RA2DLEvent e)	Receives RA2DL events with $RA2DL - Pool$ as its target
addNotify ()	Creates the peer of all the components within it
removeNotify ()	Destroys the peer of RA2DL contained within it
Insetsgetinsets()	Gets the containers current insets
list()	Useful method to find out what is inside a container

4.2 Security Mechanisms for RA2DL

To consolidate the $RA2DL - Pool$ technology, we will put a set of security-mechanisms divided into two families are described in Fig. 3 reproduced from [2]:

Authentication Mechanism. This is a critical mechanism where all users must authenticate to access to the reserved services of $RA2DL - Pool$ or RA2DL components. This mechanism is always in relation with the user table (UT), where the columns u are the identifiers of users (id_user) and lines s represent the services ($services\_user$). To implement the authentication mechanism, we use **RADIUS** *(Remote Authentication Dial-In User Service)* is a client/server protocol that runs in the application layer developed by Livingston Enterprise [22], which is a networking protocol that provides centralized Authentication, Authorization, and Accounting (AAA) management for users who connect and use a network service. The principle of the authentication of an RA2DL with RADIUS is as follows:

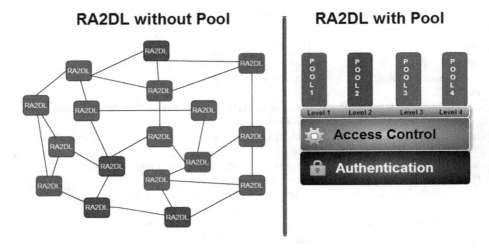

Fig. 3. Secured RA2DL method.

1. the *Controller* executes a connection request. *UT* table recovers the identification information,
2. the *Controller* transmits this information to the target service in RA2DL,
3. the target component receives the connection request from the *Controller*, controls and returns the configuration information required for the user to provide or deny access,
4. *Controller* refers to the user an error message if it fails an authentication.

Access Control Mechanism. This mechanism comes just after authentication to control the access to the RA2DL components. Two tables are used in this case: security and reconfiguration tables. The first one is the security table ST which contains in lines (p) all the user privileges ($privilege\_user$) and in columns (u) the (id_user). The second one is the reconfiguration table (RT) that contains in lines (r) reconfigurations identifiers (id_reconf) and in columns (c) the identifiers of RA2DL components (id_RA2DL).

This mechanism may be represented by a triplet (S, C, M_{sc}) where S denotes the service, C denotes the RA2DL component (or RA2DL-pool) and M_{sc} that maps each pair (C and S) to a set of access rights.

The matrix shown in Fig. 4 shows that the right of access r is associated with the service (Subject) S_j and C_j RA2DL component.

Figure 5 presents the sequencing of the interaction between the RA2DL components and the RA2DL-Pool. The main goal is to show this interaction and how to apply authentication and access control mechanisms.

Figure 6 highlights the activity of these two mechanisms and tests in order to achieve a secure RA2DL component.

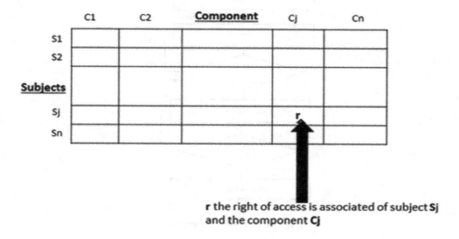

r the right of access is associated of subject **Sj**
and the component **Cj**

Fig. 4. Access control matrix.

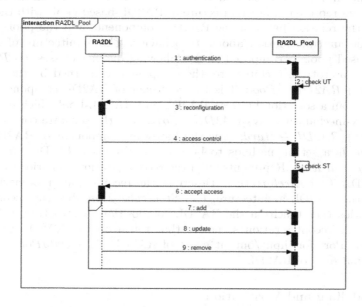

Fig. 5. Sequence diagram.

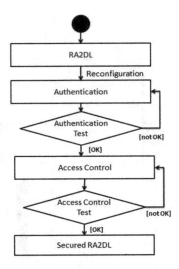

Fig. 6. Activity diagram.

4.3   Architecture of Secured RA2DL-Based Pools

We present in Fig. 7 the class diagram of the secured RA2DL-based pool. This diagram represents the architecture of RA2DL-based pools with the static aspect of the relation between the RA2DL components and the pool. It does not provide any information about its behavior. The architecture of secured RA2DL-based pools is composed of the following distinct classes: (i) *RA2DL*: The main class of the architecture, the component concerned by the security concept, (ii) *RA2DL − Pool*: It is the container of RA2DL components, (iii) *Security*: Is an association between RA2DL and RA2DL-Pool which represents the security-mechanisms, (iv) *RA2DL − Soft*: It is the software component of RA2DL, (v) *RA2DL − Hard*: It is the hardware component of RA2DL, (vi) *Algorithm*: Is a set of methods to be executed by each RA2DL component, (vii)*Reconfiguration*: Represents all of the reconfiguration scenarios to execute with RA2DL, (viii) *Architecture*: Describes the reconfiguration scenarios that touch on the RA2DL architecture, (ix) *Structure*: Describes the reconfiguration scenarios that touch on the RA2DL composition or structure, (x) *Data*: Describes the reconfiguration scenarios that touch on the RA2DL data, (xi) *EventPort*: Port for input/output event of RA2DL, (xii) *DataPort*: Port for input/output data of RA2DL.

4.4   Modelling and Verification

We propose in this section the modelling and verification of the new architecture of secured RA2DL-based pools by using UPPAAL [3]. Firstly, we model the pool with its security aspect. Secondly we check a set of properties to ensure the security of the pool.

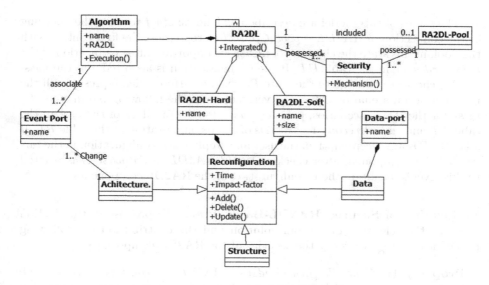

Fig. 7. Architecture of a secured RA2DL-based pool.

Modelling of Secured RA2DL-Based Pool. We propose in Fig. 8 Finite State Machine-based models of RA2DL-based Pool in order to show the interaction between the various states and to verify also some properties defined in user requirements. We present in the following a description of all the states and transitions characterizing this model. RA2DL-Pool is assumed to be a set of timed automaton, that run in parallel and communicate thanks to global variables.

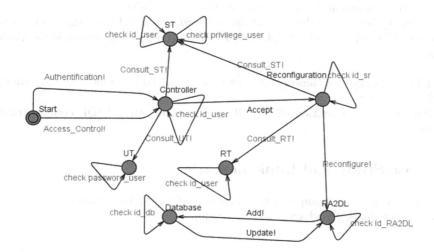

Fig. 8. Modelling of secured RA2DL-Based pools.

The states of this model are described as follows: *start* to start the querying or the connection of $RA2DL - pool$. *Controller* represents the first contact with the pool, in this state the checking of *id_user* is important after verification of the *password_user* in the table *UT*. If the authentication is accepted and the password is checked, it can go to the state *Reconfiguration* which represents all the reconfiguration scenarios. After the verification of the following parameters: (i) *id_sr* for the IDs of scenarios, *privilege_user* for the privilege of the user in the table *ST* and (iii) *id_reconf* for the IDs of the reconfiguration in the table *RT*. If all of the IDs are accepted, then the user may apply the reconfiguration in the target *RA2DL* component after checking the *id_RA2DL*. A *database* is associated to this level to facilitate the reconfiguration of the RA2DL components.

Verification of Secured RA2DL-Based Pool. We propose in this section to check the relevance of the our solution and the contribution the following properties in order to verify the security of the RA2DL components.

- **Property 1:** *(Controller[].check id_user)AND (UT[].check passeword_user):* for each connection with the pool, we should check the user authentification by using the UT table,
- **Property 2:** *(Reconfiguration[].check id_sr) AND (RT[].check id_reconf):* before the execution of any reconfiguration scenario, it is important to check if it is registered in the reconfiguration table (RT),
- **Property 3:** *(Reconfiguration[].Reconfigure!* $\Rightarrow$ *RA2DL[].check id_RA2DL) AND (ST[].check privilege_user):* this property concerns the verification of the access control mechanism,
- **Property 4:** *RA2DL[].save* $\Rightarrow$ *Database[].check id_db*: each RA2DL component should be imperatively saved in a *Database* to facilitate the use of RA2DL components and to minimize the execution time,
- **Property 5:** *(Controller[] AND Reconfiguration[] AND RA2DL[] AND Database[] AND ST[] AND RT[] AND UT[]) not deadlock:* the system is deadlock-free.

The verification of these properties is summarized in Table 2 already shown in [2].

We show the validation of the all properties of our RA2DL component in Fig. 9.

5   Case Study and Implementation

We use as a running example in the current chapter the body-monitoring system (BMS) to evaluate the chapter's contribution.

Table 2. Verification results.

Property	Result	Calculation time (sec)	Consumed memory (Mo)
Property 1	True	10.52	5.72
Property 2	True	9.12	4.82
Property 3	True	5.32	3.20
Property 4	True	13.25	6.56
Property 5	True	8.23	4.37

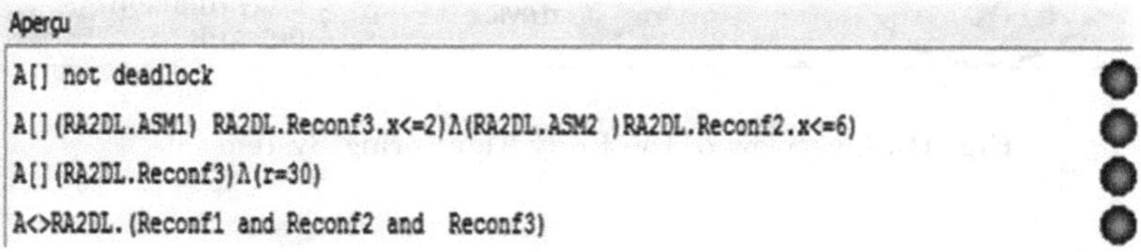

Aperçu

```
A[] not deadlock
A[] (RA2DL.ASM1)  RA2DL.Reconf3.x<=2)A(RA2DL.ASM2 )RA2DL.Reconf2.x<=6)
A[] (RA2DL.Reconf3)A(r=30)
A<>RA2DL.(Reconf1 and Reconf2 and  Reconf3)
```

Fig. 9. Validation properties.

5.1 Case Study: Body-Monitoring System (BMS)

During the last few years there has been a significant increase in the number and variety of wearable health monitoring devices ranging from simple pulse monitors, activity monitors, and portable Holter monitors, to sophisticated and expensive implantable sensors. The Body-Monitoring System (BMS) [12] is designed as a mobile device that is able to collect measured data and to act according to instructions set by a supervisor. The system consists of a body-monitoring network. In order to recognise the monitored person's state, the monitor unit connects to various body sensors and i/o devices by using either wired or wireless communication technologies. Data from all sensors are collected, stored and analysed at real-time and, according to the analysis, actions may then be performed. A computer is used as an interface to the body-monitoring network, and developed software allow a supervisor to configure the monitor unit for the monitored person, to connect sensors and i/o devices, define and upload instructions for monitoring and download collected data describe in Fig. 10 reproduced from [2].

The monitor unit software consists of a communication module (responsible for connecting and controlling sensors, and for gathering and pre-processing measured data), a storage module (for storage of collected data), and a policy interpretation module responsible of controlling the behaviour of the monitor unit according to instructions defined by a supervisor.

Two types of drivers are introduced. The role of a communication driver is to hide the way in which data is transmitted. There is one driver for every type of communication interface, e.g. a Bluetooth driver or an IEEE 802.11b driver. The communication driver does not care about the data itself; this is the role of device drivers. Each type of sensor has its own device driver. When a device

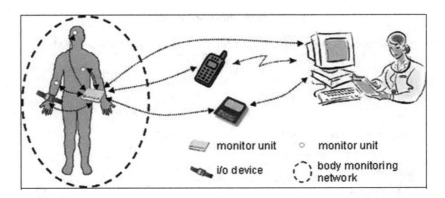

Fig. 10. Overview of the Body Monitoring System [5].

driver receives a message from one of its sensors it decodes the message and informs the policy engine about the state of the sensor. To send/receive a message to/from a sensor, the device driver uses the corresponding communication driver.

To secure this system, we must take into account these steps: (i) make the grouping of RA2DL components according to similar characteristics in RA2DL-Pool. (ii) assign for each RA2DL-pool a security level (depending on the degree of importance of the RA2DL components that they contain). (iii) allocate for each RA2DL-pool a security mechanism.

Running Example: We group the RA2DL components of BMS system in five RA2DL-Pools as shown in Fig. 11. (i) **RA2DL-Pool 1:** includes the following RA2DL components: *RA2DL-G* for the Glucose detection, *RA2DL-C* for the chloride detection and *RA2DL-W* for the water detection. (ii) **RA2DL-Pool 2:** includes the following RA2DL components: *RA2DL-L* for the lactate detection and *RA2DL-PH* for the PH detection. (iii) **RA2DL-Pool 3:** includes the following RA2DL components: *RA2DL-DM* for the Diabetes mellitus detection and the *RA2DL-BP* for the Blood pressure. (iv) **RA2DL-Pool 4:** contains the display device which is the component *RA2DL-Mobil.* (v) **RA2DL-Pool 5:** contains the *RA2DL-Soft* for the transmission of data with a protocol until *RA2DL-Mobil.*

5.2 Implementation

We present in this section the tool of the BMS system that we developed in LISI Laboratory at INSAT Institute of University of Carthage in Tunisia and CEDRIC Laboratory at National Conservatory of Arts and Crafts of Paris in France. Figure 12 reproduced from [10] shows the tool offers the possibility to create all reconfiguration scenarios of the RA2DL component (addition, removal and update of algorithms, events and data) when any problem occurs.

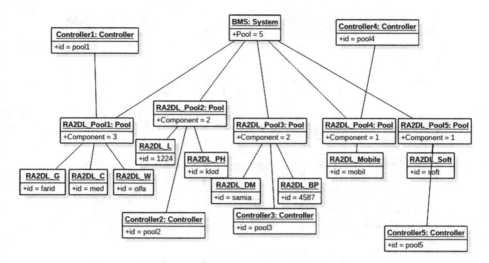

Fig. 11. Object diagram of BMS.

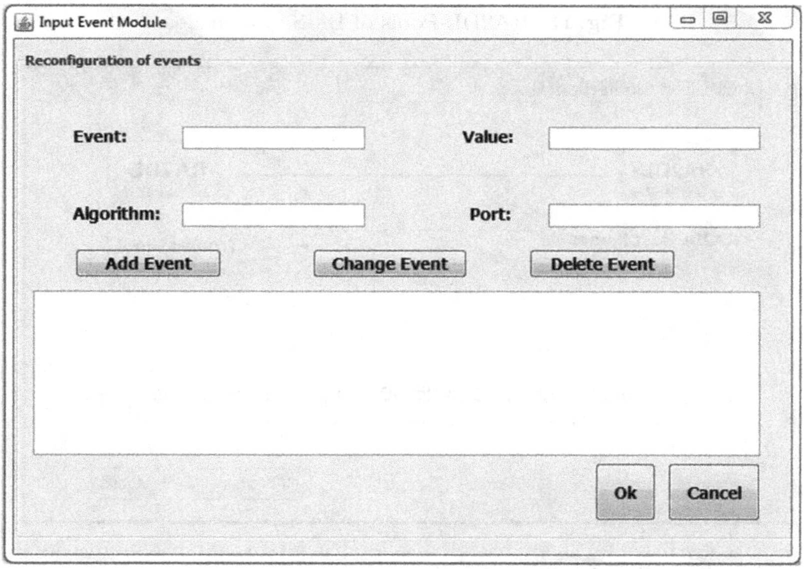

Fig. 12. Interface for reconfiguration architecture of RA2DL.

We assume five pools with their parameters such as the number of RA2DL components in pool, Worst Case Execution Time (WCET), the authentication and the access control mechanisms (Fig. 13).

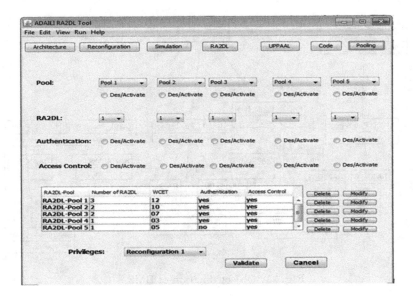

Fig. 13. RA2DL-Pools of BMS system.

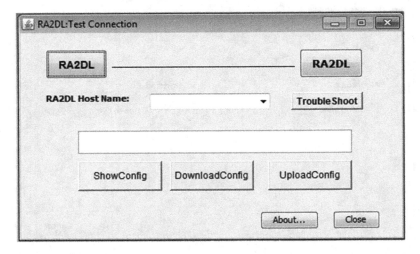

Fig. 14. Test of authentification mechanism.

Figure 14 reproduced from [2] shows the connectivity test of the different pools according to the authentication mechanisms and also to check the configuration between the various RA2DL components in each pool.

Running Example: The application of our approach to the BMS case study is illustrated in Table 3 reproduced from [2], where we give a security level (S.L)

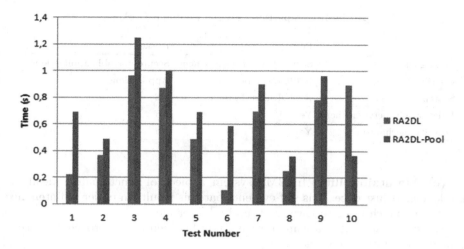

Fig. 15. Result of evaluation.

Table 3. Running example.

	Security level	Authentication mechanism	Access control mechanism	Security
Pool 1	1	No	Yes	Yes
Pool 2	2	Yes	No	Yes
Pool 3	6	Yes	Yes	Yes
Pool 4	5	Yes	Yes	Yes
Pool 5	5	Yes	Yes	Yes

for the five pools depending on the sensitivity of the comprising components. In the BMS system, the RA2DL-pool 3 is the most secured and RA2DL-pool 1 is the less secured one. Both security mechanisms are applied to the five pools.

5.3   Evaluation

This section is devoted mainly to test our approach and evaluate the execution time. Ten assessments are applied to the two mechanisms that are focused on two stolen: RA2DL without pool and RA2DL with pool of the BMS system. We show in Fig. 15 reproduced from [2] the results of the evaluation. We are interested in response time gains for secured and not secured RA2DL components.

The proposed approach has the following advantages:

(a) **Functionality:** RA2DL component in $RA2DL - Pool$ are at a functional level much more adaptable and extendable than traditional RA2DL components.

(b) **Reusability:** A reusability is an important characteristic of a high-quality RA2DL component. Programmers should design and implement RA2DL components in such a way that many different programs can reuse them.

Table 4. Comparison between Pool and Docker.

	Pool	Docker
Main goal	Secure RA2DL Component	Secure portable applications
Continent	RA2DL component	Applications
System	RA2DL-Based system	OS
Relationship between them	Yes	No
Security mechanism	Yes	No

(c) **Maintainability:** In BMS system a piece of functionality ideally is implemented just once. It is self-evident that this results in easier maintenance of system, which leads to lower cost, and a longer life.

We shows in Table 4 a comparative study between our approach *Pool* containers and *Docker* containers.

The RA2DL-Pool is a solution to secure in run-time each RA2DL component-based systems. By this solution the RA2DL component has become dynamic and secured. None of the existing works has treated the security of the RA2DL components as our method did.

6   Conclusion

Our work consisted, through this chapter, in proposing a novel approach for a required security in adaptive RA2DL control component based systems, to model and verify security control systems sharing adaptive resources. Whence, we chose to enhance RA2DL component to support security check. We proposed, then, a new and original solution to securing RA2DL component. Firstly, we define a new grouping methodology entitled RA2DL-Pool which has its own methods for the grouping of RA2DL components according to their similarities and security techniques. Secondly, we propose two crucial mechanisms to control the security in RA2DL-Pool: Authentication and access control mechanism. The relevance of our solution was proved thanks to model-checking using UPPAAL tool. This approach is original since RA2DL-Pool is a new formalism dedicated to secure RA2DL based control component.

The next step is to apply this contribution on Body-Monitoring system (BMS) by the grouping of these RA2DL components in RA2DL-Pool, we assign for each Pool a sensitivity level of these components. We plan in the future works to study the flexibility of RA2DL component in the network that links different devices of RA2DL-based systems. This work will be extended for different real-time aspects of RA2DL or in the run-time tests of components once deployed on the target devices.

References

1. Adaili, F., Mosbahi, O., Khalgui, M., Bouzefrane, S.: New solutions for useful execution models of communicating adaptive RA2DL. In: Fujita, H., Guizzi, G. (eds.) SoMeT 2015. CCIS, vol. 532, pp. 87–101. Springer, Cham (2015). doi:10.1007/978-3-319-22689-7_7
2. Adaili, F., Mosbahi, O., Khalgui, M., Bouzefrane, S.: Ra2dl-pool: new useful solution to handle security of reconfigurable embedded systems. In: Proceedings of the 11th International Conference on Evaluation of Novel Software Approaches to Software Engineering (ENASE), pp. 102–111, Rome, Italy (2016)
3. Bengtsson, J., Larsen, K., Larsson, F., Pettersson, P., Yi, W.: UPPAAL — a tool suite for automatic verification of real-time systems. In: Alur, R., Henzinger, T.A., Sontag, E.D. (eds.) HS 1995. LNCS, vol. 1066, pp. 232–243. Springer, Heidelberg (1996). doi:10.1007/BFb0020949
4. Bernstein, D.: Containers and cloud: from LXC to docker to kubernetes. IEEE Cloud Comput. 1(3), 81–84 (2014)
5. Bieliková, M.: A body-monitoring system with EEG and EOG sensors. J. ERCIM News 49, 50–52 (2002)
6. Brereton, P., Budgen, D.: Component-based systems: a classification of issues. Computer 33(11), 54–62 (2000)
7. Xia Cai, M.R., Lyu, Wong, K.-F., Ko, R.: Component-based software engineering: technologies, development frameworks, and quality assurance schemes. In: Seventh Asia-Pacific Software Engineering Conference (APSEC 2000), Proceedings, pp. 372–379 (2000)
8. Clements, P.C.: A survey of architecture description languages. In: Proceedings of the 8th International Workshop on Software Specification and Design (IWSSD 1996), p. 16, Washington, DC, USA. IEEE Computer Society (1996)
9. Rugina, A.E., Kanoun, K., Kaâniche, M.: An architecture-based dependability modeling framework using AADL. In: 10th IASTED International Conference on Software Engineering and Applications (SEA 2006) (2006)
10. Adaili, F., Mosbahi, O., Khalgui, M., Bouzefrane, S.: Ra2dl: new flexible solution for adaptive AADL-based control components. In: Proceedings of the 5th International Conference on Pervasive and Embedded Computing and Communication Systems, pp. 247–258 (2015)
11. Hansson, J., Feiler, P.H., Morley, J.: Building secure systems using model-based engineering and architectural models. CrossTalk J. Defense Softw. Eng. 21(9), 12 (2008)
12. Husemann, D., Steinbugler, R., Striemer, B.: Body monitoring using local area wireless interfaces. US Patent Ap. 10/406,865, 7 October 2004
13. Oman, P., Alves-Foss, J., Harrison, W.S., Taylor, C.: The MILS architecture for high assurance embedded systems. Int. J. Embedded Syst. 2, 239–247 (2006)
14. Jürjens, J.: UMLsec: extending UML for secure systems development. In: Jézéquel, J.-M., Hussmann, H., Cook, S. (eds.) UML 2002. LNCS, vol. 2460, pp. 412–425. Springer, Heidelberg (2002). doi:10.1007/3-540-45800-X_32
15. Kocher, P., Lee, R., McGraw, G., Raghunathan, A.: Security as a new dimension in embedded system design. In: Proceedings of the 41st Annual Design Automation Conference (DAC 2004), New York, NY, USA, pp. 753–760. ACM (2004). Moderator-Ravi, Srivaths

16. Mouratidis, H., Kolp, M., Faulkner, S., Giorgini, P.: A secure architectural description language for agent systems. In: Proceedings of the Fourth International Joint Conference on Autonomous Agents and Multiagent Systems (AAMAS 2005), New York, NY, USA, pp. 578–585. ACM (2005)

17. Anoop, M.S.: Security needs in embedded systems. Cryptology ePrint Archive, Report 2008/198 (2008). http://eprint.iacr.org/

18. Ray, A., Cleaveland, R.: A software architectural approach to security by design. In: 30th Annual International Computer Software and Applications Conference (COMPSAC 2006), Chicago, Illinois, USA, 17–21 September, vol. 2, pp. 83–86 (2006)

19. Ren, J., Taylor, R.: A secure software architecture description language. In: Workshop on Software Security Assurance Tools, Techniques, and Metrics, pp. 82–89 (2005)

20. Salem, M.O., Ben Mosbahi, O., Khalgui, M., Frey, G.: ZiZo: modeling, simulation and verification of reconfigurable real-time control tasks sharing adaptive resources - application to the medical project bros. In: Proceedings of the International Conference on Health Informatics, pp. 20–31 (2015)

21. Vergnaud, T., Pautet, L., Kordon, F.: Using the AADL to describe distributed applications from middleware to software components. In: Vardanega, T., Wellings, A. (eds.) Ada-Europe 2005. LNCS, vol. 3555, pp. 67–78. Springer, Heidelberg (2005). doi:10.1007/11499909_6

22. Yoon, E.-J., Lee, W.-S., Yoo, K.-Y.: Secure PAP-based RADIUS protocol in wireless networks. In: Huang, D.-S., Heutte, L., Loog, M. (eds.) ICIC 2007. CCIS, vol. 2, pp. 689–694. Springer, Heidelberg (2007). doi:10.1007/978-3-540-74282-1_77

AHR: Human-Centred Aspects of Test Design

Maria Spichkova[1($\boxtimes$)] and Anna Zamansky[2]

[1] School of Science (Computer Science and IT), RMIT University,
414-418 Swanston Street, Melbourne 3001, Australia
`maria.spichkova@rmit.edu.au`
[2] Information Systems Department, University of Haifa,
Carmel Mountain, 31905 Haifa, Israel
`annazam@is.haifa.ac.il`

Abstract. To apply model-based testing successfully and effectively, a complete, coherent and easy-to-read *model* of a system has to be constructed. If the model is incomplete, inconsistent or inaccurate due to human error, the corresponding test development becomes useless or even dangerous: the developers might rely on the test results that do not correctly reflect the actual system-under-test. In this chapter we discuss human-centred aspects of model-based test design, focusing on combinatorial testing. These aspects are implemented within a formal framework for combinatorial test design. The framework is called AHR by its core features: Agile, Human-centred and Refinement-oriented. The goal of the framework is to provide a human-centered iterative, refinement-based construction of system models and the corresponding test plans, as well as to supports reuse and refinement of the developed test plans at different levels of abstraction.

Keywords: Testing · Usability · Combinatorial test design · Visualisation · Formal methods

1 Introduction

The advantage of model-based testing (MBT) is that the testers can concentrate on system model and constraints instead of the manual specification of individual tests, cf. [3,7]. MBT heavily relies on *models* of a system and its environment to derive test cases for the system [30]. Thus, if the model is incomplete, inconsistent or inaccurate due to human error, the corresponding test development becomes useless or even dangerous: the developers might rely on the test results that do not correctly reflect the actual system-under-test.

A model is an *abstraction* of the system, where the goal of abstraction is to focus the core aspects of the system required for analysis at the corresponding development stage, while hiding the complexity of a system and its environment. Often it is not enough to have a single level of abstraction, i.e., several refinement steps may be required, each time using a more detailed representation of the system, cf. also [19]. Development methodologies for complex systems therefore often integrate different abstraction levels of the system representation. For each level the following crucial questions have to

© Springer International Publishing AG 2016
L.A. Maciaszek and J. Filipe (Eds.): ENASE 2016, CCIS 703, pp. 111–128, 2016.
DOI: 10.1007/978-3-319-56390-9_6

be answered: (1) Do we require the whole representation of a system to analyse its core properties? (2) What test cases are required on this particular level of abstraction? (3) How do we represent the system at this level to increase the readability and understandability of the model, as well as to increase the testability of the system?

In most cases, at different stages of the development cycle the developers have to design, analyse, implement and test different behaviour aspects of the system. This leads to the need for handling multiple abstraction levels and a systematic way of bridging between them. However, to provide an adequate model with an sufficient abstraction remains a strictly human activity, which heavily relies on the human factor. Construction of complex models at several levels of abstraction heavily relies on the knowledge of humans working in the role of software and system engineers (performing modelling and testing tasks). This task is highly complex and error-prone, as all as has a creative nature. Thus, there is a pressing need for human-centred MBT approaches, allowing not only a (semi-)automatic support but also increasing readability and understandability of the models and tests (i.e., covering the cognitive aspects of modelling and testing).

Contributions: The aim of our work is to lay the foundations for a human-centric support for the tester in model construction and test design in MBT settings. To this end we further extend and refine AHR, a formal framework which we proposed in [24–27]. The name AHR is derived from the core features of our framework: **A**gile, **H**uman-centred, and **R**efinement-oriented. The goal of the framework is to provide a human-centered iterative, refinement-based construction of system models and the corresponding test plans, as well as to support reuse and refinement of the developed test plans at different levels of abstraction by semi-automatic analysis of the model and the test plans. The framework

- allows for reusing test plans developed for an abstract level at more concrete levels;
- supports providing queries and alerts whenever the specified test plan is incomplete or invalid;
- supports analysis of constructed models.

The presented in this chapter approach extends our work introduces at the 11th International Conference on Evaluation of Novel Software Approaches to Software Engineering [24], and is also based on our recent on MBT [25] visual logical languages for system modelling in combinatorial test design [27]. In this chapter we focus on the aspect of refinement in the AHR framework and demonstrate its usefulness in the context of combinatorial test design. In the same context we further extend the framework with new features, namely visualisation of spatial parameters and traceability support.

Outline: The rest of the chapter is organised as follows. Section 2 introduces general ideas of a special kind of MBT, Combinatorial Test Design (CTD), as well as presents the corresponding formal background. Section 3 provides the formal definitions that build the core of AHR to support CTD within multiple abstraction levels. In Sect. 4 we discuss possible applications the AHR framework, including traceability support, and provide examples of use cases. Section 5 introduces the core AHR features for analysis and visualisation of spatial system properties. In Sect. 6 we discuss the related work and the corresponding motivation for the AHR development. In Section 7 we summarise the chapter and propose some directions for future research.

2   Combinatorial Test Design: Formal Background

Combinatorial Test Design (CTD, also called Combinatorial Interaction Testing) is an effective MBT approach that can be applied for testing of complex software systems, cf. also [32]. CTD focuses on testing the system-under-test (SUT) having a covering array test suite, which should cover all the combinations of the required parameter values. As highlighted by Nie and Leung [12], one of the core advantage of CTD is that this testing approach can detect failures triggered by the interactions among parameters in system-under-test.

As this approach is *model-based*, we can test only the system behaviour that is encoded in the model, and the system model has to be complete, coherent, easy-to-read and easy-to-understand for a human tester. The core artefacts in CTD to model the system behaviour are

- a finite set of parameters $\mathcal{A} = \{\mathcal{A}_1, \ldots, \mathcal{A}_n\}$,
- their respective values $\mathcal{V} = \{\mathcal{V}(\mathcal{A}_1), \ldots, \mathcal{V}(\mathcal{A}_n)\}$,
- and restrictions on the value combinations (system constraints).

In what follows we use the notion of *interactions* between the different values of the parameters and the notion of test coverage. We also assume that all the system parameters are mutually independent, i.e., none of the parameter values is determined by the value(s) of any of other parameters.

Definition 1. *An interaction for a set of system parameters $\mathcal{A}$ is an element of the form $I \subseteq \bigcup_1^n \mathcal{V}(\mathcal{A}_i)$, where at most one value of each parameter $\mathcal{A}_i$ may appear.*

Definition 2. *A test (or scenario) is an interaction of size n, where n is the number of system parameters.*

Definition 3. *A set of tests (scenarios) $\mathcal{T}$ covers a set of interactions C (denoted by $\mathcal{T} \square \mapsto C$) if for every $c \in C$ there is some $t \in \mathcal{T}$, such that $c \subseteq t$.*

Definition 4. *A combinatorial model $\mathcal{E}$ of a system with the corresponding set of parameters $\mathcal{A}$ is a set of tests (scenarios), which defines all tests over $\mathcal{A}$ that are executable in the system.*

Definition 5. *A test plan is a triple Plan $= (\mathcal{E}, C, \mathcal{T})$, where $\mathcal{E}$ is a combinatorial model, C is a set of interactions called coverage requirements, $\mathcal{T}$ is a set tests, and the relation $\mathcal{T} \square \mapsto C$ holds.*

The main challenge of CTD is to optimise the number of test cases, while ensuring the coverage of given conditions. One of the most standard coverage requirements is *pairwise testing* [12], where every (executable) pair of possible values of system parameters is considered. Experimental work shows that using tests sets with exhaustive covering of a small number of parameters (such as pairwise testing) can typically detect more than 50–75% of the bugs in a program, cf. [10,28]. This testing approach can be applied at different phases and scopes of testing, including end-to-end and system-level testing and feature-, service- and application program interface-level testing.

In the above terms, a pairwise test plan can be specified as any pair of the form

$$Plan = (\mathcal{E}, C_{pair}(\mathcal{E}), \mathcal{T})$$

where C_{pair} is the set of all interactions of size 2 which can be extended to scenarios from $\mathcal{E}$.

Example 1. For a running example scenario, let us consider a cyber-physical system with two robots R_1 and R_2 that are interacting with each other to carry an object O together. At some level of abstraction (let us call it $Level_1$), a robot can be modelled by two parameters, GM and P, representing the mode of its grippers as well as the position of the robot within the safe-work cage. The object is then modelled only by its position P_0. Thus, the system of two robots would have five parameters:

$$\mathcal{A} = \{GM_1, GM_2, P_0, P_1, P_2\}$$

The system parameters GM_1 and GM_2 specify the gripper modes (which can be either closed to hold an object or open) of robots R_1 and R_2 respectively. Let us consider that at this level of abstraction the gripper have only two modes:

$$\mathcal{V}(GM_1) = \mathcal{V}(GM_2) = \{open, closed\}$$

P_0, P_1 and P_2 represent the positions of the object and the robots. We assume at this level of abstraction that they can be only in four possible positions:

$$\mathcal{V}(P_0) = \mathcal{V}(P_1) = \mathcal{V}(P_2) = \{pos_1, pos_2, pos_3, pos_4\}$$

where the position values have the following ordering $pos_1 < pos_2 < pos_3 < pos_4$ (one-dimensional space is assumed on this level of abstraction), and

$$pos_2 = pos_1 + 1$$
$$pos_3 = pos_2 + 1 = pos_1 + 2$$
$$pos_4 = pos_3 + 1 = pos_2 + 2 = pos_1 + 3$$

In what follows let us assume *pairwise coverage requirements*. We now specify a meta-operation $Carry(A, B, O)$ to model the scenario when the robots A and B carry an object O together, where $A, B \in \{R_1, R_2\}$ and $A \neq B$. The meta-operation $Carry(A, B, O)$ can only be performed when the following constraints are satisfied:

– *Constraint 1*: The object is located exactly between the robots (i.e., the object is located between the robots, and there is no empty position between the object and any of the robots),
– *Constraint 2*: The grippers of both robots are closed.

Note that to specify the *Constraint 1* precisely, it would be not enough to have a restriction $P_A < P_0 < P_B$, as it does not exclude the situation where the object is located between the robots, but there is no empty position between the object and one of the robots, e.g., $P_A = pos_1$, $P_0 = pos_2$, and $P_B = pos_4$. Figure 1 presents four examples of

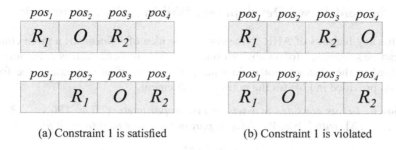

(a) Constraint 1 is satisfied   (b) Constraint 1 is violated

Fig. 1. $Level_1$: Four examples of locations of the robots in the safe-work cage.

location of the robots in the safe-work cage: two location w ith Constraint 1 satisfied, and two location with Constraint 1 violated.

Thus, the operation $Carry(R_1, O, R_2)$ can be captured on $Level_1$ in the following constraint model $M^1_{Carry(R_1,O,R_2)}$:

$$P_0 = P_1 + 1 \wedge P_2 = P_0 + 1 \ \wedge \ GM_1 = closed \ \wedge \ GM_2 = closed \tag{1}$$

where the operation $Carry(R_2, O, R_1)$ can be captured on $Level_1$ in the constraint model $M^1_{Carry(R_2,O,R_1)}$:

$$P_0 = P_2 + 1 \wedge P_1 = P_0 + 1 \ \wedge \ GM_1 = closed \ \wedge \ GM_2 = closed \tag{2}$$

Without any constraints, we would require 256 tests to cover all possible combinations of the parameter values ($2 \times 2 \times 4 \times 4 \times 4$), but considering the full coverage of both $M^1_{Carry(R_1,O,R_2)}$ and $M^1_{Carry(R_2,O,R_1)}$, we require two tests only, cf. Table 1:

– $test_1$ and $test_1 2$ cover $Carry(R_1, O, R_2)$, and
– $test_3$ and $test_4$ cover $M^1_{Carry(R_2,O,R_1)}$

At the next level of abstraction, $Level_2$, we might refine both the set of parameters $\mathcal{A}$ and their corresponding values $\mathcal{V}$ to obtain a more realistic model of the system. In the next section, we introduce the notion of parameter and value refinements, which provides an explicit specification of the relations between abstraction levels to allow traceability of the model modification and the corresponding test sets.

Table 1. Test set providing full coverage for both $Carry(R_1, O, R_2)$ and $M^1_{Carry(R_2,O,R_1)}$ on $Level_1$.

testID	P_1	P_0	P_2	GM_1	GM_2
$test_1$	pos_1	pos_2	pos_3	closed	closed
$test_2$	pos_2	pos_3	pos_4	closed	closed
$test_3$	pos_3	pos_2	pos_1	closed	closed
$test_4$	pos_4	pos_3	pos_1	closed	closed

3   Refinement-Based Development Within AHR Framework

One of the key features of AHR framework is the idea of *refinement*: a more concrete model can be substituted for an abstract one as long as its behaviour is consistent with that defined in the abstract model. In what follows we refine and extend the formal definitions provided in [24] for the notion of refinement.

Definition 6. *Let us consider two sets of system parameters* $\mathcal{A} = \{\mathcal{A}_1, \ldots, \mathcal{A}_n\}$ *and* $\mathcal{B} = \{\mathcal{B}_1, \ldots, \mathcal{B}_k\}$, *with* $k \geq n$. *We define a parameter refinement from* $\mathcal{A}$ *to* $\mathcal{B}$

$$\mathcal{A} \rightsquigarrow \mathcal{B}$$

as a function $\mathcal{R}$ *that maps each parameter* $\mathcal{A}_i$ *to a set of parameters from* $\mathcal{B}$, *so that for two distinct parameters* $\mathcal{A}_i$ *and* $\mathcal{A}_j$, $1 \leq i, j \leq n$, $i \neq j$, *the sets* $\mathcal{R}(\mathcal{A}_i)$ *and* $\mathcal{R}(\mathcal{A}_j)$ *are disjoint.*

Definition 7. *For a parameter refinement* $\mathcal{R} : \mathcal{A} \rightsquigarrow \mathcal{B}$, *a value refinement*

$$\mathcal{V}_R : \mathcal{V}(A) \rightsquigarrow \mathcal{V}(\mathcal{B})$$

maps each value $v \in \mathcal{V}(\mathcal{A}_i)$ *to the corresponding set of values* $\mathcal{V}_R(v)$, *where*

$$\mathcal{V}_R(v) \subseteq \bigcup_{\mathcal{B} \in R(\mathcal{A}_i)} \mathcal{V}(\mathcal{B})$$

such that if $\mathcal{B}_j \in \mathcal{R}(\mathcal{A}_i)$, *then for every* $v \in \mathcal{V}(\mathcal{A}_i)$, $\mathcal{V}(\mathcal{B}_j) \cap \mathcal{V}_R(v) \neq \emptyset$.

The above definitions do not exclude the case where both $\mathcal{R}$ and $\mathcal{V}_R$ are singleton functions, i.e. functions that convert each element a to a singleton $\{a\}$. For this reason we have to introduce the notion of concretisation.

Definition 8. *If there exist parameter refinement* $\mathcal{R}$ *and value refinement* $\mathcal{V}_R$ *from a set of system parameters* $\mathcal{A}$ *to a set of system parameters* B *(where at least one of the functions* $\mathcal{R}$ *and* $\mathcal{V}_R$ *is not a singleton function), we say that* $\mathcal{B}$ *is a concretisation (strict refinement) of* $\mathcal{A}$ *with respect to* $\mathcal{R}$ *and* $\mathcal{V}$. *We denote this by* $\mathcal{A} \Rightarrow \mathcal{B}$.

Example 2. Let us continue with the running example of two interacting robots. At $Level_1$, we had the set of system parameters $\mathcal{A}^{Level_1} = \{GM_1, GM_2, P_0, P_1, P_2\}$. At $Level_2$, we refine the $\mathcal{V}(GM_1)$ and $\mathcal{V}(GM_2)$ to have an additional the gripper mode *mid*, representing an intermediate position between *open* and *closed* (i.e., the position when the grippers are opening or closing, but not yet completely open or closed). We do not need to change the parameters GM_1 and GM_2, but we have to extend the sets $\mathcal{V}(GM_1)$ and $\mathcal{V}(GM_2)$.

We also refine the abstract positions to their two-dimensional coordinates: for $i \in \{0, 1, 2\}$, P_i is refined to the tuple of two new parameters X_i and Y_i, and the elements of $\mathcal{V}(P_i)$ are mapped to the tuples of the corresponding coordinates. Thus, at $Level_2$ we have

$$\mathcal{A}^{Level_2} = \{X_0, Y_0, X_1, Y_1, X_2, Y_2, GM_1, GM_2\}$$
$$\mathcal{V}(X_0) = \mathcal{V}(X_1) = \mathcal{V}(X_2) = \{x_1, x_2, x_3, x_4\}$$
$$\mathcal{V}(Y_0) = \mathcal{V}(Y_1) = \mathcal{V}(Y_2) = \{y_1, y_2, y_3, y_4\}$$
$$\mathcal{V}(GM_1) = \mathcal{V}(GM_2) = \{open, closed, mid\}$$

To represent the concretisation from $Level_1$ to $Level_2$, we specify the following relations (cf. also Figs. 2 and 3):

(1) For $j \in \{1, 2\}$, the parameter refinement $GM_j^{Level_1} \rightsquigarrow GM_j^{Level_2}$ is a singleton function. The corresponding value refinements are

$$\mathcal{V}_R(open) = \{open\}$$
$$\mathcal{V}_R(closed) = \{closed\}$$

where $mid \in \mathcal{V}(GM_i^{Level_2})$ does not have any corresponding element on $Level_1$.

(2) For $i \in \{0, 1, 2\}$, the parameter refinement $P_i \rightsquigarrow (X_i, Y_i)$ maps an abstract position to a tuple of two-dimensional coordinates, where the corresponding value refinements are

$$\mathcal{V}_R(pos_k) = \{(x_k, y_1), (x_k, y_2), (x_k, y_3), (x_k, y_4)\}$$

for any $k \in \{1, 2, 3, 4\}$.

Without any constraints on $Level_2$, we would require 16384 tests to cover all possible combinations of the parameter values ($2 \times 2 \times 4 \times 4 \times 4 \times 4 \times 4 \times 4$).

If we assume that the robots cannot be located diagonally to carry the object (i.e., the robots as well as the object should have either the same values of x-coordinates or the same values of y-coordinates, cf. Fig. 4), the operation $Carry(R_1, O, R_2)$ can be captured on $Level_2$ in the following constraint model $M_{Carry(R_1,O,R_2)}^2$:

$$(X_0 = X_1 + 1 \wedge X_2 = X_0 + 1 \wedge Y_0 = Y_1 = Y2 \vee$$
$$X_0 = X_1 = X_2 \wedge Y_0 = Y_1 + 1 \wedge Y_2 = Y_0 + 1) \qquad (3)$$
$$\wedge \ GM_1 = closed \ \wedge \ GM_2 = closed$$

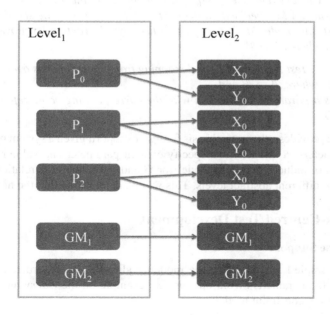

Fig. 2. Parameter refinement $\mathcal{R}$ for the concretisation from $Level_1$ to $Level_2$.

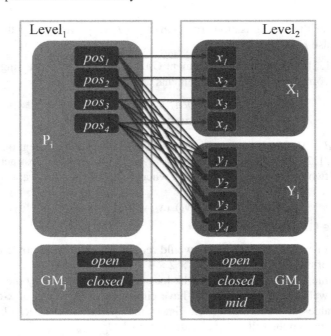

Fig. 3. Value refinement $\mathcal{V}_R$ for the concretisation from $Level_1$ to $Level_2$, $i \in \{0, 1, 2\}$ and $j \in \{1, 2\}$.

Definition 9. *A model refinement $\mathcal{M}_R$ is a mapping from the elements (conjuncts) of the constraint model M^i specified on the abstraction level i over the set of parameters $\mathcal{A}$ to the constraint model M^{i+1}, specified on the next abstraction level over the set of parameters $\mathcal{B}$, where $\mathcal{A} \Rrightarrow \mathcal{B}$.*

Definition 10. *A Test refinement $\mathcal{T}_R$ is a mapping from the set of tests over $\mathcal{A}$ to the set of tests over $\mathcal{B}$, where $\mathcal{A} \Rrightarrow \mathcal{B}$ and*
$\mathcal{R} : \mathcal{A} \rightsquigarrow \mathcal{B}$ *is a parameter refinement with the corresponding value refinement $\mathcal{V}_R$:*
$\mathcal{V}(A) \rightsquigarrow \mathcal{V}(\mathcal{B})$.

The above provides a theoretical basis for tester support: given a system model based a set of parameters $\mathcal{A}$, the user can specify explicit parameter and value refinements, which in its turn induces a system model for $\mathcal{B}$ and the refinement relations between sets of tests on different abstract levels. This will be demonstrated in the next section.

4   Human-Centred Test Development

4.1   Use Case Support

Revisiting Example 1, suppose that the modeller already has constructed a model at $Level_1$, using the parameters from our running example on the *Carry* meta-operation and providing the constraint model

$$GM_1 = closed \ \wedge \ GM_2 = closed \tag{4}$$

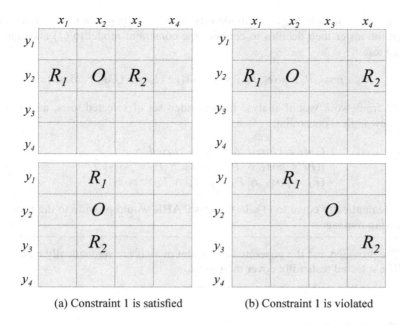

(a) Constraint 1 is satisfied   (b) Constraint 1 is violated

Fig. 4. $Level_2$: Four examples of locations of the robots in the safe-work cage.

where the information on the position is erroneously omitted, because of a human error on the modelling level. If we generate tests automatically, we obtain 64 tests to cover the model ($4 \times 4 \times 4$, i.e., 4 possible positions of each robot as well as 4 possible positions of the object).

Let us consider that the tester decided to limit the generated test set for the operation $Carry(R_1, O, R_2)$ to have one test only, e.g.,

$$\{P_1 : pos_1, P_2 : pos_3, P_0 : pos_2, GM_1 : closed, GM_2 : closed\}.$$

The proposed AHR framework would analyse these tests to come up with the corresponding logical constraint:

$$GM_1 = closed \wedge GM_2 = closed \wedge \\ P_1 = pos_1 \wedge P_2 = pos_3 \wedge P_0 = pos_2 \tag{5}$$

The AHR framework checks whether the pairwise coverage is achieved by the above two tests, and provides the corresponding alert to the tester along with the following messages:

1. The provided and the generated constraint models are semantically unequal.
2. The generated constraint is a stronger than the provided one.
3. Please check the informal specification of the operation constraints, and either refine the provided constraint or select additional tests.

This alert would help the tester to identify missing parts of the model. Let us consider that the tester then decides to changes the constraint model to (1) and select an additional test

$$\{P_1 : pos_2, P_2 : pos_4, P_0 : pos_3, GM_1 : closed, GM_2 : closed\}.$$

The AHR framework would analyse the extended set of selected tests, and come up with the new logical constraint:

$$
\begin{aligned}
&GM_1 = closed \ \wedge \ GM_2 = closed \ \wedge \\
&((P_1 = pos_1 \ \wedge \ P_2 = pos_3 \ \wedge \ P_0 = pos_2) \ \vee \\
&(P_1 = pos_2 \ \wedge \ P_2 = pos_4 \ \wedge \ P_0 = pos_3))
\end{aligned}
\tag{6}
$$

which is semantically equal to (1). In this case, AHR would provide to the tester with the following messages:

1. The provided and the generated constraint models are semantically equal.
2. The selected tests fully cover the model.

4.2 Refinement Support

Next, assume that the system model is refined as presented in Example 2. Based on the specification of the system parameters concretisation, the framework provides the following suggestion for the refinement of the constraint model $M_{Carry(R_1,O,R_2)}$:

$$
\begin{aligned}
&X_0 = X_1 + 1 \wedge X_2 = X_0 + 1 \wedge Y_0 = Y_1 + 1 \wedge Y_2 = Y_0 + 1 \ \wedge \\
&GM_1 = closed \ \wedge \ GM_2 = closed
\end{aligned}
\tag{7}
$$

To increase the readability and the traceability of the refinement steps, we the suggestion is provided in two forms: as the constructed constraint model (7) and as a mapping from the models on the previous and the current abstraction levels, cf. Table 2.

Table 2. Model refinement for $Carry(R_1, O, R_2)$.

$Level_1$	$Level_2$
$P_0 = P_1 + 1 \wedge P_2 = P_0 + 1$	$X_0 = X_1 + 1 \wedge X_2 = X_0 + 1 \wedge Y_0 = Y_1 + 1 \wedge Y_2 = Y_0 + 1$
$GM_1 = closed$	$GM_1 = closed$
$GM_2 = closed$	$GM_2 = closed$

Depending on the semantics we give to the spatial constrains in our model, we accept this suggestion or adapt it. If we assume that the robots can carry an object only while having the same x-coordinates or the same y-coordinates (i.e., the robots cannot be

Table 3. Corrected model refinement for $Carry(R_1, O, R_2)$.

$Level_1$	$Level_2$
$P_0 = P_1 + 1 \wedge P_2 = P_0 + 1$	$X_0 = X_1 + 1 \wedge X_2 = X_0 + 1 \wedge Y_0 = Y_1 = Y2 \vee$
	$X_0 = X_1 = X_2 \wedge Y_0 = Y_1 + 1 \wedge Y_2 = Y_0 + 1$
$GM_1 = closed$	$GM_1 = closed$
$GM_2 = closed$	$GM_2 = closed$

located diagonally to carry the object, cf. Fig. 4) the constraint model has to be specified on $Level_2$ as presented by (8) and Table 3.

$$(X_0 = X_1 + 1 \wedge X_2 = X_0 + 1 \wedge Y_0 = Y_1 = Y2 \vee$$
$$X_0 = X_1 = X_2 \wedge Y_0 = Y_1 + 1 \wedge Y_2 = Y_0 + 1) \wedge \qquad (8)$$
$$GM_1 = closed \wedge GM_2 = open$$

For the corrected model (8), AHR generates 16 tests to achieve the coverage (cf. also Table 4), and suggest the following mapping between sets of tests based on the value refinement:

$$test_1^{Level_1} \rightsquigarrow \{test_1^{Level_2}, test_2^{Level_2}, test_3^{Level_2}, test_4^{Level_2}\}$$
$$test_2^{Level_1} \rightsquigarrow \{test_5^{Level_2}, test_6^{Level_2}, test_7^{Level_2}, test_8^{Level_2}\}$$

Please note, that according to the provided value refinement, the following tests are not refinements of the tests specified on the previous level: $test_9^{Level_2}, \ldots, test_{16}^{Level_2}$.

To increase readability of the test table, we might follow the ideas presented in [6,9]. One of the possible optimisations would be merge of the cells with the same parameter value over the number of tests, cf. Table 5.

4.3 Traceability Support

Traceability not only between the modification in the system parameters but also between constraint models and between test plans, helps to correct possible mistakes more efficiently, as well as provides additional support if the system model is modified. For example, if at some stage a new constraint is identified that the meta-operation $Carry(R_1, O, R_2)$ is not possible when one of the robots is in the position pos_1, the required changes in the models and the corresponding test plans for all concretisations of the model can be easily identified. Moreover, the AHR framework also allows analysis of several branches of the refinement.

5   Visualisation of Spatial Parameters

In cases when system behaviour is based on spatio-temporal properties of the system, it would be very helpful to provide a visualisation of the spatial aspects of the test sets. This would

– increase readability and understandability of the test sets,

Table 4. Test set providing coverage for $Carry(R_1, O, R_2)$ on $Level_2$ under the constraint (7).

testID	X_0	Y_0	X_1	Y_1	X_2	X_2	GM_1	GM_2
$test_1$	x_2	y_1	x_1	y_1	x_3	y_1	$closed$	$closed$
$test_2$	x_2	y_2	x_1	y_2	x_3	y_2	$closed$	$closed$
$test_3$	x_2	y_3	x_1	y_3	x_3	y_3	$closed$	$closed$
$test_4$	x_2	y_4	x_1	y_4	x_3	y_4	$closed$	$closed$
$test_5$	x_3	y_1	x_2	y_1	x_4	y_1	$closed$	$closed$
$test_6$	x_3	y_2	x_2	y_2	x_4	y_2	$closed$	$closed$
$test_7$	x_3	y_3	x_2	y_3	x_4	y_3	$closed$	$closed$
$test_8$	x_3	y_4	x_2	y_4	x_4	y_4	$closed$	$closed$
$test_9$	x_1	y_2	x_1	y_1	x_1	y_3	$closed$	$closed$
$test_{10}$	x_2	y_2	x_2	y_1	x_2	y_3	$closed$	$closed$
$test_{11}$	x_3	y_2	x_3	y_1	x_3	y_3	$closed$	$closed$
$test_{12}$	x_4	y_2	x_4	y_1	x_4	y_3	$closed$	$closed$
$test_{13}$	x_1	y_3	x_1	y_2	x_1	y_4	$closed$	$closed$
$test_{14}$	x_2	y_3	x_2	y_2	x_2	y_4	$closed$	$closed$
$test_{15}$	x_3	y_4	x_3	y_2	x_3	y_4	$closed$	$closed$
$test_{16}$	x_4	y_5	x_4	y_2	x_4	y_4	$closed$	$closed$

– provide a basis for the application of the AHR framework within teaching of basic testing principles, as the cognitive load would be reduced through visualisation of the learning tasks [13].

In AHR framework we propose to have an option to separate spatial parameters from other kind of parameters (presented in tabular form) and represent them visually. If the non-spatial parameters have the same values for all tests (like in our example) or for a number of tests, then the table will be optimised correspondingly.

Thus, for our running example, both tests $test_1^{Level_1}$ and $test_2^{Level_1}$ for the meta-operation $Carry(R_1, O, R_2)$ on $Level_1$ (where one-dimensional space is assumed), can be visually represented as proposed on Fig. 5.

The sixteen tests from Table 4, where $Carry(R_1, O, R_2)$ is analysed on $Level_2$ having two-dimensional space, can be visually presented as proposed on Figs. 6 and 7.

6 Related Work

As pointed out by Pretschner in [14], MBT makes sense only if the model is more abstract than the system under test. This implies that only behaviour encoded in the model can be tested, and that different levels of abstraction must be bridged. Modelling in MBT remains a strictly human activity, and the successful employment of MBT techniques heavily relies on the human factor. As highlighted by Grieskamp in [7], one of the barriers for the adoption of MBT in industry the steep learning curve for modelling

Table 5. Optimised representation of Table 4.

testID	X_0	Y_0	X_1	Y_1	X_2	Y_2	GM_1	GM_2
$test_1$	x_2	y_1	x_1	y_1	x_3	y_1	closed	closed
$test_2$		y_2		y_2		y_2		
$test_3$		y_3		y_3		y_3		
$test_4$		y_4		y_4		y_4		
$test_5$	x_3	y_1	x_2	y_1	x_3	y_1		
$test_6$		y_2		y_2		y_2		
$test_7$		y_3		y_3		y_3		
$test_8$		y_4		y_4		y_4		
$test_9$	x_1	y_2	x_1	y_1	x_1	y_3		
$test_{10}$	x_2		x_2		x_2			
$test_{11}$	x_3		x_3		x_3			
$test_{12}$	x_4		x_4		x_4			
$test_{13}$	x_1	y_3	x_1	y_2	x_1	y_4		
$test_{14}$	x_2		x_2		x_2			
$test_{15}$	x_3		x_3		x_3			
$test_{16}$	x_4		x_4		x_4			

notations. Another barrier is the lack of state-of-the-art authoring environments, which can provide a (semi-)automatic tool support for the human tester and help minimise the number of human errors as well as their impact.

There are many approaches on model-based testing, e.g., [3,7]. Utting et al. presented a taxonomy of MBT approaches in [30]. There are also many approaches on CTD, cf. [4,5,11,17,32]. However, most of them focus on the question how to generate test cases from a model in the most efficient way also achieving full coverage of the required system properties by the generated test cases. In our approach, we combine the ideas of CTD with the idea of a step-wise refinement of the system trough the development process, also following agile modelling practices and guidelines [8,29].

Testing methodologies for complex systems often integrate different abstraction levels of the system representation [2,18]. Thus, abstraction plays a key role in the process of system modelling. An important domain in which modelling with different levels of abstraction is particularly beneficiary is *cyber-physical systems* (CPSs). Several works proposed to use a platform-independent architectural design in the early stages of system development, while pushing hardware- and software-dependent design as late as possible [1,15,20]. In our previous work [23], we suggested to use three main meta-levels of abstraction for the CPS development: abstract, virtual, and cyber-physical. The AHR framework can be applied at any of these meta-levels.

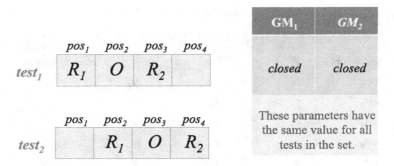

Fig. 5. Visual representation of spatial parameters for the tests on $Level_1$.

Segall and Tzoref-Brill presented in [16] a tool for supporting interactive refinement of combinatorial test plans. This tool is meant for manual modifications of existing test plans, is align with the idea of *Human-Centred Agile Test Design* [26, 31] where it is explicitly acknowledged that the tester's activity is not error-proof. This tool be a good support for the tester, but it does not cover the following point that we consider as crucial for development of complex systems: refinement-based development, where the tester is working at multiple abstraction levels. We aim to cover this point in the proposed AHR framework: If we trace the refinement relations not only between the properties but also between test plans, this might also help to correct possible mistakes more efficiently, as well as provide additional support if the system model is modified.

7   Summary

This chapter presents our ongoing work on human-centred test design, focusing on combinatorial testing and analysis of spatio-temporal properties of the systems. We propose a formal framework AHR that is *A*gile, *H*uman-centred and *R*efinement-oriented. AHR could be applied both for industrial testing of systems-under-development and for teaching of basic concepts of software and system testing, as its visualisation features would significantly reduce the cognitive load while allaying the test sets.

The proposed AHR framework

- allows us to reuse test plans developed for an abstract level at more concrete levels;
- has human-centric interface providing queries and alerts whenever the specified test plan is incomplete or invalid;
- involves analysis of the testing constraints within combinatorial testing;
- provides optimised representation of test tables to increase the readability of test suites;
- provides visualisation of spatial parameter values.

In AHR, we integrate the ideas of refinement-based development and the agile combinatorial test design. The aim of this work is to increase the readability and understandability of system models as well as the corresponding test sets, to conform with the ideas of human-oriented software development, cf. [21, 22].

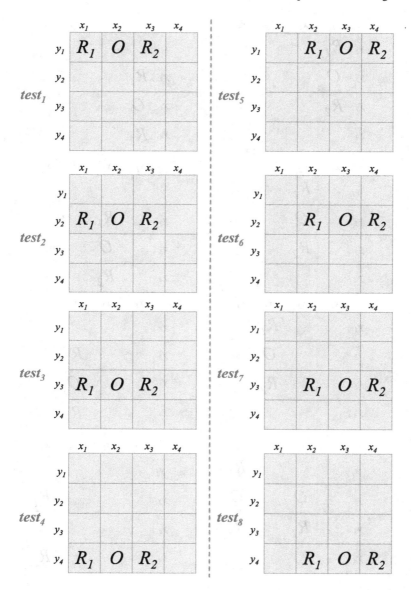

Fig. 6. Visual representation of spatial parameters for the tests on $Level_2$, $test_1, \ldots, test_8$.

Our most immediate research directions is an implementation and evaluation of a tool prototype for the proposed AHR framework. Another direction is a deeper analysis of the visualisation techniques for the spatial as well as non-spatial parameter values, as well as further optimisation strategies for the test sets representation.

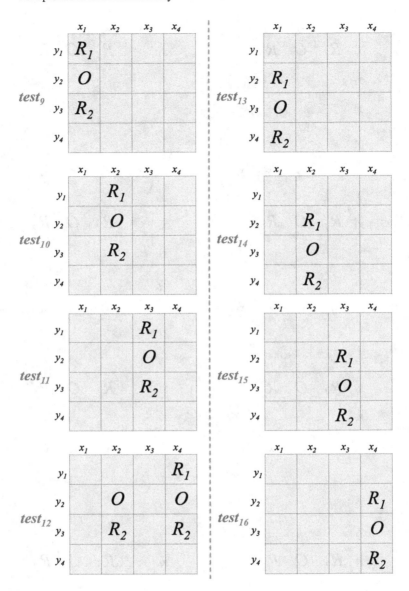

Fig. 7. Visual representation of spatial parameters for the tests on $Level_2$, $test_9, \ldots, test_{16}$.

References

1. Blech, J.O., Spichkova, M., Peake, I., Schmidt, H.: Cyber-virtual systems: simulation, validation & visualization. In: Proceedings of the 9th International Conference on Evaluation of Novel Approaches to Software Engineering (ENASE 2014) (2014)

2. Broy, M.: Service-oriented systems engineering: specification and design of services and layered architectures. In: Broy, M., Grünbauer, J., Harel, D., Hoare, T. (eds.) Engineering Theories of Software Intensive Systems. The JANUS Approach, vol. 195, pp. 47–81. Springer, Dordrecht (2005)

3. Dalal, S.R., Jain, A., Karunanithi, N., Leaton, J., Lott, C.M., Patton, G.C., Horowitz, B.M.: Model-based testing in practice. In: Proceedings of the 21st International Conference on Software Engineering, pp. 285–294. ACM (1999)

4. Farchi, E., Segall, I., Tzoref-Brill, R.: Using projections to debug large combinatorial models. In: Proceedings of the International Conference on Software Testing, Verification and Validation Workshops (ICSTW), pp. 311–320. IEEE (2013)

5. Farchi, E., Segall, I., Tzoref-Brill, R., Zlotnick, A.: Combinatorial testing with order requirements. In: Proceedings of the International Conference on Software Testing, Verification and Validation Workshops (ICSTW), pp. 118–127. IEEE (2014)

6. Feng, X., Parnas, D.L., Tse, T., O'Callaghan, T.: A comparison of tabular expression-based testing strategies. IEEE Trans. Softw. Eng. **37**(5), 616–634 (2011)

7. Grieskamp, W.: Multi-paradigmatic model-based testing. In: Havelund, K., Núñez, M., Roşu, G., Wolff, B. (eds.) Formal Approaches to Software Testing and Runtime Verification. LNCS, vol. 4262, pp. 1–19. Springer, Heidelberg (2006). doi:10.1007/11940197_1

8. Hellmann, T.D., Sharma, A., Ferreira, J., Maurer, F.: Agile testing: past, present, and future-charting a systematic map of testing in agile software development. In: Proceedings of the Agile Conference (AGILE), pp. 55–63. IEEE (2012)

9. Jin, Y., Parnas, D.L.: Defining the meaning of tabular mathematical expressions. Sci. Comput. Program. **75**(11), 980–1000 (2010)

10. Kuhn, D.R., Wallace, D.R., Gallo, A.M.: Software fault interactions and implications for software testing. IEEE Trans. Softw. Eng. **30**(6), 418–421 (2004)

11. Kuhn, R., Kacker, R., Lei, Y., Hunter, J.: Combinatorial software testing. IEEE Comput. **42**(8), 94–96 (2011)

12. Nie, C., Leung, H.: A survey of combinatorial testing. ACM Comput. Surv. **43**(2), 11:1–11:29 (2011)

13. Pane, J., Myers, B.: Usability issues in the design of novice programming systems. School of Computer Science Technical report CMU-CS-96-132 (1996)

14. Pretschner, A.: Model-based testing in practice. In: Fitzgerald, J., Hayes, I.J., Tarlecki, A. (eds.) FM 2005. LNCS, vol. 3582, pp. 537–541. Springer, Heidelberg (2005). doi:10.1007/11526841_37

15. Sapienza, G., Crnkovic, I., Seceleanu, T.: Towards a methodology for hardware and software design separation in embedded systems. In: Proceedings of the ICSEA, pp. 557–562. IARIA (2012)

16. Segall, I., Tzoref-Brill, R.: Interactive refinement of combinatorial test plans. In: Proceedings of the 34th International Conference on Software Engineering, pp. 1371–1374. IEEE Press (2012)

17. Segall, I., Tzoref-Brill, R., Zlotnick, A.: Common patterns in combinatorial models. In: Proceedings of the International Conference on Software Testing, Verification and Validation (ICST), pp. 624–629. IEEE (2012)

18. Spichkova, M.: Refinement-based verification of interactive real-time systems. Electron. Notes Theor. Comput. Sci. **214**, 131–157 (2008)

19. Spichkova, M.: Architecture: Requirements + Decomposition + Refinement. Softwaretechnik-Trends **31**, 4 (2011)

20. Spichkova, M., Campetelli, A.: Towards system development methodologies: from software to cyber-physical domain. In: Proceedings of the International Workshop on Formal Techniques for Safety-Critical Systems (2012)

21. Spichkova, M., Zhu, X., Mou, D.: Do we really need to write documentation for a system? In: Proceedings of the International Conference on Model-Driven Engineering and Software Development (MODELSWARD 2013) (2013)
22. Spichkova, M.: Design of formal languages and interfaces: formal does not mean unreadable. In: Emerging Research and Trends in Interactivity and the Human-Computer Interface. IGI Global (2013)
23. Spichkova, M., Liu, H., Schmidt, H.: Towards quality-oriented architecture: integration in a global context. In: Proceedings of the European Conference on Software Architecture Workshops, p. 64. ACM (2015)
24. Spichkova, M., Zamansky, A.: A human-centred framework for combinatorial test design. In: Proceedings of the 11th International Conference on Evaluation of Novel Software Approaches to Software Engineering, pp. 228–233 (2016)
25. Spichkova, M., Zamansky, A.: A human-centred framework for supporting model-based testing. In: CAiSE 2016, pp. 105–112. CEUR (2016). http://researchbank.rmit.edu.au/view/rmit: 38416, http://ceur-ws.org/Vol-1612/
26. Spichkova, M., Zamansky, A., Farchi, E.: Towards a human-centred approach in modelling and testing of cyber-physical systems. In: Proceedings of the International Workshop on Automated Testing for Cyber-Physical Systems in the Cloud (2015)
27. Spichkova, M., Zamansky, A., Farchi, E.: A visual logical language for system modelling in combinatorial test design. In: Krogstie, J., Mouratidis, H., Su, J. (eds.) CAiSE 2016. LNBIP, vol. 249, pp. 116–121. Springer, Cham (2016). doi:10.1007/978-3-319-39564-7_12
28. Tai, K.C., Lei, Y.: A test generation strategy for pairwise testing. IEEE Trans. Softw. Eng. **28**(1), 109–111 (2002)
29. Talby, D., Keren, A., Hazzan, O., Dubinsky, Y.: Agile software testing in a large-scale project. IEEE Softw. **23**(4), 30–37 (2006)
30. Utting, M., Pretschner, A., Legeard, B.: A taxonomy of model-based testing approaches. Softw. Test. Verif. Reliab. **22**(5), 297–312 (2012)
31. Zamansky, A., Farchi, E.: Helping the tester get it right: towards supporting agile combinatorial test design. In: Bianculli, D., Calinescu, R., Rumpe, B. (eds.) SEFM 2015. LNCS, vol. 9509, pp. 35–42. Springer, Heidelberg (2015). doi:10.1007/978-3-662-49224-6_4
32. Zhang, J., Zhang, Z., Ma, F.: Introduction to combinatorial testing. In: Zhang, J., Zhang, Z., Ma, F. (eds.) Automatic Generation of Combinatorial Test Data, pp. 1–16. Springer, Heidelberg (2014)

Software Engineering Foundations of Zoetic Data and Totally Functional Programming

Paul Bailes$^{(\boxtimes)}$ and Colin Kemp

School of ITEE, The University of Queensland, St Lucia, QLD 4072, Australia
{paul, ck}@itee.uq.edu.au

Abstract. Traditional higher-order functional programming is validated by how its logical conclusion in the shape of a "Totally Functional" style is consistent with and indeed determined by some fundamental principles of Software Engineering. The key to Totally Functional Programming is the notion of "zoetic" representations of data which embody the behaviours that we hypothesise to underlie all conventional symbolic datatypes. These representations minimise the interpretation of symbolic data at each use, and thus embody the principle of reuse. Further, we develop a scheme for formal synthesis of generator functions for zoetic data which entirely avoid the need for a separate interpretation stage. This avoidance allows us to achieve a clear separation of concerns between the creation of zoetic data objects on the one hand and their use in various applications on the other. Zoetic data are thus validated as the key enablers of the fulfilment of functional programming in its "Totally Functional" manifestation, firmly grounded in the language design consequences of software engineering principles.

Keywords: Catamorphism · Church numeral · Foldr · Functional Programming · Fusion theorem · Haskell

1 Introduction

The general purpose of this paper is to demonstrate how a new "Totally Functional" approach to programming derives from the now-well-established tradition of higher-order Functional Programming (FP) through the conscious application of software engineering principles. As a result, not only are the innovations of our Totally Functional Programming (TFP) lent a degree of legitimacy, but also is the legitimacy of traditional FP reinforced by this demonstration of its support for these principles of software engineering.

The multi-faceted advantages of FP have long been well-documented [1]. However, amid the benefits of such as lazy evaluation and referential transparency, the essential defining aspect of programmer-definable higher-order functions, seems strangely to have been under-appreciated. In particular, classic expositions of FP [2, 3] typically relegate functional ("Church") representations of data as mere curiosities.

Our specific purpose here is therefore to demonstrate the viability of these functional (or zoetic: "pertaining to life; living; vital" [4]) representations as comprehensive substitutes for conventional symbolic data, motivated by and compatible with key

© Springer International Publishing AG 2016
L.A. Maciaszek and J. Filipe (Eds.): ENASE 2016, CCIS 703, pp. 129–157, 2016.
DOI: 10.1007/978-3-319-56390-9_7

principles of software engineering [5]. The focus of the demonstration is on how zoetic data can be manipulated, and specifically created, (or "generated") independently of their symbolic counterparts, and thus form the basis of our Totally Functional Programming style where symbolic data can be superseded by these zoetic representations.

In this paper overall we: provide a basic justification of zoetic data in terms of general software engineering principles; indicate how widespread and practical zoetic data actually are; provide the conceptual and semantic bases for the synthesis of generators for a wide class of zoetic data; expose techniques for the formal synthesis of zoetic data and their generators, and demonstrate the applicability of these techniques for a range of examples; indicate how zoetic data provide a conceptual gateway into a comprehensive alternate view of programming based on total rather than partial recursion; and re-emphasise the significance of this approach through its compatibility with mainstream software engineering.

2   Applicable Principles of Software Engineering

Software engineering involves a wide range of tools, techniques and processes aimed at delivering software products with efficiency and effectiveness comparable to that of products of traditional engineering domains. As such, many issues germane to software engineering are not directly concerned with software, and indeed some of the knowledge discovered for software engineering has found applicability in systems engineering more generally [6]. For our purposes however, the relevant software-specific aspects of software engineering are:

- reuse;
- separation of concerns;
- formal methods

relevant elaborations of each of which follow below. There are of course more, but our contention is that a software technology that addresses these at least represents a serious engagement with software engineering. They will be applied as needed at the relevant points of our elaboration of zoetic data.

2.1   Reuse

Software or code reuse involves the minimisation of programming effort (and thus exposure to error) by adopting or adapting existing code for a new purpose. If the adoption/adaption is to minimise error, it should be managed through abstraction techniques supported concretely in source code rather than cut-and-paste editing. Object-orientation [7] and lambda-abstraction [8] as manifested by functions/ procedures/subroutines are key concrete abstraction mechanisms promoting reuse.

2.2   Separation of Concerns

It's useful when writing or reading any kind of document to have as few issues in mind as possible. One means is to employ powerful abstractions capable of unifying a multiplicity of concerns. If however the abstraction mechanisms at hand are inadequate for the unification of diverse concerns, then different concerns should be dealt with separately [9]. In the programming/software engineering context, this could mean specifying procedures to perform single application functions rather than a multiplicity of same. A variant of this basic theme is however the classical epistemological distinction between "what" versus "how", or in software terms between specification versus implementation. A range of techniques are available to software engineers to establish and maintain the manifestations of this distinction, including those pertaining to reuse above but also such as modularity [10] and aspect-oriented programming [11].

2.3   Formal Methods

Software is an inherently logical phenomenon, the behaviour of which can be described and analysed mathematically [12]. In particular, the correspondence between required behaviour and a putative implementation of same can just be not just proven, but an implementation corresponding to a specification can be synthesised by formal logical means. It's acknowledged that the harnessing of mathematical techniques to large-scale software remains a work in progress, but at scales where the mathematics is in place, it should be used rather than ad hoc methods to synthesise or verify source code.

3   Zoetic Data Examples

We begin by showing how zoetic data play important roles in functional programming, not just theoretically but practically also, using a range of examples of natural numbers, set data structures, and context-free grammars. The key idea in each case is that the zoetic counterpart to a conventional symbolic datatype embodies an essential characteristic behaviour.

3.1   Zoetic Naturals

Perhaps the best-known zoetic datatype in programming is the "Church numeral" [8] representation of natural numbers, whereby a natural N is represented by a counterpart function (say Ñ) such that $Ñ f x = f^N x$. That is, the characteristic behaviour Ñ of a natural number N is N-fold function composition. For example, the zoetic version of (symbolic) natural number 3 would be rendered, in Haskell [13] concrete syntax as the function:

```
(\f x -> f (f (f x)))
```

or equivalently

```
(\f -> f . f . f)
```

In particular, definitions for some basic zoetic naturals would be

```
zzero = (\f x -> x)
zone = (\f x -> f x)
ztwo = (\f x -> f (f x))
-- etc.
```

This behaviour is directly applicable as N-fold iteration. For example, assuming a successor function succ (more on which below), addition of say N1 to N2 can be implemented by

$$\tilde{N}1 \ \text{succ} \ \tilde{N}2$$

3.2 Zoetic Sets

Perhaps the best generally-known zoetic datatype is the representation of sets by (or equivalently, characterising their essential behaviour in terms of) their characteristic predicates. For example, the essence of the definition of the set of even numbers as follows:

$$\{x \mid x \ \text{modulo} \ 2 \ = \ 0\}$$

is the predicate, or Boolean-valued function (in Haskell syntax)

```
evens = (\x -> x `mod` 2 == 0)
```

Membership of such a zoetic set is tested by direct function application, e.g. (where '$\rightarrow$' denotes evaluation/reduction):

```
evens 4 → True
evens 5 → False
```

Usefully, as we shall see, the characteristic predicate is the partial application of the set membership operation to the set, as exposed by the tautology

$$S \ = \ \{x \mid x \in S\} \ = \ \{x \mid (\in S) \ x\}$$

Note the adoption of Haskell operator sectioning, where "$(\in S)$" denotes the partial application of $\in$ to S, forming the characteristic predicate of S which is then applied to putative element x.

3.3 Zoetic Grammars

The zoetic approach to context-free grammars [14] that is implicitly adopted by combinator parsing [15] is that the relevant characteristic behaviour of the grammar is the parser for the language defined by the grammar. Accordingly, the zoetic-compatible renditions of the context-free combinations of concatenation and alternation are (higher-order) functions that apply not to grammars but to parsers, and yielding not a grammar but a parser.

In its essential form, a combinator parser for a grammar G is a nondeterministic recogniser that when applied to an input string S yields the list of suffix strings that result after occurrences of sentences of G have been found as prefixes in S:

```
type CParser = String -> [String]
```

An empty list of result strings signifies failure to parse [16].

For example, assuming definitions of context-free parsing combinators "conc" and "alt" and token recogniser "tok" (see further below for these), the trivial "expression grammar"

$$\text{Exp} \rightarrow \text{Exp} + \text{Trm} \mid \text{Trm}$$

$$\text{Trm} \rightarrow x \mid y$$

can be defined in Haskell source code as

```
exp = exp `conc` ((tok "+") `conc` trm) `alt` trm
trm = (tok "x") `alt` (tok "y")
```

We then parse according it by direct functional application, e.g.

```
(1)  exp "x+y''
(2)  exp "qwe"
(3)  exp "x"
```

Each of these yields respective results

```
(1)  ["","+y"]
(2)  []
(3)  [""]
```

That is, parsing with exp respectively signifies

1. of "x + y": gives two results, one where the entirety of "x + y" is recognized with no residue, the other where only "x" is recognized leaving residue "+y"
2. of "qwe": is unrecognized
3. of "x": is uniquely and fully recognized.

4   Characteristic Methods as Basis of Zoetic Data

The key to a systematic approach to generation of zoetic data is the recognition that they embody a uniform interpretation of an underlying symbolic datatype. We use the term "characteristic method" for this interpretation, by extension from the characteristic predicate behaviour ascribed to zoetic sets. The relative advantages of zoetic data based on characteristic method interpretations of symbolic data are exposed by example in the context of natural numbers as follows.

In this exposition, it will be seen how the principles of reuse and of separation of concerns drive the key creativity and design decisions regarding our treatment of zoetic data.

4.1   Pervasive Interpretation Contravenes Reuse

The need to adopt a uniform interpretation of symbolic data is demonstrated, albeit in microcosm, by the following definitions of arithmetic operations on natural numbers, which expose how thoroughly programming is pervaded by the need to interpret symbolic data, and how potentially harmful are the effects:

```
data Nat = Succ Nat | Zero

add (Succ a) b = Succ (add a b)
add Zero b = b

mul (Succ a) b = add b (mul a b)
mul Zero b = Zero

exp a (Succ b) = mul a (exp a b)
exp a Zero = Succ Zero
```

The drawbacks inherent in these deceptively-simple definitions are profound, as follows.

- Apart from the suggestive naming of the type (Nat) and of its two constructors (Succ and Zero), there is nothing in the definition of the type that compels treatment of members of the type as numbers of any kind, never mind natural numbers specifically.
- Granted there is an obvious isomorphism between the members of Nat and the abstract entities that behave like natural numbers, but that isomorphism needs to be implemented by each usage of Nat. This implementation takes the form of an implicit interpreter that converts symbols into actions (in this case, iterative applications of other functions).
- Defining functions through interpretation of symbols using general recursion adds the burden of proving totality i.e. termination.
- Most significantly from a software engineering point of view, this implementation of the isomorphism from the symbols of Nat to the iterative behaviour of natural numbers, far from being reused, needs to be repeated at each usage: typical of failure to observe the reuse principle, inconsistent repeated usage will lead to inconsistent (erroneous) behaviour.

4.2   Explicit Interpretations Admit Reuse

The situation may be clarified somewhat by the introduction of an explicit common interpreter for the semantics (i.e. functional behaviour) of natural numbers N as N-fold iterators:

```
iter (Succ n) f x = f (iter n f x)
iter Zero f x = x
```

In the light of this, our arithmetic operation definitions can be re-expressed with explicit reuse of the "iter" interpreter:

```
add a b = iter a Succ b
mul a b = iter a (add b) Zero
exp a b = iter b (mul a) (Succ Zero)
```

The introduction of "iter" thus allows for the clarification of what interpretation is being given to the type Nat (here as iteration), and when that interpretation is being applied usefully and meaningfully.

4.3 Separation of Concerns via Zoetic Data

Despite this clarification however, the revised interpretive arithmetic definitions are still deficient in terms of inconvenience, fragility and potential inconsistency:

- inconvenience, in that the interpreter needs to be applied explicitly;
- fragility, in that the wrong interpreter could conceivably be applied;
- potential inconsistency, in that multiple interpreters with inconsistent behaviours could be defined and applied (e.g. one might assume naturals start at 0, while another might assume they start at 1, as was once a common convention).

All the above criticisms can be summarised as a failure to observe the key software design principle of separation of concerns [9]. In this case the separation is between application logic on the one hand and what we might call infrastructure logic on the other. In the above examples, the definitions (add, mul, exp) combine both the logic of the respective applications (addition, multiplication, exponentiation) with the logic of the semantics of natural numbers (iteration). Making the semantic interpreter ("iter") explicit and hiding the infrastructure logic therein ameliorates the situation somewhat but fails to consummate the separation as per the points listed above.

In order fully to achieve separation of concerns between applications and infrastructure, our solution is to require that all members of a datatype are inherently interpreted by the type's characteristic method. That is, zoetic data are in a sense self-interpreting, and the coding of the required behaviours is built into the generators from which zoetic data are themselves created. Specifically, we:

1. assume that for each (symbolic) datatype there is indeed a characteristic behaviour (such as iteration for Nat as above);
2. treat the partial application of the characteristic interpreter (for the characteristic behaviour) to the symbolic data as a conceptual zoetic unit;
3. reorganise programs around these zoetic data.

In the case of our running example of definitions of basic arithmetic operations, we replace naturals (a, b, etc.) by zoetic naturals (say za, zb, etc.) where the respective identities hold:

```
za = iter a
zb = iter b
```

et cetera. Accordingly, we rewrite arithmetic definitions on za, zb etc.:

```
addz za zb = za succz zb
mulz za ab = za (addz zb) zzero
expz za zb = zb (mulz za) zone
```

It is at once evident that the required separation of concerns has been achieved: the only information added by these definitions is with regard to how the zoetic naturals za, zb variously combine to implement the respective arithmetic operations. In particular, the iterative behaviour of za, zb is assumed to have been provided at their creation.

The remainder of this paper this focusses upon how such inherent behaviours are necessarily inbuilt when creating zoetic data, and thus achieving the further required properties of robustness (no chance of applying the wrong characteristic method) and consistency (that there indeed exists a unique characteristic method).

5   Generating Zoetic Data

To reiterate, generators embody the required behaviours of zoetic data and this effect the separation of defining and activating these behaviours from their use in applications.

The approach we shall follow is simply-stated: instead of creating zoetic data from partial applications of characteristic interpreters to symbolic data, generate the zoetic data directly with zoetic analogues of the symbolic constructors. When programming, calls to symbolic constructors are replaced by calls to the zoetic generators. In other words, we effect an isomorphism between the symbolic and zoetic type. As zoetic generators produce a member of the zoetic type, no final application of the interpreter (iter etc.) is required.

In this section, we preview the definitions of some interesting generators of zoetic data, which we later show how to derive by calculation from their specifications.

5.1   Zoetic Natural Generators

For example, the zoetic versions of natural numbers would be specified in terms of partial application of the above iterative interpreter "iter" to their usual symbolic renditions as follows:

```
zzero = iter Zero
zone = iter (Succ Zero)
ztwo = iter (Succ (Succ Zero))
-- etc.
```

Accordingly, we instead require systematic generation of zoetic naturals such as the above by application of zoetic counterparts of the symbolic constructors Zero and Succ, i.e.

```
zzero = (\f x -> x)
succz n = (\f x -> f (n f x))
```

or equivalently

```
zzero f x = x
succz n f x = f (n f x)
```

and thus

```
zone = succz zzero
ztwo = succz zone
zthree = succz ztwo
-- etc.
```

In particular, it is straightforward to show (by simple term rewriting from the definitions of zzero and succz) that these correctly yield the expected Church numerals, e.g.

```
zthree
=
succz (succz (succz zzero))
=
(\f x -> f (f (f x)))
```

5.2   Zoetic Set Generators

For zoetic sets it's possible to intuit generators that apply to appropriate elements or (sub-)sets yielding characteristic predicates that test the membership or otherwise of a putative element x:

```
empty x = False
singleton e x = x==e
union zs1 zs2 x = zs1 x || zs2 x
complement zs x = not (zs x)

-- etc…
```

5.3   Zoetic Grammar Generators

Following our example above, combinator parsers are generated, as are context-free grammars, from alternation of grammars/parsers, or concatenation of grammars/parsers, or tokens. Alternation accordingly builds a combinator parser from two components p1 and p2, by appending the results of parsing s with each of p1 and p2:

```
alt :: CParser -> CParser -> CParser
alt p1 p2 s = p1 s ++ p2 s
```

Concatenation accordingly builds a combinator parser from two components p1 and p2, by parsing s with p1 and then parsing each of the results with p2:

```
conc :: CParser -> CParser -> CParser
conc p1 p2 s = concat (map p2 (p1 s))
```

A token t parses string s by removing prefix t from s:

```
tok :: String -> CParser
tok t s = if prefix t s then [chop t s] else []
```

where

- "prefix t s" tests if string t is a prefix of s;
- "chop t s" removes prefix t from s.

6 Generator Synthesis for Primary Zoetic Types

In the context of the above, our (related) problem is:

- to discover the zoetic generators that correspond to symbolic constructors in a systematic way, as opposed to the mere intuitions that have led to the examples above;
- which then enables us to replace the partial applications to symbolic data of characteristic methods/interpreters with direct applications of these generators to zoetic data.

In the solution of this problem, we rely upon formal methods to derive generator implementations from their specifications.

In this section, we deal with the simplest kind of zoetic datatype - the Primary Zoetic Type (1ZT) - which correspond to regular algebraic types [17].

6.1 Catamorphic Expressibility of 1ZTs

We recognise the generic catamorphic pattern [18] on the regular algebraic type (more widely-known as the foldr operation in the list context, and represented by iter above for naturals) as the characteristic behaviour of its zoetic counterparts.

This choice is made on the basis of:

- category-theoretic justifications of catamorphisms as capturing the essence (categorically-speaking, "initiality") of a regular algebraic type;
- the practical capability of catamorphic patterns to express a wide range of subrecursive operations [19];
- the above capability including the ability to express other more apparently-sophisticated recursion patterns [20].

6.2 Specification of Generators for 1ZTs

Just as with Naturals above, zoetic versions of these types in general are specified by the partial application of the relevant catamorphism pattern for that type to the symbolic data.

For example, for the types of lists and rose trees:

```
data List a = Cons t (List a) | Nil
data Rose a = Tip a | Branch (List (Rose a))
```

we have:

1. Catamorphism patterns:

```
catL Nil c n = n
catL (Cons x xs) c n = c x (catL xs c n)

catR (Tip x) t b = t x
catR (Branch rs) t b = b (mapL (\r -> catR r t b) rs)
mapL f xs =
-- corresponds to Haskell prelude ''map'', but on List t
instead of [t]
  catL xs (\x xs' -> Cons (f x) xs') Nil
```

where that the usual order of operands (e.g. to "foldr") is changed (consistently with "iter" above) to facilitate partial application of the catamorphic pattern to symbolic data, in particular

```
catL xs op b = foldr op b xs
```

Note also how in the case of rose trees, where the recursion is not a simple polynomial, that some additional complexity is entailed in that the structure of the n-ary recursion has to be processed by the relevant map function (in this case over Lists). The resulting list is processed by some combining function b which could well be a (List) catamorphism also. For these 1ZTs, synthesis of the generators proceeds by straightforward equational reasoning, as exemplified by the following.
And we correspondingly have

2. Specifications of zoetic counterparts zL, zR of respective symbolic lists L and rose trees R:

```
zL = catL L
zR = catR R
```

Generally:

- the specification of a zoetic counterpart Z of a symbolic datum D of type T will be
  `Z = catT D`
- the specification of generators Gi for the zoetic counterpart of symbolic type T with constructors Ci will follow case analysis of the foregoing, of the schematic form
  `Gi argsZ = catT (Ci argsD)`
  where argsD are the symbolic operands to Ci from which datum D is constructed, and argsZ are the zoetic operands to Gi from which the zoetic counterpart Z to D is generated.

6.3   Synthesis of Generators for Zoetic Naturals

For example, for zoetic Naturals as defined above, from the specifications of the isomorphism between Nat and our zoetic Naturals, we specify the generators as follows, i.e. as partial applications of the interpreter for the required characteristic behaviour - the relevant catamorphism pattern "iter". Observe how the zoetic operand to generator succz is consistently specified as the partial application of "iter" to the corresponding symbolic natural:

```
zzero = iter Zero

succz (iter n) = iter (Succ n)
```

To calculate their implementations, we proceed respectively, in each case adding sufficient relevant parameters to the specifications in order to allow the expansion of the application of iter and then simplification according to the definition of iter in the course of which the interpreter (iter) is eliminated, i.e.:

```
zzero f x
```

= (supplying additional parameters to the RHS also)

```
iter Zero f x
```

= (by definition of iter)

```
x
```

and

```
succz (iter n) f x
```

= (supplying additional parameters to the RHS also)

```
iter (Succ n) f x
```

= (by definition of iter)

```
f (iter n f x)
```

Thus, recognizing the partial application "iter n" as the zoetic natural zn, we have the Haskell function declarations for the zoetic natural generators:

```
zzero f x = x
succz zn f x = f (zn f x)
```

6.4   Synthesis of Generators for Zoetic Lists

Lists are treated similarly, from the specification of generators in terms of partial application of the characteristic symbolic interpreter - in this case the catamorphism pattern for lists "catL":

```
znil = catL Nil
zcons x (catL xs) = catL (Cons x xs)
```

We proceed respectively by adding parameters and simplifying according to the defining equations of catL:

```
znil c n = catL Nil c n = n
```

and (in detail)

```
zcons x (catL xs) c n
```

= (supplying additional parameters to the RHS also)

```
catL (Cons x xs) c n
```

= (by definition of catL)

```
c x (catL xs c n)
```

Thus, recognizing the partial application "catL xs" as the zoetic list zxs, we have the Haskell function declarations to implement the zoetic list generators:

```
znil c n = n
zcons x zxs c n = c x (zxs c n)
```

6.5   Synthesis of Generators for Zoetic Rose Trees

Again, we follow the principle that the specification of generators is in terms of partial application of the characteristic symbolic interpreter - in this case the catamorphism pattern for rose trees "catR". Note especially in this case how the zoetic operand to zbranch is specified as the list of the partial applications of "catR" to each of the symbolic rose trees in the branch, as effected by "mapL".

```
ztip x = catR (Ztip x)

zbranch (mapL catR rs)) = catR (Branch rs)
```
To calculate the implementation we as usual proceed respectively
```
ztip x t b
```
= (supplying additional parameters to the RHS also)
```
catR (Ztip x) t b
```
= (by definition of catR)
```
t x
```
and
```
zbranch (mapL catR rs)) t b
```
= (supplying additional parameters to the RHS also)
```
catR (Branch rs) t b
```
= (by definition of catR)
```
b (mapL (\r -> catR r t b) rs)
```
= (abstracting "catR r")
```
b(mapL(\r->(\zr->(zr t b))(catR r))rs)
```
= (identifying function composition)
```
b(mapL(\r->((\zr->(zr t b)).catR) r)rs)
```
= (removing r by eta-reduction)
```
b (mapL ((\zr -> (zr t b)).catR) rs)
```
= (distributing mapL over composition)
```
b (mapL (\zr -> zr t b)(mapL catR rs))
```

Thus, recognizing the list of partial applications "mapL catR rs" as the list of zoetic rose trees zrs, we have the Haskell function declarations for the zoetic rose tree generators:

```
ztip x t b = t x
zbranch zrs t b = b (mapL (\zr -> zr t b) zrs)
```

If the n-ary recursive structure of rose trees is represented not by a symbolic list zrs but rather is zoetic, then the effect of mapL on zrs is simply achieved by its direct application as a list catamorphism:

```
zbranch zrs t b = b (zrs (\zr zrs' -> zcons (zr t b)
zrs') znil)
```

7 Secondary Zoetic Types

The above systemic approach to 1ZT generator synthesis is however only part of the story. A wider class of zoetic types than 1ZTs is formed by the partial application of specific characteristic methods rather than the generic catamorphic patterns on the relevant symbolic algebraic types. In other words, while catamorphic patterns represent the most general behaviours, specialisations may be required in specific circumstances. Examples of these as seen so far in this presentation are combinator parsers and characteristic predicates.

Regarding the latter, consider for example the following type of trees with a mixture of binary and unary subtrees:

```
Bt a = Nul | Lf a | Brn (Bt a)(Bt a)| One(Bt a)
```

This algebraic type has a default interpretation in terms of its catamorphic pattern:

```
catBt Nul n l b o = n
catBt (Lf x) n l b o = l x
catBt (Brn t1 t2) n l b o = b(catBt t1 n l b o)(catBt t2
n l b o)
catBt (One t) n l b o = o t
```

Generators for the consequent 1ZT, derived using the above methods are:

```
nul n l b o = n
lf x n l b o = l x
brn t1 t2 n l b o = b (t1 n l b o) (t2 n l b o)
one t n l b o = o t
```

A different interpretation however of these trees as sets is given by the characteristic method "member":

```
member Nul e = False
member (Lf x) e = x==e
member (Brn t1 t2) e = member t1 e || member t2 e
member (One t) e = not (member t e)
```

Obviously, zoetic sets that behave as characteristic predicates are given by partial applications

```
member bt    -- NB bt :: Bt a
```

The challenge now facing us, in order to widen the practical range of zoetic data beyond pure catamorphic behaviours, is synthesis of the generators for such secondary zoetic types (2ZTs). With respect to the above example, this means empty, singleton, union, complement as further above corresponding respectively to Bt constructors Nul, Lf, Brn and One. This is more complex than that of generic catamorphism-based 1ZTs, and hence first requires the conceptual infrastructure of the following section.

8 Principles of Generator Derivation for 2ZTs

Derivation of generators for 2ZTs depends upon some further properties common to zoetic data and catamorphisms. Again, formal methods are the basis of derivation of implementations from specifications.

8.1 Schematic Catamorphism

Demonstration of key properties common to catamorphisms is facilitated by a scheme of catamorphisms captured in Haskell source code by definitions as follows [21].

First, identify some general algebraic abstractions:

```
type Algebra f a = f a -> a

-- as per Haskell prelude
class Functor f where fmap :: (a -> b) -> f a -> f b
```

The key to a generic definition of the catamorphic pattern is the pattern functor that defines the shape of the data for a (recursive) type. In order to isolate the (non-recursive) pattern functor, direct recursion in type definitions is not appropriate. Recursive types are instead the explicit fixed-point of their pattern functor, thus we need a fixpoint operator for data types:

```
newtype Mu f = InF { outF :: f (Mu f) }
```

(The respective constructor and extractor functions for Mu - Inf and outF - are artefacts of the Haskell type system.)

For example, the pattern functor type of the polymorphic list type (with elements of type 'a') is:

```
data Lf a lf = Nl | (Cns a lf)
instance Functor (Lf a) where
    fmap g Nl = Nl
    fmap g (Cns x xs) = Cns x (g xs)
```

Thus, the actual recursive polymorphic List type is the least fixed point of "Lf a":

```
type List a = Mu (Lf a)
```

The catamorphic recursion pattern for any type is the most general homomorphism from the algebra given by the pattern functor of the type to any other result algebra (i.e. the polymorphic target type of the recursion pattern). A generic rendition in Haskell is

```
cata :: Functor f => Algebra f a -> Mu f -> a
cata f = f . fmap (cata f) . outF
```

where 'f' embodies the embedded operation that characterises the catamorphism in terms of the pattern algebra of the type. Observe how the recursive application of "cata f" by fmap ensures the desired recursive operation of the catamorphism.

So in order to define specific catamorphic operations, all that is required is to define the embedded operation (the 'f' parameter of cata). For example:

- the catamorphic definition of the length of a list is now

```
length xs = cata phi where
    phi Nl = 0
    phi (Cns _ xs) = 1+xs
```

- the list catamorphism pattern (catL) as above can be written simply by passing its parameters to the catamorphism's characteristic operation:

```
catL xs o b = cata phi where
    phi Nl = b
    phi (Cns x xs) = o x xs
```

8.2 Fusion Theorem

Just as catamorphisms exemplify how the programming of recursion can be packaged and simplified, so fusion [19] is an example of how reasoning about recursive programs can be packaged and simplified.

In terms of the schematic catamorphism above, fusion is the implication:

$$h\,(phi\,x) \;=\; chi\,(fmap\,h\,x) \to h\,(cata\,phi\,x) \;=\; cata\,chi\,x$$

where phi and chi are the embedded operations of type-compatible catamorphisms

Fusion for individual types can be derived from the above schema, typically with the antecedent of the implication as: the conjunction of the instantiation of the schema with the particulars of each of the constructors for the relevant pattern functor.

For example, for list catamorphisms the two characteristic operations are typified by

```
phi Nl = B1
phi (Cns x xs) = O1 x xs

chi Nl = B2
chi (Cns x xs) = O2 x xs
```

Thus for some base values Bi and binary operations Oi, we instantiate the fusion theorem for lists as follows.

- The antecedent condition, case Nl, is:

```
h (phi Nl)= chi (fmap h Nl)
```
⇔
```
h (phi Nl)= chi Nl
```
⇔
```
h B1 = B2
```
- The antecedent condition, case Cns x xs, is

```
        h (phi (Cns x xs))= chi (fmap h (Cns x xs))
```
        ⇔
```
        h (phi (Cns x xs)) = chi (Cns x (h xs))
```
        ⇔
```
        h (O1 x xs) = O2 x (h xs)
```

- There is a single consequent:
```
h (cata phi xs) = cata chi xs
```
⇔
```
h (catL xs O1 B1) = catL xs O2 B2
```

Thus, conjunction of the consequents gives the single implication:
```
h B1 = B2 • h (O1 x xs) = O2 x (h xs)
```
→
```
h (catL xs O1 B1) = catL xs O2 B2
```

8.3   Identity Property and Constructor Replacement

The Identity property for Catamorphisms [17] (IC) is crucial in our development. Its simplest typical form is:

```
(IC) catT D C1 ... Cn = D
```

where the C_i are the (symbolic) constructors for (symbolic type) T and (of course) D :: T. That is, applying a catamorphism to a structure with the structure's own constructors yields the same structure.

IC follows from how a catamorphism can be thought of as implementing constructor replacement with the catamorphism operands. In terms of the schematic catamorphism, observe how the embedded operation 'f' is applied by cata recursively to and across each level of substructure. At each level the embedded operation is applied to an instance of the pattern algebra where the constructors are replaced according to the programming of the embedded operation.

In the case of 1ZTs with generators G_i, a corollary of IC is

```
Z = catT D G1...Gn = Z G1...Gn
```

8.4   Catamorphic Expressibility of 2ZTs

The continuing central role played by catamorphisms in zoetic data is reflected in the critical assumption that the characteristic functions of specific zoetic data are all expressible as catamorphisms, i.e. as the generic catamorphic patterns themselves (for 1ZTs) or, as well shall see, specialisations by applying these patterns to appropriate operands to the generic catamorphic patterns on the underlying types (for 2ZTs).

The basis for this assumption relates to one of the basic premises for zoetic data, i.e. the liberation of programming from the burden of interpretation. Thus, if interpreters don't need to be written, then programming languages don't need to be so complex as to express interpreters. Rather, the expressiveness of catamorphisms a.k.a. "fold" [19] seems to provide a sufficient basis for all practically-imaginable applications (i.e. other than a Universal Turing Machine or equivalent programming language interpreter). Formally-speaking, the iterative aspect of any function provably terminating in second-order arithmetic [22] is expressible as a catamorphism.

Accordingly, our derivations of 2ZT generators are limited to those for which holds what we call the "Catamorphic-Expressible property" (CE) - that the characteristic behaviour B on some symbolic data D of type T can be expressed as a catamorphism:

    (CE)   B D = catT D A1 … An

where

- cataT is the catamorphism on type T
- Ai are the arguments/operands to cataT that implement B (which as we see below, are actually the zoetic generators we seek).

Note that CE for 2ZTs is a generalization of the specification of 1ZTs as follows:

- recall the behaviour of a 1ZT is the catamorphism on the type
  Z = catT D
- but applying IC to the above yields
  catT D = catT D G1…Gn
  for 1ZT generators Gi

In other words, the only difference between 1ZTs and 2ZTs is that for the former the zoetic behaviour is constrained to be actual catamorphism on the type, whereas for the latter the zoetic behaviour is any operation provided that it can be expressed in terms of that catamorphism.

8.5   Identifying and Deriving 2ZT Generators

The values Ai used in CE above, as operands to the relevant catamorphic pattern catT to express 2ZT behaviours B, can be demonstrated to have the critical role, of 2ZT generators as follows. For each distinct case of CE, typically (note renaming of Ai as Gi)

    B D = catT D G1…Gn

we first use IC to expand the LHS systematically, in what we identify as a Derivative of Catamorphic-Expressibility (DCE):

(DCE) `B (catT D C1...Cn) = catT D G1...Gn`

or, in terms of the schematic catamorphism

$$B\,(cata\,phi\,D) \,=\, cata\,chi\,D$$

where embedded phi and chi as usual replace constructors Ci, in this case for phi by themselves and for chi by the Gi.

At this point, fusion is applicable, i.e. to establish the above identity, we need schematically

$$chi\,(fmap\,B\,x) \,=\, B\,(phi\,x)$$

or typically

`Gi (B args' ...) = B (Ci args ...)`

where "args ..." are the operands to which Ci applies to produce some D :: T, and "args'..." are the args ... but with Ci uniformly replaced throughout by Gi.

Thus, the operands Gi (that are used to express the behaviours of 2ZTs) are not only calculable by fusion, but they are also the zoetic generators (as with 1ZTs corresponding to the symbolic constructors). From this point equational reasoning yields implementations of Gi just as for 1ZTs as above. Illustrative examples now follow.

9 Generator Derivations for Exemplar 2ZTs

Examples of the formal derivations of 2ZT generators from specifications, following the above pattern, now follow.

9.1 Derivation of Zoetic Set Generators

Recall the type of trees with a mixture of binary and unary subtrees:

`Bt a = Nul | Lf a | Brn(Bt a)(Bt a)| One(Bt a)`

for which the relevant catamorphic pattern is catBt (as defined above).

The relevant fusion law (derivable from the earlier fusion schema) is

$h\,n_a = n_b$

$\wedge$

$h\,(l_a\,x) = l_b\,x$

$\wedge$

$h\,(b_a\,t_1\,t_2) = b_b\,(h\,t_1)\,(h\,t_2)$

$\wedge$

$h\,(o_a\,t) = o_b\,(h\,t)$

$\rightarrow$

$h\,(catBt\,t\,n_a\,l_a\,b_a\,o_a) = catBt\,t\,n_b\,l_b\,b_b\,o_b$

Now, if these trees are to be interpreted as zoetic sets by the characteristic method "member" above, the relevant expression of DCE in this case is:

```
member (catBt bt Nl Lf Brn One) = catBt bt m s u c
```

Application of fusion gives:

```
(1)  member Nul = m
(2)  member (Lf x) = s x
(3)  member (Brn t1 t2) = u (member t1) (member t2)
(4)  member (One t) = c (member t)
```

From this point, equational reasoning respectively proceeds in each case:

```
(1)  m e = member Nul e = False
(2)  s x e
     = member (Lf x) e
     = x==e
(3)  u (member t1) (member t2) e
     = member (Brn bt1 bt2) e
     = member t1 e || member t2 e
(4)  c (member t) e
     = member (One t) e
     = not (member t e)
```

Thus, recognising in particular the partial applications "member ti" as zoetic sets zsi, we have derived implementations for zoetic generators of empty, singleton, union and complement of sets respectively m, s, u and c:

```
m e = False
s x e = x==e
u zs1 zs2 e = zs1 e || zs2 e
c zs e = not (zs e)
```

which are identical (modulo names) to the intuitive definitions offered originally far above.

9.2   Derivation of Zoetic Grammar Generators

Based on an interpretation of two-flavoured Rose trees (where the different "flavours" are distinguished by respective constructors B1 and B2), we can specify and derive implementations for n-ary versions of the parsing combinators conc and alt from far above. The basic infrastructure is as follows. (For simplicity of presentation, native Haskell lists are used to implement the n-ary subtree structure.)

```
data Rose2 = Tip String | B1 [Rose2] | B2 [Rose2]

catR2 (Tip s) t b1 b2 = t s
catR2 (B1 r2s) t b1 b2 = b1 (map (\r2 -> catR2 r2 t b1
b2) r2s)
catR2 (B2 r2s) t b1 b2 =
  b2 (
    map (\r2 -> catR2 r2 t b1 b2) r2s
  )
```

The relevant fusion law (again derivable from the earlier fusion schema) is

$h (t_a\ x) = t_b\ x$

$\wedge$

$h (b1_a\ rs) = b1_b (map\ h\ rs)$

$\wedge$

$h (b2_a\ rs) = b2_b (map\ h\ rs)$

➔

$h (catR2\ rs\ t_a\ b1_a\ b2_a) = catR2\ rs\ t_b\ b1_b\ b2_b$

Then the following interpretation (by "parse") ascribes behaviours

- to Tip: the behaviour of a token
- to B1: the behaviour of n-ary alternation
- to B2: the behaviour of n-ary concatenation:

```
parse (Tip tk) str =
  if prefix tk str
  then [chop tk str]
  else []
-- prefix, chop as before

parse (B1 r2s) str = concat (map (\p -> p str)(map parse
r2s))

parse (B2 r2s) str =
  foldr
  (\p ss -> concat (map p ss))         -- op
  (head (map parse r2s) str)           -- b
  (reverse (tail (map parse r2s)))     -- xs
```

The required n-ary generators tok, nalt and nconc are specified by the relevant expression of DCE:

```
parse (catR2 rs Tip B1 B2) = catR2 rs tok nalt nconc
```

From the above, fusion yields:

```
(1) parse (Tip tk) = tok tk
(2) parse (B1 r2s) = nalt (map parse r2s)
(3) parse (B2 r2s) = nconc (map parse r2s)
```

Equational reasoning respectively proceeds

```
(1)  tok tk str
     = parse (Tip tk) str
     = if prefix tk str
       then [chop tk str]
       else []

(2)  nalt (map parse r2s) str
     = parse (B1 r2s) str
     = concat (map(\p-> p str)(map parse r2s))

(3)  nconc (map parse r2s) str
     = parse (B2 r2s) str
     = foldr
        (\p ss -> concat (map p ss))
        (head (map parse r2s) str)
        (reverse (tail (map parse r2s)))
```

Finally, recognising "parse (Tip ts)" as "tok ts" and "map parse r2 s" as the list of zoetic grammars gs, and p(arser) as zoetic g(rammar) yields implementations as follows. The implementation of tok repeats the intuitive definition above:

```
tok tk str =
  if prefix tk str
  then [chop tk str]
  else []
```

The respective implementations of nalt and ncat are evident generalisations of the intuitive definitions of binary alt and conc of traditional combinator parsers above:

```
nalt gs str = concat (map (\g -> g str) gs)

nconc gs str =
   foldr
   (\g ss -> concat (map g ss))
   (head gs str)
   (reverse (tail gs))
```

10   Related Work

Earlier versions of the formal derivation of zoetic types are available [23, 24]. A complementary view of the significance to Software Engineering of catamorphic patterns is also available [25].

We have already emphasised how zoetic data, while not recognised or identified distinctively as such, are not uncommon to functional programming in general (e.g. characteristic predicates, combinator parsers). Some other connections (different and/or more specific) are as follows.

10.1   Zoetic Data Reflected in Mainstream Programming Languages and Software Engineering

It's interesting to note that the earliest high-level programming language control construct (the DO-loop of FORTRAN) is precisely the catamorphism on natural numbers.

Backus' later language design (FP [26]) extended the fixed set of control constructs to include catamorphisms on lists and other list operations expressible as catamorphisms.

The "structured programming" [27] school does not limit itself to catamorphisms, but nonetheless echoes our approach in advocating a fixed set of program composition or "control" constructs.

10.2   Subrecursive Programming - Turner's TFP

Our grounding of zoetic data in catamorphic recursion patterns establishes a further link, to Turner's "Total Functional Programming" [28] which emphasises the use of subrecursive program structuring mechanisms to ensure that its programs avoid unproductive non-termination (i.e., are total functions). The basis for the link is that our grounding of zoetic data in catamorphic recursion patterns also ensures functional totality.

Thus, our "Totally Functional" programming develops Turner's, as follows.

1. For every datatype there is posited a characteristic method, so that symbolic data are completely ("totally") replaced by functional representations.
2. However, these characteristic methods are all ultimately definable totally as catamorphisms: in the case of 1ZTs, directly in terms of the catamorphic pattern that can be thought of as characterising the type; in the case of 2ZTs, by application of an underlying catamorphic pattern to operands (that turn out to be the generators for the 2ZT).

Note that not every function of interest to us is expressible as a (single) catamorphism. For example the catamorphic pattern catR for Rose trees requires mapL on the list of subtrees, itself definable in terms of the list catamorphism pattern catL. Also, other operations (as basic as inserting an element into a sorted list) may involve non-iterative post-processing of the results of catamorphisms - see Bailes and Brough [20] for a summary. However, the essential iterative behaviour of non-trivial zoetic data seems to remain amenable to our methods as above.

10.3   Constructive Type Theory

We acknowledge that programming based on the catamorphisms implicit in regular recursive type definitions is not original e.g. Coq [29]; however we take the further step of attempting to treat all data as behaviour, i.e. "totally functional".

11   Future Directions

A range of obstacles and or opportunities remain to be exploited before our TFP is a practical alternative for conventional symbolic-data-based interpretive programming.

11.1   Revisit 2ZT Derivation

Our scheme for deriving 2ZT generators is based on symbolic data. A re-presentation based purely on 1ZTs would better demonstrate the self-consistency of the zoetic universe.

11.2   Anamorphic Duals to Zoetic Data

In view of the evident usefulness of the categorical dual of list catamorphisms (for lists the "unfold" [30], or "anamorphisms" more generally), zoetic versions of these as embraced by Turner in his Total Functional Programming (above), need exploration. We anticipate that for every 1ZT there would be a dual, i.e. primary zoetic co-datatype, and that from these specific zoetic co-datatypes would be derivable.

11.3   Connection with Object-Oriented Programming

It's apparent that zoetic types possess by definition only a single method i.e. their characteristic behaviours. There exist however discernible hierarchies of related behaviours (some kind of "super" and "sub" types) together with the means to program connections. This is that application of a 1ZT zoetic datum to the generators of a 2ZT (derived from that 1ZT) yields the corresponding value of the 2ZT. Consider for example binary trees "BT a" above. Thus, for the 1ZT values "nl", "lf X", "brn T1 T2" and "one T" (for some Bts T, T1, T2), applying each to the set-as-characteristic-predicate 2ZT generators m, s, u, c evaluates to the corresponding 2ZT values:

```
nl m s u c ➔ m
lf X m s u c ➔ s X
brn T1 T2 m s u c ➔ u (T1 m s u c) (T2 m s u c)
one T m s u c ➔ c (T m s u c)
```

Further recognizing that "Ti m s u c" is in turn a zoetic set Si gives

```
brn T1 T2 m s u c ➔ u S1 S2
one T m s u c ➔ c S
```

where Si is the 2ZT counterpart of the 1ZT Ti. That is, a 2ZT value can be obtained by applying a 1ZT value to the 2ZT generators.

It remains to be exposed how multi-level hierarchies of such super- and sub-types can be developed.

11.4 Type-Checking

Automatic type inference is not available for zoetic data, because they require functional types that transcend the expectations, implicit in Milner [31] and its derivatives such as the Haskell type regime, of automatic type inference rather than providing explicit type signatures for function declarations.

For example, the simple application

```
expz ztwo ztwo
```

fails (spectacularly) to type-check, with 28 lines of error message from WinGHCi [32]. A cleverer definition of expz solves the problem in this case:

```
expz za zb = zb za
```

However, replacement of straightforward definitions by such subtleties does not seem to be the basis of a sustainable solution. Higher type systems [33] offer apparent remedies, but the cost of the loss of the convenience of inference remains to be understood.

11.5 "Zoe" Language Design and Implementation

Work has begun on the design and agile implementation in parallel of the Zoe programming language [34] that embodies our Totally Functional Programming approach. Zoe superficially resembles a subset of Haskell, with the key distinction that instances of regular types are zoetic i.e. behave catamorphically. For example, the declaration

```
TYPE bintree = branch @ INT @ | nil;
```

defines a type of binary tree "bintree" with ternary generator "branch" and nullary generator "nil". The type is recursive on the first and third operands of "branch", the second operand being a member of the builtin "INT" type.

Continuing this example, we can construct a "bintree" in the obvious way, e.g.

```
b = branch (branch nil 1 (branch nil 2 nil)) 3 (branch
nil 4 nil);
```

Operations on b are by direct application with the required catamorphic behaviour, e.g. to sum the elements of the tree it suffices to apply

```
b (\ r1 i r2 -> r1+i+r2) 0
```

In anticipation of the dominant role of catamorphism application in Zoe programming, special syntax is supplied for catamorphism application, e.g. the above can also be rendered as

```
FOLD b :: bintree {
   branch r1 i r2 = r1+i+r2;
   nil = 0
}
```

The potential merits of this notation (not without at least some degree of precedent [35]) are:

- highlighting of the catamporphism application by keyword and block structure;

- signification of catamorphism operands by name of the corresponding generator rather than position.

Other interesting features of Zoe include:

- predefined list and natural number types with the obvious catamorphic behaviours;
- overloading of the zoetic behaviour of natural numbers with arithmetic operators;
- a simple pattern-matching behaviour for character strings that foreshadows their use in lexical analysis in the Zoe self-implementation.

The prototype implementations of Zoe to date have all involved straightforward preprocessing into Haskell. The eventual self-implementation will as ever provide a useful validation of Zoe's pragmatics.

11.6 Program Synthesis and Analog Computation

The whole point of zoetic data is that programs are built around the behaviours of their components and not about their representations, thus finessing the linguistic schism between "program" and "data". But construction of programs based on the behaviours (not representations) of components is in effect analog computation. Even though classical analog computation [36] involves the behaviours of electronic components, whereas our TFP involves the behaviours of functions, there may well be useful parallels so that the long-dormant field of analog computing might be able to offer insights to support a comprehensive discipline of program synthesis of zoetic-data-based totally Functional Programming.

11.7 Zoetic Data as Refactoring Targets

Further to the above, if zoetic-data-based totally Functional Programming were to emerge as a viable alternative to conventional symbolic-data-based programming, then reverse engineering of conventional programs into TFP would be a desirable step in the evolution of existing applications. See [37] for some initial ideas about how to exploit zoetic data as targets for source code refactoring in this way.

12 Conclusions

Zoetic data exploit the key characteristic of functional languages - support for higher-order functions - to embody functional representations that embody the characteristic behaviours inherent to each datatype. The reusability implicit in this representation allows us to avoid repeated interpretation of otherwise symbolic data at each use in source code. Our "Totally Functional" approach to programming further separates the decoupling of the definition of datatypes from their various applications by replacing constructors of symbolic data with data generators that produce these zoetic representations. Two kinds of zoetic data/functional behaviours are recognized: primarily the catamorphism on the underlying regular types; and secondarily the behaviours that can be expressed in terms of these catamorphisms. In each of these cases the zoetic generators are derived formally by program transformation of their specifications.

The significance of our work is two-fold. Firstly, we have demonstrated a fulfilment of functional programming in a "zoetic" treatment of data that is faithful to the original vision of Church as foreshadowed by "Church numerals" in his lambda-calculus. Secondly and moreover, we have thus demonstrated the foundation in Software Engineering principles of this fulfilment of functional programming through these zoetic data, as follows:

- the idea of zoetic data arises from applying the **reuse** principle to the problem of multiple occurrences of interpreters of intended behaviours from symbolic data;
- zoetic data *per se* arise from **separating the concerns**, on the one hand of ascribing particular behaviours when generating zoetic data, from the other of using those behaviours in various applications;
- the implementations of zoetic data generators are calculated from their specifications using **formal methods** of mathematical program transformation.

Acknowledgements. We gratefully acknowledge our various colleagues' contributions over the years to our ongoing work reflected here, especially those of Leighton Brough. Also, Tim Westcott, William Woodward and Khoa Tran made useful contributions to the implementation of the Zoe language prototypes.

References

1. Hughes, J.: Why functional programming matters. Comput. J. **32**(2), 98–107 (1989)
2. Bird, R., Wadler, P.: Introduction to Functional Programming. Prentice-Hall International, Upper Saddle River (1988)
3. Abelson, H., Sussman, G.J., Sussman, J.: Structure and Interpretation of Computer Programs, 2nd edn. MIT Press, Cambridge (1996)
4. Collins English Dictionary. http://www.collinsdictionary.com. Accessed 4 July 2014
5. Sommerville, I.: Software Engineering, 8th edn. Addison Wesley, Boston (2007)
6. Sommerville, I.: Software Engineering, 10th edn. Pearson, Essex (2015)
7. Meyer, B.: Object-Oriented Software Construction. Prentice Hall, Englewood Cliffs (1997)
8. Barendregt, H.: The Lambda Calculus - Its Syntax and Semantics, 2nd edn. North-Holland, Amsterdam (1984)
9. Dijkstra, E.: On the role of scientific thought. In: Dijkstra, E.W. (ed.) Selected writings on Computing: A Personal Perspective. Texts and Monographs in Computer Science, pp. 60–66. Springer-Verlag, New York (1982)
10. Scott, M.: Programming Language Pragmatics, 3rd edn. Morgan Kaufmann, San Francisco (2009)
11. Kiczales, G., Lamping., J., Mendhekar, A., Maeda, C., Lopes, C., Loingtier, J. M., Irwin, J.: Aspect-oriented programming. In: Proceedings of the 11th European Conference on Object-Oriented Programming ECOOP'97. LNCS 1241, pp. 220–242 (1997)
12. Hinchey, M., Bowen, J., Vassev, E.: Formal Methods. In: Laplante, P.A. (ed.) Encyclopedia of Software Engineering, pp. 308–320. Taylor & Francis, New York (2010)

13. Haskell Programming Language. http://www.haskell.org. Accessed 4 July 2014
14. Hopcroft, J., Ullman, J.: Introduction to Automata Theory, Languages, and Computation. Addison-Wesley, Boston (1979)
15. Hutton, G.: Higher-order functions for parsing. J. Funct. Program. **2**, 323–343 (1992)
16. Wadler, P.: How to replace failure by a list of successes a method for exception handling, backtracking, and pattern matching in lazy functional languages. In: Jouannaud, J.-P. (ed.) FPCA 1985. LNCS, vol. 201, pp. 113–128. Springer, Heidelberg (1985). doi:10.1007/3-540-15975-4_33
17. Backhouse, R., Jansson, P., Jeuring, J., Meertens, L.: Generic programming - an introduction. In: Swierstra, S., Henriques, P., Oliveira, J. (eds.) Advanced Functional Programming. LNCS, vol. 1608, pp. 28–115 (1999)
18. Meijer, E., Fokkinga, M., Paterson, R.: Functional programming with bananas, lenses, envelopes and barbed wire. In: Hughes, J. (ed.) FPCA 1991. LNCS, vol. 523, pp. 124–144. Springer, Heidelberg (1991). doi:10.1007/3540543961_7
19. Hutton, G.: A tutorial on the universality and expressiveness of fold. J. Funct. Program. **9**, 355–372 (1999)
20. Bailes, P., Brough, L.: Making sense of recursion patterns. In: Proceedings of 1st FormSERA: Rigorous and Agile Approaches, pp. 16–22. IEEE (2012)
21. Uustalu, T., Vene, V., Pardo, A.: Recursion schemes from comonads. Nordic J. Comput. **8** (3), 366–390 (2001)
22. Reynolds, J.C.: Three approaches to type structure. In: Ehrig, H., Floyd, C., Nivat, M., Thatcher, J. (eds.) CAAP 1985. LNCS, vol. 185, pp. 97–138. Springer, Heidelberg (1985). doi:10.1007/3-540-15198-2_7
23. Bailes, P., Kemp, C.: Fusing folds and data structures into zoetic data. In: Proceedings of 23rd IASTED International Multi-Conference on Applied Informatics (AI 2005), pp. 299–306 (2005)
24. Bailes, P., Kemp, C.: Zoetic data and their generators. In: Proceedings of 11th International Conference on Evaluation of Novel Software Approaches to Software Engineering (ENASE 2016), pp. 260–271 (2016)
25. Bailes, P., Brough, L., Kemp, C.: From computer science to software engineering – a programming-level perspective. In: Fujita, H., et al. (eds.) New Trends in Software Methodologies. Tools and Techniques. IOS Press, Amsterdam (2014)
26. Backus, J.: Can programming be liberated from the von Neumann style?: A functional style and its algebra of programs. Commun. ACM **21**(8), 613–641 (1978)
27. Dahl, O.-J., Dijkstra, E.W., Hoare, C.A.R.: Structured Programming. Academic Press, Cambridge (1972)
28. Turner, D.A.: Total functional programming. J. Univers. Comput. Sci. **10**(7), 751–768 (2004)
29. Coq proof assistant. https://coq.inria.fr/. Accessed 22 Feb 2016
30. Gibbons, J., Hutton, G., Altenkirch, T.: When is a function a fold or an unfold? Electron. Notes Theor. Comput. Sci. **44**(1), 2001 (2001)
31. Milner, R.: A theory of type polymorphism in programming. J. Comput. Syst. Sci. **17**, 348–375 (1977)
32. Haskell platform. http://www.haskell.org/platform/. Accessed 4 July 2014
33. Vytiniotis, D., Weirich, S., Jones, S.L.P.: Boxy types: inference for higher-rank types and impredicativity. In: Proceedings of ICFP, pp. 251–262 (2006)
34. Bailes, P.: Recursion patterns and their impact on programming language design. In: Proceedings of IASTED International Conference Advances in Computer Science (ACS 2013), pp. 450–459 (2013)

35. Swierstra, S.D., Azero Alcocer, P.R., Saraiva, J.: Designing and implementing combinator languages. In: Swierstra, S.D., Oliveira, J.N., Henriques, P.R. (eds.) AFP 1998. LNCS, vol. 1608, pp. 150–206. Springer, Heidelberg (1999). doi:10.1007/10704973_4
36. Jackson, A.: Analog Computation. McGraw-Hill, New York (1960)
37. Bailes, P., Brough, L., Kemp, C.: Higher-order catamorphisms as bases for program structuring and design recovery. In: Proceedings of IASTED International Conference Software Engineering (SE 2013), pp. 775–782 (2013)

Towards Modelling and Implementation of Reliability and Usability Features for Research-Oriented Cloud Computing Platforms

Maria Spichkova[1]([✉]), Heinz W. Schmidt[1,2], Iman I. Yusuf[2],
Ian E. Thomas[2], Steve Androulakis[3], and Grischa R. Meyer[3]

[1] School of Science, RMIT University, 414-418 Swanston Street,
Melbourne 3001, Australia
{maria.spichkova,heinz.schmidt}@rmit.edu.au
[2] eResearch, RMIT University, 17-23 Lygon Street, Carlton 3053, Australia
{iman.yusuf,ian.edward.thomas}@rmit.edu.au
[3] eResearch, Monash University, Wellington Road, Clayton 3800, Australia
{steve.androulakis,grischa.meyer}@monash.edu

Abstract. Usability and readability features are crucial on all phases of software development process as well as while applying the developed software. A hard-to-read and hard-to-understand model of a complicated system might provide more confusion that clarification and development support. A hard-to-use technology or system might lead to its misuse or even to hazardous accidents. In this chapter, we present an approach on modelling and implementation of research-oriented cloud computing platforms, focusing on the reliability and usability features. The proposed formal framework provides an easy-to-read templates for modelling of core platform components. The proposed cloud computing platform allows researchers to conduct experiments requiring complex computations over big data. The core feature of the platform is that the users do not require to a deep technical understanding of cloud computing, HPC, fault tolerance, or data management in order to leverage all the benefits of cloud computing.

Keywords: Usability · Reliability · Modelling · Cloud computing · Visualisation

1 Introduction

Formal models allow comprehensive analysis of system properties in the early phases of software and system development, to identify possible faults as well as discrepancies between requirements and the system-under-development as early as possible to decrease the production costs. The lack of understandability and readability features might be an obstacle for adoption of formal models in industrial development process [44], as these features are crucial on all phases

© Springer International Publishing AG 2016
L.A. Maciaszek and J. Filipe (Eds.): ENASE 2016, CCIS 703, pp. 158–178, 2016.
DOI: 10.1007/978-3-319-56390-9_8

of software development as well as while applying the developed software. If the model of a complicated system is not easy-to-read and easy-to-understand, it might provide even more confusion about system properties instead of providing their clarification and the corresponding development support.

For these reasons, we developed a formal framework and the corresponding model of a cloud-based platform, focusing on the usability and readability features as they are defined in [32,36]. The framework allows (1) formal analysis of properties of composed processes within a cloud-based platform, and (2) estimation of the worst case execution time of these processes.

Cloud computing provides a great opportunity for scientists, as it enables large-scale experiments that are too complicated to run them on local desktop machines. Conduction experiments on big data and applying complex computational methods demands using cluster or cloud computing [4,10]. Cloud-based computations can be highly parallel, long running and data-intensive, which is desirable for many kinds of scientific experiments.

However, to unlock this power, we need a user-friendly interface and an easy-to-use methodology for conducting these experiments. For most users, both present new technologies, either computationally and in data management, and both require learning non-standard data management, programming languages and libraries. In the case of cloud computing, the users have to learn how to work within a cloud-based environment, e.g., how to create and set up virtual machines (VMs), how to collect the results of their experiments, and finally destroy the VMs, etc. Thus, the users have to obtain a new set of skills (e.g., knowledge of fault tolerance), which might distract from focusing on the domain specific problems of the experiment, where scientific experiments can be very challenging from a domain point of view, even in the case the computation can be done on a local desktop machine. Failure while setting up a cloud-based execution environment or during the execution itself may be an obstacle for an inexperienced user, if the cloud-based platform does not provide corresponding user-support and is not user-friendly enough.

Contributions: We propose a user-friendly open-source platform supported by the corresponding formal model. The proposed platform hides the above problems from the user by incapsulating them in the platform's functionality. On this stage, we focus on scientific computations, i.e., we assume that the users of the platform would be researchers working in the fields of physics, chemistry, biology, etc. Our solution enables researchers to focus on domain-specific problems, and to delegate to the tool to deal with the detail that comes with accessing high-performance and cloud computing infrastructure, and the data management challenges it poses. Moreover, the platform implements various fault tolerance strategies to prevent the failed execution from causing a system-wide failure, as well as to recover a failed execution.

In the current version of the platform, we have focused on biophysics and structural chemistry experiments, based on the analysis of big data from synchrotrons and atomic force microscopy. We conducted a number of case studies across Theoretical Chemical and Quantum Physics group at the RMIT university. The domain experts noted the time savings for computing and data management, as well as user-friendly interface.

The presented in this chapter approach extends our work introduced at the 11th International Conference on Evaluation of Novel Software Approaches to Software Engineering [39], and is also based on our recent work on scalability and fault-tolerance of Cloud computations [35,43].

Outline: The rest of the paper is structured as follows. Section 2 presents the formal background for our framework. Section 3 introduces the proposed formal model of a cloud-based platform. Section 4 presents implementation of the proposed model as an open-source *Chiminey* platform, focusing on the reliability aspects. In Sect. 5, we discuss the usability and visualisation features of *Chiminey* and how they are reflected in the conducted case studies. Section 6 overviews the related work. Section 7 concludes the paper by highlighting the main contributions, and introduces the future work directions.

2   Background

In this approach, we follow the ideas on reconciling component and process views [31,38], where any process P its entry and exit points by $Entry(P)$ and $Exit(P)$ respectively, and represent a process P (elementary or composed) by the corresponding component specification $PComp$, thus, $[P] = PComp$. For any process P with syntactic interface $(I_P \triangleright O_P)$, where I_P and O_P are sets of input and output data streams respectively, we can specify

$$I_{[P]} = \{Entry(P)\} \cup I_P$$

and

$$O_{[P]} = \{Exit(P)\} \cup O_P.$$

A process can be defined as an elementary or a composed one, where the composition of any two processes P_1 and P_2 can be sequential $P_1; P_2$, alternate $P_1 \oplus P_2$ or parallel $P_1 \| P_2$, and for any process P we can define repetitively composed process $P \circlearrowright_{lpspec}$, where *lpspec* denotes a loop specifier. In this paper we use the following operators to present examples of process/component specifications:

$\langle\rangle$	an empty stream
$\langle x \rangle$	one element stream consisting of the element x
ft.l	the first element of an untimed stream l
s^i	the ith time interval of the stream s
$\mathsf{msg}_n(s)$	s can have at most n messages at each time interval
$\#l$	number of elements in an untimed stream l

We treat a process as a special kind of a component that has additionally two extra channels (one input and one output channel) which are used only to activate the process and to indicate its termination, i.e., to represents the entry and exit points of the process. All the control channels (representing entry and exit points of a process) are drawn as orange dashed lines, the corresponding auxiliary components over these channels are also drawn in orange.

An elementary process corresponds to an elementary specification that has $m + n$ special channels, where $m \geq 1$ and $n \geq 1$ (i.e., if $m > 1$, the process has more than one entry point, and if $n > 1$, it has more than one exit point):

- input channels $start_1, \ldots, start_m$ of type *Event* consisting of one element *;
  these are entry points of the process that corresponds to an activation signal
  process is started;
- output channels $stop_1, \ldots, stop_n$ of the same type; these are exit points of the
  process that corresponds to the signals *process is finished with the result i*,
  where $1 \leq i \leq n$.

The framework allows us

- to analyse properties of composed processes by applying a well-developed
  theories of composition [7, 34], and
- to estimate the worst case execution time (WCET) of the composed processes
  on the base of following rules:

$$wcet(P \; ; \; Q) = wcet(P) + wcet(Q)$$
$$wcet(P \circlearrowleft_{lpspec}) = wcet(P)$$
$$wcet(P \,||\, Q) = max\{wcet(P), wcet(Q)\} + wcet(\&)$$
$$wcet(P \oplus Q) = max\{wcet(P), wcet(Q)\} + wcet(@) + wcet(+)$$

where $wcet(A)$ denotes the WCET of the process A.

To avoid the omission of assumptions about the environment of the system, we specify every component in terms of an assumption and a guarantee: whenever input from the environment behaves in accordance with the assumption, the specified component is required to fulfil the guarantee.

3   Formal Model of a Cloud-Based Platform

The proposed *Chiminey* platform provides access to a distributed computing infrastructure. On the logical level it is modelled as a dynamically built set of *Smart Connectors* (SCs), which handle the provision of cloud-based infrastructure. SCs vary from each other by the type of computation to be supported and/or the specific computing infrastructure to be provisioned. An SC interacts with a cloud service (Infrastructure-as-a-Service) on behalf of the user. Figure 1 presents the corresponding workflow.

With respect to the execution environment, the only information that is expected from the user is to specify the number of computing resources she wishes to use, credentials to access those resources, and the location for transferring the output of the computation. Thus, the user does not need to know about how the execution environment is set up (i.e., how VMs are created and configured for the upcoming simulation), how a simulation is executed, how the

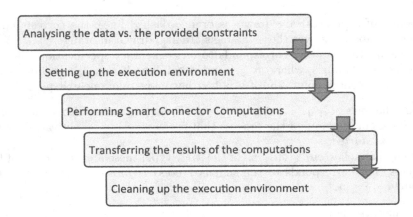

Fig. 1. Cloud service: Workflow.

final output is transferred and how the environment is cleaned up after the computation completion (i.e., how the VMs are destroyed).

Figure 2 shows the logical architecture of an SC. Each SC consist of five logical components, which can also be seen as processes within the framework workflow, presented on Fig. 1.

An execution of an SC is called a *job*. An SC executes a user requested process cP, which consists of tasks $Task_1, \ldots, Task_{NT}$, which could be executed in iterative manner. In the simplest case, cP consists of a single task that should be executed once only.

A concrete SC is build from a general template by configuration its parameters:

- *DataConstraints* specifies constraints on the user provided input *dataInput*;
- *ExecParamVM* specifies parameters of the job, e.g., which compilers should be installed on the generated VMs;
- *ExecParamT* is a list of the task execution parameters $ExecParamT_1, \ldots,$ $ExecParamT_{NT}$. These parameters specify for each task which data are required for its execution, what is a convergence criterion and whether there is any for that task, which scheduling constrains are required, etc.;
- *TCode* presents an actual executable code for the corresponding tasks, in general case it consists of NT elements.
- *Sweep* is a list of values to sweep over: With respect to configuring and executing the simulation, the user may set the value and/or ranges of domain specific parameters, and subsequently automatically creating and executing multiple instances of the given SC to sweep across ranges of values.

The first three parameters can be partially derived from *TCode* on the development stage for a concrete SC.

In the rest of this section we will discuss the core subprocesses (subcomponents) of an SC presented on Fig. 1. We also provide formal specifications of two subprocesses, *DataAnalysis* and *EnvSetUpVM*, to illustrate how the formal framework can be used.

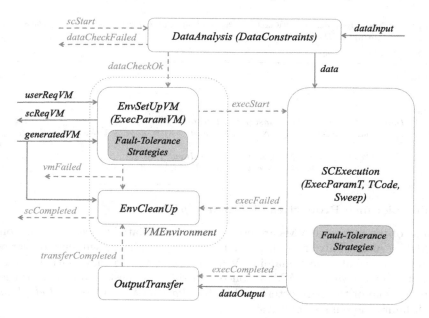

Fig. 2. Logical architecture of a *Smart Connector*, reproduced from [39].

3.1 Data Analysis

The *DataAnalysis* process (component) is responsible for the preliminary check whether the user *dataInput* satisfies the corresponding *DataConstraints*, both on syntactical and on semantical level. The *DataAnalysis* process is started by receiving an *scStart* signal from the user. If the data check was successful, the *VMEnv* component is activated by signal *dataCheckOk* and the data are forwarded to the *SCExecution* component, otherwise the process is stopped and the user receives an error message *dataCheckFail*.

Below we provide a formal specification of the process *DataAnalysis* on a high level of abstraction. This process has one entry and two exit points.

3.2 Environment SetUp and CleanUp

The *EnvSetUpVM* process (component) is responsible for the communication with the cloud to obtain a number of VMs that is enough for the task according to the user requests *userReqVM*. The user request *userReqVM* is a pair of numbers (iN, mN), where iN is an ideal and mN is a minimal (from the user's point of view) number of VMs required for the experiment. The *EnvSetUpVM* component requests from the cloud iN VMs.

Below we provide a formal specification of the *EnvSetUpVM* process on a high level of abstraction. This process has one entry and two exit points.

process DataAnalysis [scStart ; dataCheckOk, dataCheckFail] (DataConstraints) ————— timed —

in	$dataInput : DataInputType$
out	$data : dataType$

asm   true

- -

gar

1 $DataCheckSucessful(DataConstraints, dataInput^t) \rightarrow$
     $dataCheckOk^t = \langle * \rangle \ \wedge \ dataCheckFail^t = \langle \rangle \ \wedge \ data^t + 1 = dataInput^t$

2 $\neg DataCheckSucessful(DataConstraints, dataInput^t) \rightarrow$
     $dataCheckOk^t = \langle \rangle \ \wedge \ dataCheckFail^t = \langle * \rangle \ \wedge \ data^t + 1 = \langle \rangle$

Fault-Tolerance Properties of *EnvSetUpVM*

If some of the requested VMs are not created/instantiated successfully (i.e. only j VMs are successfully created, where $0 \leq j < mN$. The SC will employ various strategies to create the remaining VMs: it will retry to make either a block request to create $mN - j$ VMs at once or a single request at a time. For these purposes, one of the parameters within *ExecParamVM* have to be *RetryLimit*, which limits the number of retries.

The number of VMs generated by cloud (the list *generatedVM* represents the list of the corresponding identifiers, e.g., IP addresses) has to fulfil the following property

$$mN \leq length(generatedVM) \leq iN \tag{1}$$

If Eq. 1 is not fulfilled (more precisely, if $length(generatedVM) < mN$, because the cloud never provides a number of VMs larger than requested), the process is stopped and the user receives an error message *vmFail*. The message *vmFailed* is also activates the *EnvCleanUp* component, which is responsible for final clean up of the system and the destruction of corresponding VMs. When the clean up is completed, the *EnvCleanUp* component generated the message *scCompleted*, which also indicates that the whole process chain is completed.

If Eq. 1 is fulfilled, our platform preforms bootstrapping of generated VMs, and the required compilers are installed according to *ExecParamVM*. If the bootstrapping was successful, the *SCExecution* component is activated by the signal *execStart*.

EnvSetUpVM and *EnvCleanUp* can also be logically composed into a meta-component *VMEnv*, which is responsible for any communication with the cloud and the corresponding environment manipulations.

The *EnvCleanUp* process has three entry and a single exit points: this process can be initiated in three cases:

- failure of the VMs set up process, indicated by *vmFailed*,
- failure of the SC execution, indicated by *execFailed*,
- successful completion of the output transfer (i.e., successful completion of the whole process chain), indicated by *transferCompleted*.

3.3   Execution of a Smart Connector

The *SCExecution* component (cf. Fig. 3) is the main part of a smart connector. It is responsible for the actual execution of the task and provides a number of the task execution options, defined by parameters *ExecParamT*. The corresponding process has one entry point *execStart* and two exit points, *execFailed* and *execCompleted*.

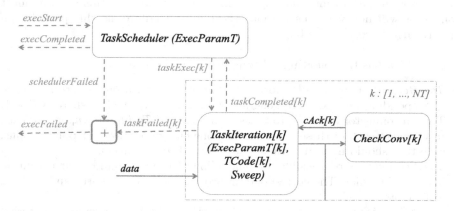

Fig. 3. *SCExecution* subcomponent of Smart Connector, reproduced from [39].

When the *SCExecution* component is activated, we could have two cases:

(1) The smart connector execution was successful. Then, the *SCExecution* component
   - forwards the results of the computations *dataOutput* to the *OutputTransfer* component;
   - generates the signal *execCompleted* that indicates that the *SCExecution* process is completed, and activates *OutputTransfer*.

   The *OutputTransfer* component is responsible for the transfer of the output data to the corresponding server and to a data management system. When the data transfer is completed, the message *transferCompleted* is generated to activate the *EnvCleanUp* component.
(2) The smart connector execution failed on the stage of scheduling or during execution of a task. Then, the *SCExecution* component generates the signal *execFailed*, to activate *EnvCleanUp* for the final clean up of the system and the destruction of corresponding VMs.

Fault-Tolerance Properties of *SCExecution*

The computation might fail due to network or VM failure, i.e., the VM that hosts some of the processes cannot be reached. To avoid an endless waiting on the output from the processes on the unreachable VM, the smart connector will identify the processes that are hosted there, and then execute the appropriate fault tolerance strategy, e.g.,

(i) marking the processes that are hosted on the unreachable VM as failed beyond recovery and then collecting the output of processes from the other VMs, or

(ii) re-running the failed processes on a different VM until maximum re-run limit is reached.

However, we do not implement any strategies to recover a failed process if the failure was due to an internal bug within the task code. In this case, a smart connector will notify the user about the detected failure, as this provides an opportunity to correct the bug.

SCExecution has the following subcomponents (subprocesses):

- *TaskIterarion* is responsible for execution of task iterations according to the corresponding task code. In general case we have NT tasks, where $NT \geq 1$. Thus, a connector has NT processes (components) *TaskIterarion*, one for each task, where each of these processes has one entry and two exit points. Thus, each task should have at least one iteration of its execution.
- *TaskScheduler* is responsible for scheduling of the tasks and their execution in the right order. The corresponding process has $NT + 1$ entry and $NT + 2$ exit points;
- *CheckConv* is an optional component, to check whether convergence criterion of a multi-iterational execution is met.

3.4   Advantages of the Model

Our model allows us not only to have a precise and concise specification of the cloud-based platform on a logical level but also provides a basis for a formal analysis of its properties, including security properties, as well as of the core computation properties. For the formal analysis we suggest to use an interactive semi-automatic theorem prover Isabelle/HOL [6,26] and the corresponding methodologies [33,34,37], as the provided specification is compatible to these methodologies. Moreover, the purposed representation gives a basis for the resource management and performance prediction, cf. [5], as it allows a straightforward analysis of the worst case execution time (WCET) of the composed processes.

4   Implementation

The *Chiminey* platform is implemented using a number of Docker containers [23]. Docker is a linux containerisation technology that creates lightweight virtual machines that share access to the underlying host operating system. We chose to use this approach due its benefits in deployment, flexibility, reproducibility and maintainability for our platform. The resulting composition of components can be deployed on hosts ranging from laptops through to large clusters of cloud nodes, the later destination being ideal for our focus of cloud infrastructure.

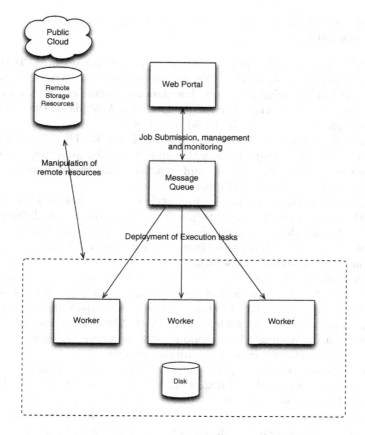

Fig. 4. Architecture of the *Chiminey* platform.

Figure 4 shows the simplified architecture of *Chiminey*. The main components of interest are:

Portal: This component provides the user interface as described in Sect. 5. Is is implemented within a container running a Django/Python application. Python was chosen as the development language due to its rapid prototyping features, integration with our data curation system, and due to its increasing uptake by researchers as a scientific software development language.

Message Queue: This component provides the store of messages created by the portal to query and manage jobs. It is implemented within a Redis container [12].

Workers: Each worker listens on the message queue for instructions to process and hence advance the execution of jobs that have been scheduled from the portal. The workers coordinate access to external resources such as cloud nodes, HPC nodes, etc., as described by the specific smart connector. Each worker is implemented within a container running a Python application using Celery tasks [13].

The current version of the *Chiminey* platform provides a set of APIs to create new and customise existing SCs. We do not restrict our system to be build using a single programming language. The domain-specific calculations could be written in any language. The choice of the language depends on the domain and the concrete research task which should be solved.

For the case studies conducted in collaboration with Theoretical Chemical and Quantum Physics group at the RMIT university, the following two types of Smart Connectors are specified and implemented: cloud-based iterative MapReduce connector (MRSC) and PBS-based connector.

MRSC was developed for MapReduce style of computation. This connector executes the same computation multiple times, each time with different input data. MRSC is suitable for long-running data-parallel programs like Monte Carlo simulations. In our case study, the Monte Carlo based simulations were applied for modelling of a material's porosity and the size distribution of its pores (industrial applications of these research are in diverse areas such as filtration and gas adsorption). One such modelling methodology is the Hybrid Reverse Monte Carlo (HRMC), cf. [28]. HRMC characterises a material's microstructure by producing models consistent with experimental diffraction data, while at the same time ensuring accurate local bonding environments via energy minimisation using an accurate empirical interatomic potential.

The PBS-based connector provisions high-performance computing (HPC) resources that are managed by Portable Batch System (PBS), cf. [2]. This connector is used to execute VASP [16] calculations on the Australia's National Computing Infrastructure [24]. The VASP code contains many options that may be turned on or altered, depending on the physics the researcher is going to explore. Thus, it involves setting up input files describing the desired structure and setting various model parameters or options within the calculation, before running the software on an appropriately sized computation platform, and analysing the resulting output.

An alternative class of connectors that was investigated, acts as a mediator for an *existing* remote computation resource. Such connectors copy initial inputs to existing resources, perform calculations, and collate resources, but do not manage provision of the possibly shared resource.

We have implemented a number of these connectors that have this architecture: connecting to head node of a HPC cluster to submit and monitor PBS jobs, execute multiple parameterised models from a PRISM model checking server [18], and managing execution of big data jobs on a Hadoop cluster. Such connectors automate the process of execution parameterisation, execution monitoring, and curation of output data; tasks that can be error prone if performed manually.

5   Usability Aspects

The proposed open-source platform has been applied across two research disciplines, physics (material characterisation) and structural biology (understanding materials at the atomic scale), to assess its usability and practicality. The domain experts noted the following advantages of the *Chiminey* platform:

- time savings for computing and data management,
- user-friendly interface for the computation set up,
- visualisation of the calculation results as 2D or 3D graphs.

In the rest of this section we will discuss in more details how the above mentioned features are implemented within the platform.

5.1   Chiminey: Overview

The menu has the following sections: *Logout, Create Job, Jobs, Admin, Settings*. After logging in, the users are in the *Jobs* section, where they can see the status of current and previous jobs (executions of SCs), when they were created and

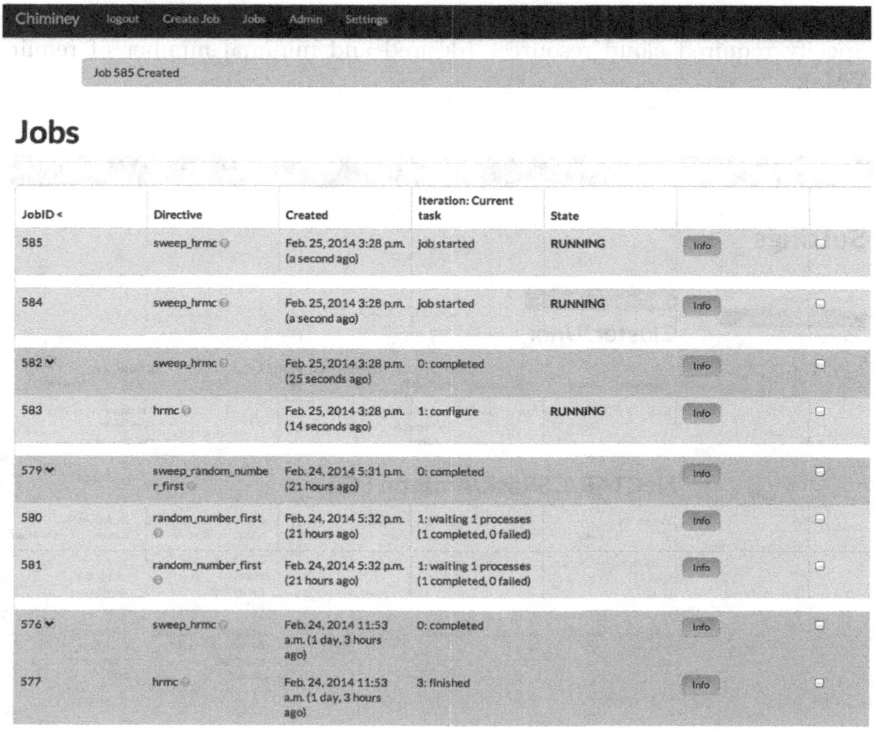

Fig. 5. *Jobs* section of the platform, reproduced from [39].

under what directive. Some of the jobs may be processing (i.e., have the status *Running*), have been completed or had errors, cf. Fig. 5. When we click the *Info*-button, a more detailed information on the particular job is provided.

5.2   Chiminey: Settings

In the *Settings* section, cf. Fig. 6, we can

- set up general account properties,
- change settings of computation platforms as well as add new computation platforms,
- change settings of storage platforms as well as add new storage platforms.

5.3   Chiminey: Creating New Jobs

When we select *Create Job* in the menu, we will see the job submission page, which has a set of available SCs currently registered. The user has to complete the following simple seven steps:

1. Define a name of the SC,
2. Select the computational platform from a given list,
3. Specify required cloud resources (desired and minimal number of required VMs),

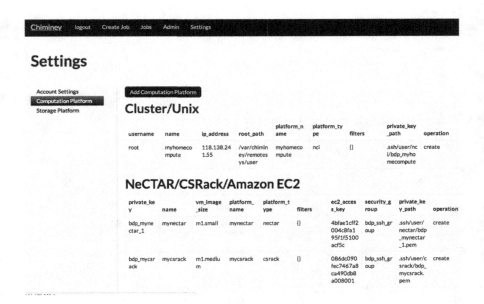

Fig. 6. *Settings* section of the platform, reproduced from [39].

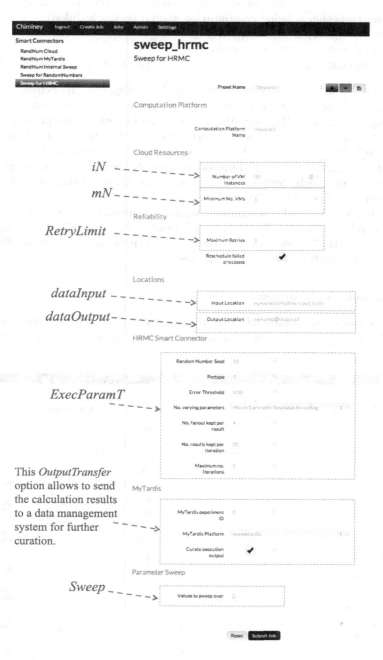

Fig. 7. *Create Job* section of the platform, reproduced from [39].

4. Specify reliability requirements (max. number of retries of a failed computation and whether a failed computation should be rescheduled),
5. Select input/output locations, and
6. Specify domain specific characteristics,
7. Select whether the execution output should be curated and where.

The execution of the smart connector can be configured. To achieve this the following steps are required: (1) set domain specific parameters and the corresponding values, and (2) automatically create and execute multiple instances of the given smart connector to sweep across the specified ranges of values.

Figure 7 shows how to create a job on example of execution of Monte Carlo simulations, which was a part of one of our case studies, cf. Sect. 4. We extended the print screens with the comments to show the match of these parameters to the model from Sect. 3.

The process for such an example within the platform is to provision new virtual machines from a cloud tenancy, transfer and install required software and input for the simulation, and then execute programs, collate results, and finally decommission the virtual machines.

5.4   Chiminey: Visualisation

The user interface, combined with the MyTardis [3] data curation module, allows for flexible handling of data according to its completion and significance.

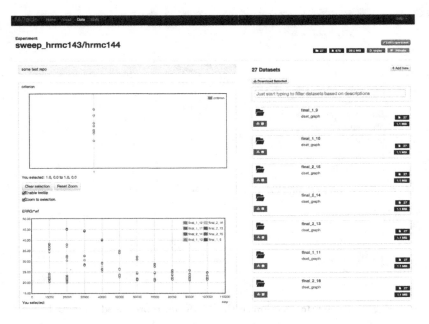

Fig. 8. Visualisation of calculation results, reproduced from [39].

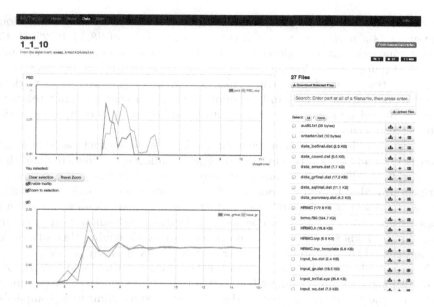

Fig. 9. Visualisation of calculation results as 2D graphs, reproduced from [39].

The results of the calculation can be visualised as 2D or 3D graphs using a plug-in developed to provide better readability of the obtained data.

Figure 8 shows the result of an execution of one complete Hybrid Reverse Monte Carlo (HRMC) run. On the right side you can see the datasets generated during that execution and on the left side graphs generated automatically from inspection of key features of from those datasets. The main utility of these graphs is that they regenerated from each new dataset as it arrives. For a long running calculation, a researcher can observe the trend of these interim results graphically to see whether key criterion are being achieved (for this example, convergence of results). If the criterion is being invalidated (in this case divergence of results), then the user can immediately decide whether to abandon this long running task.

Figure 9 shows the contents of one of these datasets. Here we see on the right the individual files that made up this specific execution and on the left domain specific graphs generated from these data files. The curated experiments and datasets are fully accessible and shareable online and the generated graphs can easily be used for presentations or in written documents.

6   Related Work

While developing the model, we focused on its understandability and readability aspects. There are several approaches on model readability, e.g., [22,40,46]. We aimed to incorporate their core principles within our formal framework.

The development of formal models and architectures for system involved in cloud computing, is a more recent area of system engineering, cf. [8, 11, 19, 29, 41, 45]. Several approaches have proposed the data stream processing systems for clouds, e.g., Martinaitis et al. [21] introduce an approach towards component-based stream processing in clouds, Kuntschke, and Kemper [17] present a work on data stream sharing. Yusuf and Schmidt have shown that the fault-tolerance is best achieved by reflecting the computational flow in such complex scientific system architectures, cf. [42].

There are different types of scientific workflow systems such as Kepler [20], Taverna [27] and Galaxy [1], which are designed to allow researchers to build their own workflows. The *contribution of the work presented in this paper* is that our platform provides drop-in components, Smart Connectors, for existing workflow engines: (*i*) researchers can utilise and adapt existing Smart Connectors; (*ii*) new types of Smart Connectors would be developed within the framework if necessary. From our best knowledge, there is no other framework having this advantage. SCs are geared toward providing power and flexibility over simplicity.

Nimrod [9] is a set of software infrastructure for executing large and complex computational, contains a simple language for describing sweeps over parameter space and the input and output of data for processing. Nimrod is compatible with the Kepler system [20], such that users can set up complex computational workflows and have them executed without having to interface directly with a high-performance computing system.

There are a number of applications which aims are similar to *Chiminey*'s aims. However, we believe that Chiminey is more user-friendly and provides more features crucial to increase efficiency of scientific experiments. In contrast to VIVO, a semantic web application for the discovery of research outputs within an institution [15], the data management component of Chiminey focuses on curating data from *instruments*, visualising and publishing these data, and making the research data itself accessible. In contrast to Chorus, a web application for managing spectrometry files [14], Chiminey is not restricted to managing a specific type of files. Chiminey not only manages any type of files but also allows the addition of filters to the files for automatic generation of domain-specific metadata. Furthermore, Chiminey provisions a reliable computing capability for data processing. Unlike ReDBox, a software platform for curating and publishing experimental results [30], Chiminey curates and publishes metadata and data collected from instruments. Furthermore, *Chiminey* provides a reliable computing and data visualisation capability.

7   Conclusions and Future Work

In this chapter, we present an approach on modelling and implementation of research-oriented cloud computing platforms. Our approach focuses on the reliability and usability features, both of the model and its implementation.

Cloud computing provides a great opportunity for scientists, as it enables large-scale experiments that cannot are too long to run on local desktop machines. To unlock all the benefits of cloud computing, we require a platform with a user-friendly interface and an easy-to-use methodology for developing new processes/components and conducting the experiments. Usability and reliability features are crucial for such systems. This paper presents (1) a formal framework that we used to develop a model of a cloud-based platform, (2) the developed formal model, and (3) the latest version of its open-source implementation as the *Chiminey* platform. The proposed *Chiminey* platform allows to conduct the experiments without having a deep technical understanding of cloud-computing, fault tolerance, or data management in order to leverage the benefits of cloud computing.

To assess its usability and practicality of the platform, we conducted a number of case studies within two research disciplines, physics (material characterisation) and structural biology (understanding materials at the atomic scale). The domain experts noted the following advantages of the *Chiminey*: (1) time savings for computing and data management, (2) user-friendly interface, and (3) visualisation of the calculation results as 2D or 3D graphs. We believe that the proposed platform will have a strong positive impact on the research community, because it give an opportunity to focus on the main research problems and takes upon itself solving of the major part of the infrastructure problems.

Future Work. One of the directions of our future work is incorporation Nimrod [9] into our open-source platform for the execution of its Smart Connectors. A further direction of our future work is application of the platform for an efficient testing based on analysis of system architecture.

Acknowledgements. The Bioscience Data Platform project acknowledges funding from the NeCTAR project No. 2179 [25]. We also would like to thank our colleagues Dr Daniel W. Drumm (School of Applied Sciences, RMIT University), Prof Salvy P. Russo (School of Science, RMIT University), Dr George Opletal (School of Science, RMIT University), and Prof Ashley M. Buckle (School of Biomedical Sciences, Monash University) for the fruitful collaboration within the Bioscience Data Platform project.

References

1. Afgan, E., Baker, D., Coraor, N., et al.: Harnessing cloud computing with Galaxy Cloud. Nat. Biotechnol. **29**(11), 972–974 (2011)
2. Altair, P.W.: http://www.pbsworks.com/
3. Androulakis, S., Schmidberger, J., Bate, M.A., et al.: Federated repositories of X-ray diffraction images. Acta Crystallogr. Sect. D **64**(7), 810–814 (2008)
4. Armbrust, M., Fox, A., Griffith, R., et al.: A view of cloud computing. Commun. ACM **53**(4), 50–58 (2010)
5. Aversa, R., Di Martino, B., Rak, M., Venticinque, S., Villano, U.: Performance Prediction for HPC on Clouds, pp. 437–456. John Wiley & Sons, Inc. (2011)
6. Blanchette, J.C., Popescu, A., Wand, D., Weidenbach, C.: More SPASS with isabelle – Superposition with hard sorts and configurable simplification. In: Beringer, L., Felty, A. (eds.) ITP 2012. LNCS, vol. 7406, pp. 345–360. Springer, Heidelberg (2012). doi:10.1007/978-3-642-32347-8_24

7. Broy, M.: Time, abstraction, causality and modularity in interactive systems: extended abstract. Electr. Notes Theor. Comput. Sci. **108**, 3–9 (2004)
8. Buyya, R., Sulistio, A.: Service and utility oriented distributed computing systems: challenges and opportunities for modeling and simulation communities. In: Proceedings of the 41st Annual Simulation Symposium, ANSS-41 2008, pp. 68–81. IEEE (2008)
9. Buyya, R., Abramson, D., Giddy, J.: Nimrod/G: An Architecture for a Resource Management and Scheduling System in a Global Computational Grid (2000)
10. Buyya, R., Yeo, C.S., Venugopal, S., Broberg, J., Brandic, I.: Cloud computing and emerging IT platforms: vision, hype, and reality for delivering computing as the 5th utility. Future Gener. Comput. Syst. **25**(6), 599–616 (2009)
11. Cafaro, M., Aloisio, G.: Grids, clouds, and virtualization. In: Cafaro, M., Aloisio, G. (eds.) Grids, Clouds and Virtualization. Computer Communications and Networks, pp. 1–21. Springer, London (2011)
12. Carlson, J.L.: Redis in Action. Manning Publications Co., Greenwich (2013)
13. Celery Project: The Celery Distributed Task Queue. http://www.celeryproject.org/
14. Chorus. https://chorusproject.org/pages/index.html
15. Krafft, D., Cappadona, N., Caruso, B., Corson-Rikert, J., Devare, M., Lowe, B.: VIVO: enabling national networking of scientists. In: WebSci10: Extending the Frontiers of Society On-Line (2010)
16. Kresse, G., Furthmüller, J.: Efficient iterative schemes for ab initio total-energy calculations using a plane-wave basis set. Phys. Rev. B **54**(16), 11169–11186 (1996)
17. Kuntschke, R., Kemper, A.: Data stream sharing. In: Grust, T., Höpfner, H., Illarramendi, A., Jablonski, S., Mesiti, M., Müller, S., Patranjan, P.-L., Sattler, K.-U., Spiliopoulou, M., Wijsen, J. (eds.) EDBT 2006. LNCS, vol. 4254, pp. 769–788. Springer, Heidelberg (2006). doi:10.1007/11896548_58
18. Kwiatkowska, M., Norman, G., Parker, D.: PRISM 4.0: verification of probabilistic real-time systems. In: Gopalakrishnan, G., Qadeer, S. (eds.) CAV 2011. LNCS, vol. 6806, pp. 585–591. Springer, Heidelberg (2011). doi:10.1007/978-3-642-22110-1_47
19. Leavitt, N.: Is cloud computing really ready for prime time? Computer **42**(1), 15–20 (2009)
20. Ludscher, B., Altintas, I., Berkley, C., et al.: Scientific workflow management and the Kepler system. Concurrency Comput. Pract. Experience **18**(10), 1039–1065 (2006)
21. Martinaitis, P.N., Patten, C.J., Wendelborn, A.L.: Component-based stream processing in the cloud. In: Proceedings of the 2009 Workshop on Component-Based High Performance Computing, CBHPC 2009, pp. 16:1–16:12. ACM (2009)
22. Mendling, J., Reijers, H.A., Cardoso, J.: What makes process models understandable? In: Alonso, G., Dadam, P., Rosemann, M. (eds.) BPM 2007. LNCS, vol. 4714, pp. 48–63. Springer, Heidelberg (2007). doi:10.1007/978-3-540-75183-0_4
23. Merkel, D.: Docker: lightweight linux containers for consistent development and deployment. Linux J. **2014**(239), Article No. 2, March 2014. Belltown Media, Houston. http://dl.acm.org/citation.cfm?id=2600241
24. National Computational Infrastructure. http://nci.org.au/
25. NeCTAR: the National eResearch Collaboration Tools and Resources (2015). http://www.nectar.org.au/
26. Nipkow, T., Paulson, L.C., Wenzel, M.: Isabelle/HOL - A Proof Assistant for Higher-Order Logic. LNCS, vol. 2283. Springer, Heidelberg (2002)

27. Oinn, T., Greenwood, M., Addis, M., et al.: Taverna: lessons in creating a workflow environment for the life sciences. Concurr. Comput. Pract. Exper. **18**, 1067–1100 (2006)
28. Opletal, G., et al.: Hrmc: Hybrid reverse monte carlo method with silicon and carbon potentials. Comput. Phys. Commun. **178**, 777–787 (2008)
29. Ostermann, S., Iosup, A., Yigitbasi, N., Prodan, R., Fahringer, T., Epema, D.: A performance analysis of EC2 cloud computing services for scientific computing. In: Avresky, D.R., Diaz, M., Bode, A., Ciciani, B., Dekel, E. (eds.) CloudComp 2009. LNICST, vol. 34, pp. 115–131. Springer, Heidelberg (2010). doi:10.1007/978-3-642-12636-9_9
30. ReDBox-Mint. http://www.redboxresearchdata.com.au/
31. Spichkova, M.: Focus on processes. Technical report TUM-I1115, TU München (2011)
32. Spichkova, M.: Design of formal languages and interfaces: "formal" does not mean "unreadable". In: Blashki, K., Isaias, P. (eds.) Emerging Research and Trends in Interactivity and the Human-Computer Interface. IGI Global (2013)
33. Spichkova, M.: Stream Processing Components: Isabelle/HOL Formalisation and Case Studies. Archive of Formal Proofs (2013)
34. Spichkova, M.: Compositional properties of crypto-based components. Archive of Formal Proofs (2014)
35. Spichkova, M., Thomas, I., Schmidt, H., Yusuf, I., Drumm, D., Androulakis, S., Opletal, G., Russo, S.: Scalable and fault-tolerant cloud computations: modelling and implementation. In: Proceedings of the 21st IEEE International Conference on Parallel and Distributed Systems (2015)
36. Spichkova, M., Zhu, X., Mou, D.: Do we really need to write documentation for a system? In: International Conference on Model-Driven Engineering and Software Development (2013)
37. Spichkova, M.: Formalisation and analysis of component dependencies. Archive of Formal Proofs (2014)
38. Spichkova, M., Schmidt, H.: Reconciling a component and process view. In: 7th International Workshop on Modeling in Software Engineering (MiSE) at ICSE 2015 (2015)
39. Spichkova, M., Schmidt, H.W., Thomas, I.E., Yusuf, I.I., Androulakis, S., Meyer, G.R.: Managing usability and reliability aspects in cloud computing. In: Proceedings of the 11th International Conference on Evaluation of Novel Software Approaches to Software Engineering, pp. 288–295 (2016)
40. Spichkova, M., Zamansky, A., Farchi, E.: Towards a human-centred approach in modelling and testing of cyber-physical systems. In: 21st International Conference on Parallel and Distributed Systems. IEEE (2015)
41. Vaquero, L.M., Rodero-Merino, L., Caceres, J., Lindner, M.: A break in the clouds: towards a cloud definition. SIGCOMM Comput. Commun. Rev. **39**(1), 50–55 (2008)
42. Yusuf, I., Schmidt, H.: Parameterised architectural patterns for providing cloud service fault tolerance with accurate costings. In: Proceedings of the 16th International ACM Sigsoft Symposium on Component-Based Software Engineering, pp. 121–130 (2013)
43. Yusuf, I., Thomas, I., Spichkova, M., Androulakis, S., Meyer, G., Drumm, D., Opletal, G., Russo, S., Buckle, A., Schmidt, H.: Chiminey: reliable computing and data management platform in the cloud. In: Proceedings of the International Conference on Software Engineering (ICSE 2015), pp. 677–680 (2015)

44. Zamansky, A., Rodriguez-Navas, G., Adams, M., Spichkova, M.: Formal methods in collaborative projects. In: 11th International Conference on Evaluation of Novel Approaches to Software Engineering (ENASE). IEEE (2016)
45. Zhang, Q., Cheng, L., Boutaba, R.: Cloud computing: state-of-the-art and research challenges. J. Internet Serv. Appl. **1**(1), 7–18 (2010)
46. Zugal, S., Pinggera, J., Weber, B., Mendling, J., Reijers, H.A.: Assessing the impact of hierarchy on model understandability – a cognitive perspective. In: Kienzle, J. (ed.) MODELS 2011. LNCS, vol. 7167, pp. 123–133. Springer, Heidelberg (2012). doi:10.1007/978-3-642-29645-1_14

An Improved Method Level Bug Localization Approach Using Minimized Code Space

Shanto Rahman$^{(\boxtimes)}$, Md. Mostafijur Rahman, and Kazi Sakib

Institute of Information Technology, University of Dhaka, Dhaka, Bangladesh
{bit0321,bit0312,sakib}@iit.du.ac.bd

Abstract. In automatic software bug localization, source code classes and methods are commonly used as the unit of suggestions. However, existing techniques consider whole source code to find the buggy locations, which degrades the accuracy of bug localization. In this paper, a Method level Bug localization using Minimized code space (MBuM) has been proposed which improves the accuracy by only considering bug specific source code. Later, this source code is used for identifying the similarity to the bug report. These similarity scores are measured using a modified Vector Space Model (mVSM), and based on that scores MBuM ranks a list of source code methods. The validity of MBuM has been checked by providing theoretical proof using formal methods. Case studies have been performed on two large scale open source projects namely Eclipse and Mozilla, and the results show that MBuM outperforms existing bug localization techniques.

Keywords: Method level bug localization · Search space minimization · Retrieval and ranking

1 Introduction

In general, bug fixing is initiated when the Quality Assurance (QA) team or user reports against a faulty scenario. Developer receive the reports and try to find the buggy locations into the source code. Generally developers use their experiences on the source code, or debug the code using the debugger of an Integrated Development Environment (IDE). A source code project often contains millions of lines (e.g., Eclipse version 3.0.2 contains 1,86,772 nonempty lines) from which identifying the actual buggy location is always challenging. In case of automatic software bug localization, developers usually provide the bug reports and corresponding buggy project to an automated tool, which provides a ranked list of buggy locations. Developer traverse the list from the beginning until they find the actual one. Hence, the accurate ranking of buggy locations is needed to reduce the searching time.

Automatic software bug localization is commonly performed using static, dynamic or both analysis of the source code by which failure locations of a software can be identified [1–3]. Most of the bug localization techniques follow

© Springer International Publishing AG 2016
L.A. Maciaszek and J. Filipe (Eds.): ENASE 2016, CCIS 703, pp. 179–200, 2016.
DOI: 10.1007/978-3-319-56390-9_9

static analysis where Information Retrieval (IR) techniques are used [4,5]. Static analysis uses probabilistic approach, so the more the unnecessary information is considered, the more the biasness will be introduced, and the biasness lead to inaccuracies. Dynamic analysis based techniques analyze the execution trace of the source code with suitable test suites to identify the executed methods for a bug. As dynamic analysis only provides method call sequences except method contents, the solution search space has become very small. And using this small search space, it is hard to find the buggy locations.

In recent years, several researches on bug localization have been conducted using static analysis where buggy locations are identified using bug reports and source code [6,7]. In static analysis, authors create two lists of corpora from the source code and bug report. Then corpora are processed so that proper similarities between source code and bug report can be measured. Finally, IR based techniques are applied for ranking probable buggy files [4,5]. Zhou et al. [5] propose such a technique named as BugLocator where Vector Space Model (VSM) is modified by proposing tf-idf formulation. As BugLocator only uses static information of the whole source code, this considers irrelevant information for a bug. An extended version of BugLocator is proposed by assigning special weights on structural information (e.g., class names, method names, variable names and comments) of the source code which also ranks classes as buggy [4]. Similar to BugLocator, this technique also considers the whole source code, as a consequence biasness may be raised. Several dynamic analysis based bug localization techniques have already been proposed [8,9]. Wilde et al. introduce a technique where source code execution traces are considered using passing and failing test cases [8]. However, due to considering passing test cases, irrelevant features may be included in the domain of search space which may hamper the accuracy of bug localization. Poshyvanyk et al. propose PROMISER which suggests methods as buggy by combining both static and dynamic analysis of the source code [9]. Unfortunately, this technique considers whole source code in static analysis which may produce biasness on the ranking.

This paper proposes an a automatic software bug localization technique, namely Method level Bug localization using Minimized code space (MBuM) where buggy locations of the source code are identified by eliminating irrelevant source code (Code space and search space basically represent the same thing. That is why, in this article, code space and search space are used interchangeably; a preliminary version of this work can be found in [10]). At first, MBuM identifies a relevant search space by tracing the execution of the source code for a bug. As dynamic analysis provides a list of executed methods without method contents, static analysis is performed to extract those. Several pre-processing techniques are applied on these relevant source code along with the bug report, which produce code and bug corpora. During the creation of bug corpora, pre-processing techniques such as stop words removal, multiwords splitting, semantic meaning extraction and stemming are applied on the bug report. In addition, programming language specific keywords removal is applied for generating scenario specific code corpora. Finally, to rank the buggy methods, similarity scores are measured between the code corpora of the methods and bug corpora of the bug report by applying mVSM. It modifies existing VSM by providing more priority to be buggy to the larger sized methods than the small sized methods [5].

The effects of search space on ranking is formulated as a proposition, which has been proved using formal methods. To evaluate the results of the proposed solution, the experiments (i.e., Sect. 5) contain three case studies where Eclipse and Mozilla are used as the subject. Results are compared with four existing bug localization techniques namely PROMISER [9], BugLocator [5], LDA [11] and LSI [12]. In Eclipse, MBuM ranks the actual buggy method at the first position in three (60%) among five bugs, while other techniques rank no more than one (20%) bug at the top. Similarly in case of Mozilla, LDA, LSI and BugLocator rank none of the bugs at the top whereas MBuM ranks three (60%) and PROMISER ranks two (40%) bugs at the first position. Above results show that, MBuM outperforms other existing state-of-the-art bug localization techniques.

Rest of the paper is structured as follows. In Sect. 2, existing literature on bug localization are given. Section 3 presents the model of the proposed technique, and the implementation of that model is described in Sect. 4. The result is analyzed in Sect. 5, and later several kinds of threats are discussed in Sect. 6. Finally, Sect. 7 concludes the contribution with future remarks.

2 Related Work

This section focuses on the researches which are conducted to increase the accuracy of bug localization. Following discussion first holds some of the static analysis based bug localization techniques. Later, dynamic analysis based techniques are depicted.

2.1 Source Code Static Analysis Based Techniques

Brent D. Nichols proposes a method level bug localization technique [6] using source code static analysis. At first, the semantic meanings of each method has been extracted by applying several text processing techniques such as stop words removal, separation of identifiers and stemming. In the second phase, authors add extra information from the previous bug history to the methods. When a new bug is arrived, Latent Semantic Indexing (LSI) is applied on the method documents to identify the relationships between the terms of the bug report and the concepts of the method documents. Based on that relationships, a list of buggy methods has been suggested. Due to depending on the predefined dictionary keywords and inadequate previous bug reports, this greedy approach may fail. Furthermore, the accuracy of this technique may not be satisfactory enough due to considering the whole source code information rather than the bug specific information.

Zhou et al. propose BugLocator where buggy locations are identified at the class level using static analysis of the source code [5]. At first authors process bug report and source code separately, resulting two sets of corpora, one for bug report and another for source code. These corpora are processed using several text processing techniques such as stop words removal, programming language specific keywords removal, multi-words identification and stemming. Later, these two sets of corpora are compared using a revised Vector Space Model (rVSM). For a specific bug, BugLocator suggests a list of classes as buggy where developers need to manually investigate the source code for finding more granular buggy locations (e.g., buggy methods of the source code). As this technique considers whole source code during static analysis, accuracy may be hampered because large unnecessary information creates more biasness in the ranking.

An improved version of BugLocator [5] is addressed (titled as BLUiR) by Ripon et al. where structural information including class names, method names, variable names and comments of the source code get more priority than others [4]. All identifiers and comments are tokenized using above mentioned text processing approaches except the removal of programming language specific keywords. However, most of the cases the consideration of programming language specific keywords may introduce irrelevant information. Along with this, BLUiR may increase unnecessary information by considering whole source code. And these large irrelevant information for a bug may increase false positive rate in the ranking of buggy locations.

Alhindawi et al. [13] introduce another method level feature location based technique by enhancing source code with stereotypes. Stereotypes represent the details of each word which is commonly used in programming. For example, the stereotype named as 'get' means that a method returns a value. Similarly, the stereotype 'set' represents that the value of a data member has been set. In this approach, the corpus of the source code is enriched with the combination of stereotypes which describes the abstract role of the source code method. These stereotype information are derived automatically from the source code via program analysis. After adding stereotype information with the source code methods, Information Retrieval (IR) based technique is used to run queries for feature location. The basic assumption is that adding stereotype information to the source code corpus will improve the results of bug localization.

Wang et al. introduce another bug localization technique, where similar bug reports, version history and structure of the source code are amalgamated [7]. This technique also suggests file level buggy locations and so developers have to spend lots of searching time to identify more granular level (i.e., methods of the source code). Here, the accuracy may be deteriorated significantly because of the consideration of large and irrelevant source code for a bug. Recently, Rahman et al. consider version histories and structural information of the source code to identify buggy files [14]. Here, the scores of rVSM [5] are combined with the frequently changed files information. Later, the source code files whose structural information (such as class names, method names) are available in the bug report get more priority. Based on the above assigned scores, a list of buggy files are ranked. Unfortunately, due to using whole source code in static analysis, the accuracy of this technique may also be biased.

2.2 Source Code Dynamic Analysis Based Techniques

In dynamic analysis based techniques, the run time behavior of the source code is obtained using proper test suits. Using source code dynamic analysis, data flow of the execution are recorded and irrelevant source code are discarded.

The first dynamic analysis based bug localization technique is proposed by Wilde et al. where source code execution traces are analyzed using multiple test cases [8]. Authors consider two types of test cases such as passing and failing test cases. Using the passing test cases, desired features are extracted. Similarly, failing test case provides the features which are not desirable. To identify the buggy locations, these two types of test cases are considered which provide a large volume of features. However, due to using passing test cases, irrelevant features may be included in the domain of search space.

Eisenbarth et al. propose an improved version of [8] where both dynamic and static analysis of the source code are combined [15]. Here, static analysis identifies the dependencies among the data to locate the features in a program while dynamic analysis collects the source code execution traces for a set of scenarios. These traces are analyzed with a view to categorizing the subroutines based on the degree of a feature. However, here during static analysis whole source code is used which degrades the accuracy of the technique.

PROMESIR is another source code dynamic analysis based technique, addressed by Poshyvanyk et al. [9]. Through dynamic analysis, executed buggy methods are extracted for a bug. Meanwhile, static analysis is also applied here which collects the whole source code. Initially, these two analysis techniques produce bug similarity scores differently without interacting with one another. Finally, these two scores are combined and obtained a weighted ranking score for each source code method. Although this technique uses dynamic information of the source code, it fails to discard the irrelevant source code for a bug. Rather the whole source code is considered during static analysis which may increase the biasness. As a consequence, the accuracy of bug localization is declined.

From the above discussions, it is clear that the existing bug localization techniques commonly follow static, dynamic or combination of both analysis of the source code and all of the existing techniques consider whole source code rather than discarding irrelevant source code for a bug. As a result, the accuracies of the existing bug localization techniques hamper significantly.

3 Does Minimized Code Space Can Improve the Accuracy of Bug Localization Techniques?

To answer this question, a model named as Method level Bug localization using Minimized code space (MBuM) has been developed. At first, the elements of the model are defined. Source code and bug report act as the input, while a ranked list of buggy methods is the system output. The input are processed using a bug localizer, and the buggy methods are ranked. During the processing of input, it is assumed that a bug report and source code share some common information. Since the size of a software project is too large (with respect to the total statements of the source code), it is quite difficult to find the actual buggy locations. The details of the model is described below using Z notations [16].

MBuM _____

D : *Dictionary*
M : *List of methods*
B : *Bug report*
S : *whole source code*
b_i : *terms of the bug report*
m : *accurate set of buggy methods*
s_i : *terms of the source code*
_____

$B \leftarrow b_i \mid b_i \in D$
$S \leftarrow s_i \mid s_i \in D$
$m \leftarrow$ *find accurate relation between* $b_i \bigwedge s_i$

Here, D represents the set of Dictionary words of bug report and source code. b_i and s_i are the number of the terms of bug report and source code respectively. As the main objective is to increase the suggestion of accurate numbers of buggy methods (m), an accurate relationship should be established between the bug report and source code terms. However, it is difficult to find exact buggy locations from the whole source code, and so removal of irrelevant source code is desired. Moreover, to find the list of buggy methods, a good source code terms and bug report processing technique is needed.

Now, a new proposition is developed by which valid search space can be extracted. The proof of the proposed proposition is described in the followings using Z notations [16].

A small and relevant search space can increase the accuracy of bug localization because localization follows a probabilistic way and accuracy depends on the volume of search space. The relevant search space may be obtained by executing the source code for a specific bug. Since only the bug specific source code is considered, it ensures that the actual buggy methods must reside within the relevant extracted domain. After discarding the irrelevant source code, more accurate bug localization techniques can be obtained. This hypothesis is described in **Lemmas 1** and **2**.

Lemma 1: In bug localization, the selection of relevant domain can produce more accurate ranking than considering the whole-domain.

For developing a software, a large number of source code files or classes are created. The number of selected source code class can significantly affect the ranking score of bug localization. In case of accurate bug localization, to show the number of classes' effects, a representative ranking model namely Vector

Space Model (VSM) can be used [17]. VSM depends on the inverse document frequency (*idf*), and *idf* also depends on the number of documents or source code files which is used to increase the weights of rare terms as Eq. 1.

$$idf = \log(\frac{\sharp docs}{n_t})$$ (1)

Here, $\sharp docs$ and n_t are the total number of documents and the number of documents containing the term t respectively. Equation 1 shows that *idf* increases with the increment of $\sharp docs$. The VSM depends on the *idf* and the final score of VSM is calculated using Eq. 2.

$$VSM(q, d) = cos(q, d) = (\sum_{t \in q \cap d} (\log f_{tq} + 1) \times (\log f_{td} + 1) \times idf^2)$$

$$\times \frac{1}{\sqrt{\sum_{t \in q}((\log f_{tq} + 1) \times idf)^2}} \times \frac{1}{\sqrt{\sum_{t \in d}((\log f_{td} + 1) \times idf)^2}}$$ (2)

In Eq. 2, t, q and d represent the term, query and document respectively. f_{tq} and f_{td} are the term frequencies within the query and documents respectively. In this study, inverse method frequency (*imf*) has been used instead of *idf* to give more priority to rare terms in methods. So, the consideration of large number of irrelevant methods can deteriorate the ranking scores significantly. The effect of *imf* is illustrated by the following mathematical model when whole source code is considered for finding buggy locations.

Rare Term Priority _____
$weight(x) : x$ *gets weight*
$r? :$ *Rare Term*
$b? :$ *Bug Report*
$t? :$ *Term*
$v :$ *Buggy Methods*
$\psi :$ *Non Buggy Methods*

$\exists t? \in b? : (t? \in r?) \wedge (t? \in v) \wedge (t? \notin \psi)$
• $weight(v) \Rightarrow rank_{high}(v)$ (a)
$\exists t? \in b? : (t? \in r?) \wedge (t? \notin v) \wedge (t? \in \psi)$
• $weight(\psi) \Rightarrow rank_{high}(\psi)$ (b)

The above model shows the impact of rare terms in bug localization. Here, two scenarios may be occurred such as *RareTermPriority(a)* and *RareTermPriority(b)* which represent the weight of buggy and non-buggy methods respectively. The detail is described below.

1. The methods which hold rare terms and related to a bug, get more priority to be buggy which is desired (shown in *RareTermPriority(a)*).

2. Similarly, rare terms exist in methods which have no relation with the occurrence of reported bugs, get more *imf* weights which is repulsive (shown in *RareTermPriority(b)*). When the solution search space is large, the situation of *RareTermPriority(b)* may be occurred which deteriorates the ranking accuracy significantly. So, if the total number of methods can be restricted by only considering valid and relevant methods, *imf* cannot create large negative impacts on the ranking.

Another problem may be occurred due to considering large solution search space and that is the actual buggy location may be suggested in the *Tth* position in the worst case where the total number of available methods are T. It is noteworthy that an automated bug localization technique provides a list of buggy locations according to the descending order of ranking scores, where developers traverse from the beginning of the suggested list one by one. If the actual buggy location is suggested in *Tth* position, the developers need to inspect T number of suggestions to find the actual one. On the other hand, if it can be ensured that the bug is obtained in the targeted domain (e.g., $T - \psi$), developers have to inspect only $(T - \psi)$ buggy locations in the worst case.

SearchSpaceMinimization _____
$b?$: *Bug Report*
$m_t?$: *Total methods in source code*
$m_d?$: *Methods relevant to bug*
$m_u?$: *Methods irrelevant to bug*
ϑ : *seq bugs*
$\kappa!$: *Minimized search space*

$m_d? \in \mathbb{P}\, m_t?$
$m_d? \subseteq m_t?$
$m_d? = m_t? \setminus m_u?$
$m_t? = m_d? \cup m_u?$
$\forall\, b? \in \vartheta \bullet (b? \in m_d?) \wedge (b? \notin m_u?) \Rightarrow \kappa! = m_d?$ (c)

In the above *SearchSpaceMinimization* model, b is a bug report. m_t, m_d and m_u represent total, relevant and irrelevant methods of source code for a bug respectively. This model states that the relevant methods can be obtained by discarding the irrelevant methods from the source code. From this model, it is clear that the bug must reside into the dynamically traced methods m_d according to *SearchSpaceMinimization(c)*.

Lemma 2: Large information domain can increase False Positive Rate of bug localization

In case of software bug localization, False Positive Rate (FPR) means that the identification of non-buggy methods as buggy which misguides developers to identify buggy methods. The large unnecessary information can produce large FPR. The situation of the increment of FPR with respect to the unnecessary information is illustrated using the following mathematical model.

In this model, m is a module which is common within p_1, p_2 and p_3 packages of a project whose basic functionalities are same but implementations are different. b is a bug associated to m, which is actually related to package p_1. Due to obtaining the same feature in three different packages, it may happen that p_2 and p_3 get more ranking scores than p_1. This situation could be raised when the whole source codes have been considered to locate a single bug because the size (that is, terms) of p_2 and p_3 may be larger than p_1. And according to VSM, the small but relevant document will get more priority than others which leads to the following theorem.

$$\begin{array}{l}
\underline{FPR} \\
Package : \{p_1, p_2, p_3, \ldots\ldots, p_n\} \\
p? : Package \\
m? : Module \\
b? : Bug\ report \\
Buggy(x) : x\ is\ buggy \\
pr_{rank}(x) : Ranking\ score\ of\ x \\
f(p?) : Feature\ of\ p? \\
Imp(p?) : Implementation\ of\ p? \\
\beta! = Buggy\ package \\
\hline
m? \in f(p_1) \cap f(p_2) \cap f(p_3) \\
b? \in m? \wedge b? \in p_1 \\
(f(p_1(m?)) = f(p_2(m?)) = f(p_3(m?))) \wedge \\
(Imp(p_1)! = Imp(p_2)! = Imp(p_3)) \Rightarrow \\
(pr_{rank}(p_2) \geq pr_{rank}(p_1)) \vee (pr_{rank}(p_3) \geq pr_{rank}(p_1)) \\
\beta! = p_2 \vee p_3
\end{array}$$

Theorem 1: A small but relevant search space can increase the accuracy of bug localization.

Lemma 1 illustrates that *VSM* may incur negative impacts in case of large solution search space and **Lemma 2** shows the effects of using whole source code in case of FPR. From **Lemmas 1** and **2**, it can be derived that a small number of relevant search space can increase the accuracy of bug localization.

4 Method Level Bug Localization Using Minimized Code Space

In this section, a model described in Sect. 3 has been implemented by devising a methodology which increases the ranking accuracy because of considering only relevant search space from the source code for a bug. The methodology of the proposed bug localization technique is described in the following subsections.

The overall process of improving the bug localization accuracy is briefly discussed as follows. From Sect. 3, it is observed that if relevant information domain

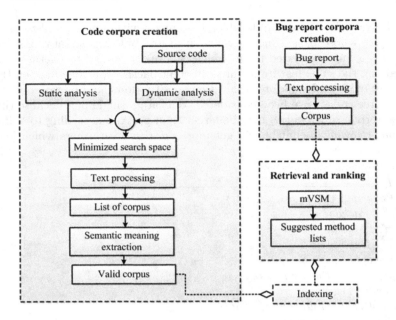

Fig. 1. Functional block diagram of MBuM (N.B. reproduced from [10]).

can be extracted by ignoring irrelevant methods from the large solution space, the accuracy of bug localization can be increased dramatically. At the beginning of bug localization, source code dynamic analysis is performed to minimize the solution search space which extracts only the related methods for generating a specific bug. Static analysis is done with a view to getting the contents of extracted methods. After applying dynamic and static source code analysis, valid and relevant information can be obtained. The contents of extracted methods are processed to create code corpora using static analysis. Since bug report only contains textual information related to a specific buggy scenario, again static analysis is performed to process the bug report. Finally, generated corpora from the bug report and source code are matched with each other to rank the source code methods. The whole process for localizing bugs can be divided into four steps and those are Code corpora creation, Indexing, Bug corpora creation and Retrieval and ranking. Each of the steps follow series of tasks as shown in Fig. 1.

4.1 Code Corpora Creation

Code corpora are the collection of source code words which are used to check the similarity with bug report corpora [4–7]. So, the more accurate the code corpora generation is, the more accurate matching can be obtained which may increase the accuracy of bug localization. For generating valid code corpora, two approaches are conducted and those are dynamic and static analysis [18]. Dynamic analysis produces relevant search space by considering source code execution trace (e.g., source code methods) for a specific bug by despising the codes which are not responsible for generating the bug. Although dynamic analysis provides relationships between methods or classes, it cannot provide method or class contents. On the other hand, static analysis is related to the code analysis which considers whole source code information and extracts method contents. So, to get the method contents for only relevant methods, the output from dynamic and static analysis are combined and the common methods of those analysis are considered. The code corpora creation can be divided into multiple granular levels which are described below.

For the purpose of dynamic analysis, initially developers need to reproduce the bug after getting the information from the bug report's title, summary and description. Here, execution traces are recorded and analyzed to extract executed methods. From these traces, method call graphs are generated and parsed to obtain the structure of the executed source code. It is noteworthy that the method call graph does not contain the method contents rather it stores the sequentially executed method names. Hence using static analysis, source code is parsed by maintaining the code structures. This is done by traversing the Abstract Syntax Tree (AST)[1] to extract different program structures such as package, class, method and variable names.

Contents of the above minimized search space are processed to get the relevant code corpora as shown in Fig. 1. This is needed because buggy locations are identified by measuring similarity between the contents of bug report and minimized search space. So, trade-off is needed between bug report and source code contents such as the format of all words should be the same (e.g., base form). Minimized source code are pre-processed because source code may contain lots of unnecessary keywords such as programming language specific keywords (e.g., public, static, void, int, string, etc.), stop words (e.g., has, is, a, the, etc.) which do not provide any bug specific information rather may create impacts on ranking and thus stop words are discarded.

Within source code, one word may consist of multiple terms such as 'beginHeader' consists of 'begin' and 'Header' terms. Therefore, multiword identifiers are also used for creating singular value decomposition. Porter Stemming [19] is applied to get the original form of the word so that 'searching', 'searched' and 'search' are identified as the same word. Moreover, statements are splitted based on some syntax specific separators such as '.', '=', '(', ')', '{', '}', ';', '/', etc. After completing all the aforementioned pre-processing, source code corpora are produced.

The last step for generating code corpora is semantic meaning extraction as shown in Fig. 1. During this step, semantic information of each word is extracted because one word may have multiple synonyms. For example, to describe a single case, developers and QA teams often use different words. Although the semantic meanings of developers and QA described scenarios are the same, the only difference is in their vocabulary choice. Bug localization usually follows IR based

---

[1] Abstract Syntax Tree, for details - https://eclipse.org/jdt/core/r2.0/dom%20ast/ast.html.

techniques by performing word matching. So, the accuracy depends on the matching of the words. For improving the accuracy, semantic word matching is done. For example, 'close' word has many synonyms such as 'terminate', 'stop', etc. To describe a scenario if a developer uses 'close' and QA uses 'terminate', the system cannot identify the similar words without using semantic meanings of those words. Thus semantic meaning extraction plays vital role in accurate ranking of buggy methods.

4.2   Indexing

In this paper, indexing has been performed according to Fig. 2 where within each package, multiple classes are available with different id, and within each class several methods are stayed with unique id. Each method contains multiple words and each word within a method is stored sequentially. Here, the synonymous words of each word are also stored. Later, each method code corpora and bug corpora is compared by searching only the indices.

Figure 2 is an example of a source code index (taken from, Eclipse project). To better understand about the indexing only one package (that is, *org.eclipse.swt.graphics*) contents are expanded. At first, that package is defined and later the class name, method name of the source code are accumulated in Fig. 2. Here, two classes such as Rectangle and Point are available in package *org.eclipse.swt.graphics*. Among these classes, two methods are stored. As this technique provides a method level ranking, the contents of each method is stored within the method.

```
1   <?xml version="1.0" encoding="UTF-8" standalone="no"?>
2   <Source_Code>
3       <Package name="org.eclipse.swt.graphics">
4           <Class name="Rectangle">
5               <Method lineNo="66" name="Rectangle">
6                   <Word content="rectangl"/>
7                   <Word content="width"/>
8                   <Word content="width"/>
9                   <Word content="height"/>
10                  <Word content="height"/>
11                  <Word content="rectangl"/>
12              </Method>
13          </Class>
14          <Class name="Point">
15              <Method lineNo="53" name="Point">
16                  <Word content="point"/>
17                  <Word content="point"/>
18              </Method>
19          </Class>
20      </Package>
21  </Source_Code>
```

Fig. 2. Example of source code indexing.

4.3   Bug Report Corpora Creation

Software bug report contains the details of a programs' error. The bug report is usually prepared by Quality Assurance (QA) team or users. A software bug report contains bug title, summary and description which provide important information about a bug.

In bug report, the information may contain some common and irrelevant words such as stop words which do not provide any bug specific information rather create biasness for localizing the bugs. Moreover, words of bug report may be in present, past or future tenses. Bug report needs to be processed to remove these noisy information. At the beginning, stop words (e.g., am, is, are, etc.) are removed from the bug report. Then multiword splitting (if needed) and porter stemming [19] are applied (as used for code corpora generation) to get the base form of the words. After completing these pre-processing, valid bug corpora are generated which provide only the relevant words.

4.4   Retrieval and Ranking of Buggy Methods

In this step, each bug corpus is searched in the minimized solution space. For ranking the source code methods, the proposed technique applies modified Vector Space Model ($mVSM$) [5]. $mVSM$ calculates the similarity between each query (bug corpora) and methods as the cosine similarity with their corresponding vector representations according to Eq. 3.

$$Similarity(q, m) = cos(q, m) = \frac{\overrightarrow{V_q} \times \overrightarrow{V_m}}{\mid \overrightarrow{V_q} \mid \times \mid \overrightarrow{V_m} \mid} \tag{3}$$

Here, $\overrightarrow{V_q}$ and $\overrightarrow{V_m}$ are the vectors of terms for the query (q) and method (m) respectively. $\mid \overrightarrow{V_q} \mid \times \mid \overrightarrow{V_m} \mid$ is the inner product of two vectors. Term weight is calculated by multiplying tf (term frequency) and imf (inverse method frequency). $mVSM$ uses the logarithm of term frequency of a method. The imf ensures that rare or unique terms in the methods are given more importance. tf and imf are calculated using Eqs. 4 and 5 respectively.

$$tf(t, m) = \log f_{tm} + 1 \tag{4}$$

$$imf = \log(\frac{\sharp methods}{n_t}) \tag{5}$$

f_{tm} is the number of occurrences of a term (t) in a method (m), $\sharp methods$ refers to the total number of methods in the minimized search space, and n_t refers to the total number of methods containing the term t. MBuM also considers method length because previous studies showed that larger files are more likely to contain bugs due to carrying many features of a software [5]. The function used to model the method length is provided in Eq. 6.

$$g(terms) = \frac{1}{1 + e^{-Norm(\sharp terms)}} \tag{6}$$

$\sharp terms$ is the number of terms in a method and $Norm(\sharp terms)$ is the normalized value of $\sharp terms$. The normalized value of a is calculated using Eq. 7.

$$Norm(a) = \frac{a - a_{min}}{a_{max} - a_{min}} \tag{7}$$

where, a_{max} and a_{min} are the maximum and minimum value of a. Now this normalized value is multiplied with the cosine similarity score to calculate final $mVSM$ score which is calculated by Eq. 8.

$$mVSM(q, m) = g(terms) \times cos(q, m) \tag{8}$$

After measuring $mVSM$ score of each method, a list of buggy methods has been ranked according to the descending order of scores. The method with maximum score is suggested at the top of the ranking.

5   Case Study

The effectiveness of MBuM has been evaluated by conducting several research questions followed by multiple case studies. The case studies are similar to the existing bug localization techniques such as PROMISER [9], LSI [12] and LDA [11]. For this purpose, Top N Rank, Mean Reciprocal Rank (MRR) and Mean Average Precision (MAP) are used as the measurement metrics.

5.1   Elements of the Case Studies

Here, two well-known open-source projects named as Eclipse and Mozilla are considered as the subject of case study. Eclipse is a widely used open source Integrated Development Environment (IDE) which is used for developing Java applications. Meanwhile, Mozilla is a web browser which is used in most of the hardware and software platforms [9]. Different versions of Eclipse (e.g., version 2.1.0, 3.0.1, 3.0.2 and 3.1.0) and Mozilla (e.g., version 1.5.1, 1.6 and 1.6 (a)) are chosen which contain large volume of source code. As an example, 12,863 classes and 95,341 methods are available in Eclipse 3.0.2, while Mozilla 1.5.1 contains 4,853 classes and 53,617 methods [9].

5.2   Objectives of the Case Studies

Since MBuM performs method level bug localization, methods are chosen as the level of granularity in all the case studies. The actual buggy classes and methods corresponding to the bugs are identified from the published patches. Theses are used to evaluate the bug localization techniques where each patch specifies which methods were actually changed to fix a specific bug. In case of a bug, more than one published patches, the union of the most recent and earlier patches are considered. A brief overview of bug title, description and the generated queries for Eclipse and Mozilla are provided in [20]. The considered bugs are well-acquainted and reproducible which meet the following criteria.

(i) Bugs are often categorized as resolved or verified or fixed. So, only the valid bugs that have been fixed are considered.

(ii) The bugs having large similarity with multiple scenarios are chosen. For example, a similar feature is implemented in multiple packages where the implementations are different in every packages. Here, a bug may be occurred in one package. This criterion supports **Lemma 2** (Sect. 3).

5.3 Evaluation Metrics

To measure the performance of MBuM, Top N Rank, MRR (Mean Reciprocal Rank) and MAP (Mean Average Precision) are used as metrics. These are widely-used for measuring the effectiveness of a retrieval and ranking system [17, 21]. For all of these, the higher the value, the better the performance is. These metrics are briefly described as follows.

(i) Top N Rank: This is the number of bugs that are localized in the top N ranks ($N = 1, 5, 10, \ldots$ for this system). For an example, $N = 5$ means that the buggy statements ranked within top 5 suggestions. If one of the fixed files of a bug is in the result set, it is marked as localized [14].

(ii) MRR: A reciprocal rank is the multiplicative inverse of the first correct results' rank of a query [14]. For example, if a bug is localized in rank position 4, the reciprocal rank is $\frac{1}{4}$. So, the range of MRR will be $0 \leq MRR \leq 1$. MRR is the average of all the reciprocal ranks of a set of queries. MRR is calculated using Eq. 9. Here, n and r_i are the number of queries and rank of a query i, respectively.

$$MRR = \frac{1}{n} \sum_{i=1}^{n} \frac{1}{r_i} \tag{9}$$

(iii) MAP: MAP indicates how successfully the system is able to locate all the buggy locations unlike MRR [14]. MAP is the mean of the average precision values of a set of query [5].

5.4 Research Questions

In MBuM, probable buggy methods are ranked by conducting static analysis followed by dynamic analysis of the source code. Hence, few research questions have been emerged such as **RQ1** and **RQ2**. **RQ1** is introduced to validate that, the minimization of search space can improve the localizing accuracy. It is also needed to prove that the actual buggy methods get large similarity scores for a bug. To validate this, **RQ2** is introduced.

RQ1: Does the minimization of search space can improve the accuracy of bug localization?

To answer this question, bug report ♯74149[2] has been introduced which searches from 'Help' in Eclipse titled as "the search words after ''" will be

---

[2] https://bugs.eclipse.org/bugs/show_bug.cgi?id=74149.

ignored". For this case, the following scenario is executed to retrieve the relevant methods.

(i) Expand the 'Help' menu from Eclipse and click on the search option.
(ii) Enter a search query within the search field.
(iii) Finally, click on 'Go' button or press enter.

In this case, MBuM finds only 20 classes and 100 methods as relevant to this bug, shown in Fig. 3. Here, two source code packages namely *org.eclipse.help.internal.search* and *org.eclipse.help.internal.base* are executed. Within the first package, 14 classes are available and only 6 relevant classes are extracted from *org.eclipse.help.internal. base* package. Each extracted class also contains one or more methods. After despising the large irrelevant search space, static analysis is applied only on the relevant information. If a query contains lots of ambiguous keywords (e.g., very few bug related information), MBuM may suggest the actual buggy method at most $100th$ position while all other existing bug localization techniques will suggest buggy method in $53,617th$ position in the worst case. This is because by discarding irrelevant source code methods, MBuM only uses these 100 methods for finding buggy methods while other techniques consider total (i.e., $53,617$) methods of Eclipse.

```xml
<?xml version="1.0" encoding="UTF-8" standalone="no"?>
<source>
<Package name="org.eclipse.help.internal.search">
    <Class name="SearchProgressMonitor">
        <Method name="getProgressMonitor"/>
        <Method name="SearchProgressMonitor"/>
        <Method name="DummySearchQuery"/>
    </Class>
    <Class name="SearchManager">
        <Method name="SearchManager"/>
        <Method name="search"/>
        <Method name="getIndex"/>
        <Method name="getAnalyzer"/>
        <Method name="ensureIndexUpdated"/>
        <Method name="updateIndex"/>
    </Class>
    <Class name="SearchQuery">
        <Method name="getLocale"/>
        <Method name="getSearchWord"/>
        <Method name="getFieldNames"/>
        <Method name="isFieldSearch"/>
    </Class>
    <Class name="AnalyzerDescriptor">
        <Method name="AnalyzerDescriptor"/>
        <Method name="createAnalyzer"/>
        <Method name="getLang"/>
    </Class>
    <Class name="SearchIndexWithIndexingProgress">
        <Method name="SearchIndexWithIndexingProgress"/>
        <Method name="getProgressDistributor"/>
    </Class>

    <Class name="SearchIndex">
        <Method name="SearchIndex"/>
        <Method name="tryLock"/>
        <Method name="needsUpdating"/>
        <Method name="getDocPlugins"/>
        <Method name="getIndexedDocs"/>
        <Method name="getTocManager"/>
        <Method name="addDocument"/>
        <Method name="beginAddBatch"/>
        <Method name="endAddBatch"/>
        <Method name="exists"/>
        <Method name="search"/>
        <Method name="registerSearch"/>
        <Method name="openSearcher"/>
    </Class>
    <Class name="HTMLDocParser">
        <Method name="HTMLDocParser"/>
    </Class>
    <Class name="ProgressDistributor">
        <Method name="ProgressDistributor"/>
        <Method name="addMonitor"/>
    </Class>
    <Class name="IndexingOperation">
        <Method name="IndexingOperation"/>
        <Method name="execute"/>
        <Method name="getRemovedDocuments"/>
        <Method name="getIndexableURL"/>
        <Method name="getAddedDocuments"/>
        <Method name="getAllDocuments"/>
        <Method name="removeDocuments"/>
        <Method name="checkCancelled"/>
        <Method name="addDocuments"/>
    </Class>

    <Class name="LazyProgressMonitor">
        <Method name="LazyProgressMonitor"/>
        <Method name="beginTask"/>
    </Class>
    <Class name="QueryBuilder">
        <Method name="QueryBuilder"/>
        <Method name="getLuceneQuery"/>
        <Method name="tokenizeUserQuery"/>
        <Method name="analyzeTokens"/>
        <Method name="buildLuceneQuery"/>
        <Method name="getLuceneQuery"/>
        <Method name="createLuceneQuery"/>
        <Method name="getRequiredQueries"/>
        <Method name="getRequiredQuery"/>
        <Method name="getHighlightTerms"/>
    </Class>
    <Class name="QueryWordsToken">
        <Method name="word"/>
        <Method name="phrase"/>
        <Method name="createLuceneQuery"/>
    </Class>
    <Class name="SearchResults">
        <Method name="addHits"/>
    </Class>
    <Class name="QueryWordsPhrase">
        <Method name="addWord"/>
    </Class>
</Package>
<Package name="org.eclipse.help.internal.base ">
}
</Package>
</source>
```

Fig. 3. Extracted methods for Eclipse Bug Id-74149.

A query is formulated using the bug description which contained 'search query quote token'. The actual buggy method is manually retrieved from the published patch which is 'org.eclipse.help.internal.search.QueryBuilder.tokenizeUserQuery'. MBuM suggests 'tokenizeUserQuery' method at the 1st position of its ranking (shown in Table 1). Same query is applied on PROMISER, LSI and BugLocator to find the buggy location. PROMISER and LSI rank the actual buggy method at the $5th$ and $8th$ position respectively (shown in Table 1). So,

Table 1. The suggestion of buggy methods using different bug localization techniques in Eclipse (reproduced from [10]).

♯Bug	BugLocator	PROMISER	LSI	LDA	Proposed MBuM
5138	7	2	7	2	1
31779	4	1	2	2	1
74149	12	5	8	1	1
83307	6	5	13	7	2
91047	4	6	9	5	3

comparing with PROMISER and LSI, the effectiveness of MBuM is 5 and 8 times better respectively. On the other hand, BugLocator suggests buggy class at $12th$ position which shows that MBuM performs m times faster where m represents total number of methods in the suggested 12 buggy classes because BugLocator suggests buggy classes. LDA is not implemented because same bug reports are also used in LDA and that is why the results are taken from that paper [11]. In this case, LDA creates a different query as 'query quote token' which discards the 'search' term from the query due to obtaining 'search' query in multiple scenarios. That is the reason for suggesting the buggy method at the 1st position. Hence, it can be concluded that static analysis followed by dynamic execution trace of the source code reduces the search space which improves the ranking accuracy of bug localization technique.

RQ2: How much effectively MBuM can suggest buggy methods?

The effectiveness of MBuM can be measured by considering the ranking of buggy methods. If the buggy method is ranked at the 1st position, the effectiveness is 100%. To answer **RQ2**, two case studies are conducted on Eclipse and Mozilla where the ranking of buggy methods provided by MBuM are compared with BugLocator, PROMISER, LSI and LDA. These case studies consider five different bugs which were also studied in PROMISER [9] and LDA [11].

Case Study 1: Bug Localization in Eclipse. In this case study, five different bugs in Eclipse are considered for making a comparison with state-of-the-art bug localization techniques named as BugLocator, LDA, PROMISER and LSI. The chosen bugs are described as follows.

- Bug ♯74149[3], titled as "The search words after '"' ' will be ignored", exists in the versions 3.0.0, 3.0.1, 3.0.2, and fixed in the version 3.1.1.
- Bug ♯5138[4], titled as "Double-click-drag to select multiple words doesn't work", exists in version 2.1.3 and fixed in the version 3.3.
- Bug ♯31779[5], titled as "UnifiedTree should ensure file/ folder exists", presents in version 2.0.0 and fixed in the version 2.1.0.

---

[3] https://bugs.eclipse.org/bugs/show_bug.cgi?id=74149.
[4] https://bugs.eclipse.org/bugs/show_bug.cgi?id=5138.
[5] https://bugs.eclipse.org/bugs/show_bug.cgi?id=31779.

– Bug ♯83307[6], titled as "Unable to restore working set item", presents in version 3.1.0 and fixed in the version 3.4.
– Bug ♯91047[7], titled as "About dialog buttons seemingly not responsive", exists in version 3.1.0 and fixed in the version 3.4.

Table 1 presents the ranking of the aforementioned bug localization techniques. It is noteworthy that, BugLocator did not suggest methods rather suggest files or classes. Figure 4 represents the ranking provided by different techniques for five different considered bugs in Eclipse.

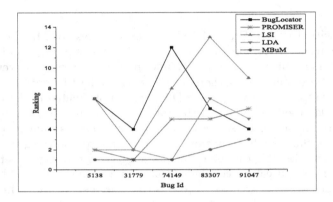

Fig. 4. Ranking provided by different bug localization techniques in Eclipse (reproduced from [10]).

These results show that MBuM ranks the actual buggy methods at the 1st position for three (60%) of the five bugs. Table 1 and Fig. 4 present that for bugs ♯5138, ♯83307 and ♯91047, MBuM performs better than four other techniques. For bug ♯31779, PROMISER only provides equal result as MBuM. In case of bug ♯74149, although LDA ranks equal as MBuM, the term 'search' is omitted from the query which helps for providing better ranking because 'search' is a common term in Eclipse and might create biasness. However, it is not desired because 'search' may be a good candidate for finding buggy locations. From this case study, it can be concluded that the proposed bug localization technique performs better results than others.

Case Study 2: Bug Localization in Mozilla. Similar to the previous case study, here also five mostly used bugs are taken from Mozilla bug repository and the selected bugs are described in [20] and only the title of these bugs are presented in the followings.

---

[6] https://bugs.eclipse.org/bugs/show_bug.cgi?id=83307.
[7] https://bugs.eclipse.org/bugs/show_bug.cgi?id=91047.

- Bug ♯182192[8], titled as "quotes (') are not removed from collected e-mail addresses", presents in Mozilla version 1.6 and fixed in the version 1.7.
- Bug ♯216154[9], titled as "Anchors in e-mails are broken - clicking anchor doesn't go to target in an email", exists in version 1.5.1 and patched in the version 1.6.
- Bug ♯225243[10], titled as "Page appears reversed (mirrored) when printed", exists in the version 1.6 (a) and fixed in the version 1.7. This bug does not exist in version the 1.6 rather actually presents in the version 1.6(a) [11].
- Bug ♯209430[11], titled as "Ctrl+Delete and Ctrl+BackSpace delete words in the wrong direction", located in version 1.5.1 and fixed in the version 1.6.
- Bug ♯231474[12], titled as "Attachments mix contents", presents in the version 1.5.1 and fixed in the version 1.6.

The results demonstrate that MBuM provides better ranking accuracy over BugLocator, LDA, PROMISER and LSI techniques (shown in Table 2). These results show that three (60%) out of five bugs are located at the 1st position and another two are ranked at the 2nd position by MBuM. On the other hand, among the other four techniques only PROMISER suggests two (40%) of five bugs at the 1st position and other three techniques' results are far away from the 1st position (according to Table 2).

Table 2. The suggestion of buggy methods using different bug localization techniques in Mozilla (N.B. reproduced from [10]).

♯Bug	BugLocator [5]	PROMISER [9]	LSI [12]	LDA [11]	Proposed MBuM
182192	4	2	37	3	1
216154	7	6	56	4	2
225243	5	6	24	9	2
209430	6	1	49	9	1
231474	3	1	18	4	1

Figure 5 presents the ranking provided by different techniques for five different bugs in Mozilla. Although for bugs ♯209430 and ♯231474, PROMISER provides the same ranking as MBuM, it produces noticeably poor ranking in other three bugs as shown in Table 2 and Fig. 5. In case of ♯182192, ♯216154 and ♯225243, MBuM ranks the actual buggy methods more accurately than other four techniques. This comparative analysis of results also shows the significant improvement of ranking by MBuM.

---

[8] https://bugzilla.mozilla.org/long_list.cgi?buglist=182192.
[9] https://bugzilla.mozilla.org/show_bug.cgi?id=216154.
[10] https://bugzilla.mozilla.org/show_bug.cgi?id=225243.
[11] https://bugzilla.mozilla.org/show_bug.cgi?id=209430.
[12] https://bugzilla.mozilla.org/show_bug.cgi?id=231474.

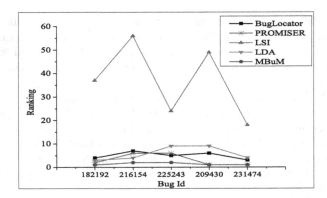

Fig. 5. Ranking provided by different bug localization techniques in Mozilla (reproduced from [10]).

6   Threats to Validity

This section discusses the threats which can affect the validity of the proposed technique. The threats are identified from three perspectives - internal threats, external threats and construct threats.

Internal Threats: The internal threats refer threats that affect the validity of the results which depend on the implementation of the technique and the environmental set up of the experimental procedure. The proposed technique as well as the experimental projects are implemented in Java programming language. Therefore, the result gained through analyzing the experimental projects may differ when experimented in platforms other than java.

External Threats: MBuM requires proper quality of the bug reports. As bug report is one of the important means from which the buggy locations can be identified, the quality of the bug report should contain the bug related information. For example, if a buggy scenario is related to the 'file import' module and the bug report holds another bug modules' information, the quality of the bug report will be significantly deteriorated. In practice, non-informative bug report can also delay to fix a bug. Similarly, if a bug report does not provide enough information, or provides misleading information, the performance of MBuM may be adversely affected. The slight modification is handled by the proposed technique using the semantic meaning extraction from WordNet. However, if the source code is not similar to the bug report, the localization may fail, though it is a common problem in all bug localization schemes.

Finally, if the bug report does not contain proper reproducible approach, it may be hard for developers to find the accurate source code dynamic tracing.

Another factor is the quality of source code, and the accuracy of bug localization depends on the good programming practices in naming variables, methods and classes. If a developer uses meaningless names, the performance of the proposed technique may be affected. However, in most of the well-managed projects, developers follow good naming conventions and programming practices.

Construct Threats: Construct threats are related to the metrics which are used to analyze the effectiveness of the proposed technique. The results are analyzed based on Top N Rank, MRR and MAP. Therefore, analyzing the results with other metrics can affect the generalization of the results.

7 Conclusion

This paper presents an approach to rank Method level Bug localization using Minimized search space (MBuM). For ranking buggy methods, it discards irrelevant search space by taking the execution trace considering method call sequences of the source code. To retrieve the content of the methods static analysis has been performed. Finally, similarity is measured between the method contents of the source code and bug report which provides a rank list of the methods.

MBuM has been evaluated both theoretically and experimentally. Theoretical evaluation is done using formal methods, and for the purpose of experiments case studies are conducted using two large scale open-source projects named as Eclipse and Mozilla. The case studies show that MBuM ranks buggy methods at the 1st position in most of the cases.

In this research, although fine grained suggestions such as method level bug localization has been conducted, statement level bug localization can be addressed in near future. In addition, since MBuM outperforms other existing techniques for open source projects, it will be applied in industrial projects to assess its effectiveness in practice.

Acknowledgment. This research is supported by the fellowship from ICT Division, Ministry of Posts, Telecommunications and Information Technology, Bangladesh. No - 56.00.0000.028.33.028.15-214 Date 24-06-2015.

References

1. Dit, B., Revelle, M., Gethers, M., Poshyvanyk, D.: Feature location in source code: a taxonomy and survey. J. Softw. Evol. Process **25**(1), 53–95 (2013)
2. Hovemeyer, D., Pugh, W.: Finding bugs is easy. ACM Sigplan Not. **39**(12), 92–106 (2004)
3. Saha, R.K., Lawall, J., Khurshid, S., Perry, D.E.: On the effectiveness of information retrieval based bug localization for c programs. In: IEEE International Conference on Software Maintenance and Evolution (ICSME 2014), pp. 161–170. IEEE (2014)
4. Saha, R.K., Lease, M., Khurshid, S., Perry, D.E.: Improving bug localization using structured information retrieval. In: Proceedings of the 28th International Conference on Automated Software Engineering (ASE 2013) IEEE/ACM, pp. 345–355. IEEE (2013)

5. Zhou, J., Zhang, H., Lo, D.: Where should the bugs be fixed? more accurate information retrieval-based bug localization based on bug reports. In: Proceedings of the 34th International Conference on Software Engineering (ICSE 2012), pp. 14–24. IEEE (2012)

6. Nichols, B.D.: Augmented bug localization using past bug information. In: Proceedings of the 48th Annual Southeast Regional Conference, p. 61. ACM (2010)

7. Wang, S., Lo, D.: Version history, similar report, and structure: putting them together for improved bug localization. In: Proceedings of the 22nd International Conference on Program Comprehension, pp. 53–63. ACM (2014)

8. Wilde, N., Gomez, J.A., Gust, T., Strasburg, D.: Locating user functionality in old code. In: Proceerdings of the Conference on Software Maintenance, pp. 200–205. IEEE (1992)

9. Poshyvanyk, D., Gueheneuc, Y.-G., Marcus, A., Antoniol, G., Rajlich, V.C.: Feature location using probabilistic ranking of methods based on execution scenarios and information retrieval. IEEE Trans. Softw. Eng. $33(6)$, 420–432 (2007)

10. Rahman, S., Sakib, K.: An appropriate method ranking approach for localizing bugs using minimized search space. In: Proceedings of the 11th International Conference on Evaluation of Novel Software Approaches to Software Engineering, pp. 303–309 (2016)

11. Lukins, S.K., Kraft, N., Etzkorn, L.H., et al.: Source code retrieval for bug localization using latent dirichlet allocation. In: Proceedings of the 15th Working Conference on Reverse Engineering (WCRE 2008), pp. 155–164. IEEE (2008)

12. Deerwester, S.C., Dumais, S.T., Landauer, T.K., Furnas, G.W., Harshman, R.A.: Indexing by latent semantic analysis. JAsIs $41(6)$, 391–407 (1990)

13. Alhindawi, N., Dragan, N., Collard, M.L., Maletic, J.I.: Improving feature location by enhancing source code with stereotypes. In: 2013 IEEE International Conference on Software Maintenance, pp. 300–309. IEEE (2013)

14. Rahman, S., Ganguly, K., Kazi, S.: An improved bug localization using structured information retrieval and version history. In: Proceedings of the 18th International Conference on Computer and Information Technology (ICCIT) (2015) (accepted)

15. Eisenbarth, T., Koschke, R., Simon, D.: Locating features in source code. IEEE Trans. Softw. Eng. $29(3)$, 210–224 (2003)

16. Woodcock, J., Davies, J.: Using z. specification, refinement, and proof (1996)

17. Manning, C.D., Raghavan, P., Schütze, H., et al.: Introduction to information retrieval, vol. 1. Cambridge University Press, Cambridge (2008)

18. Kim, D., Tao, Y., Kim, S., Zeller, A.: Where should we fix this bug? a two-phase recommendation model. IEEE Trans. Softw. Eng. $39(11)$, 1597–1610 (2013)

19. Frakes, W.B.: Stemming algorithms, pp. 131–160 (1992)

20. Rahman, S.: shanto-rahman/mbum: (2016). https://github.com/shanto-Rahman/MBuM. 4/1/2016

21. Pareek, H.H., Ravikumar, P.K.: A representation theory for ranking functions. In: Advances in Neural Information Processing Systems, pp. 361–369 (2014)

How Interesting Are Suggestions of Coupled File Changes for Software Developers?

Jasmin Ramadani[(✉)] and Stefan Wagner

Institute of Software Technology, University of Stuttgart,
Universitätstraße 38, Stuttgart, Germany
{jasmin.ramadani,stefan.wagner}@informatik.uni-stuttgart.de
http://www.iste.uni-stuttgart.de/en/se.html

Abstract. Software repositories represent a data source from which we can extract interesting information to be presented to the developers working on their maintenance tasks. Various studies use the software repositories to extract sets of files that changed frequently in the past. However, they do not consider feedback from developers on whether they would like to use this kind of information. The aim of our research is to support developers in maintenance tasks using suggestions which other files they should also change. We investigate three software repositories to find coupled file changes to support the software developers. We also propose a set of attributes from the versioning system, the issue tracking system and the project documentation. We contrast our findings with the feedback gathered using survey and interviews with the developers. According to our results, small repositories make an insightful analysis difficult. Both from experienced and inexperienced developers, the feedback was mostly neutral. Most of the attributes we proposed were accepted as interesting by the developers. Furthermore, developers also suggested other additional issues to be relevant, e.g. the context of the coupled changes. Generally, developers did not reject the coupled file changes suggestions. However, the presentation form of coupled changes and context information need to be taken into account.

Keywords: Data mining · Coupled file changes · Usefulnesses

1 Introduction

Software product development produces large amounts of data which is stored in software repositories. They contain the artifacts developed during software evolution. These repositories include different data sources like version control systems, issue tracking systems and project documentation archives. After some time, this data becomes a valuable information source for bug fixing or maintenance tasks. To learn from it, we need a technique to extract relevant details from the source code history and search for valuable information. One of the most used techniques is data mining which has become popular for analyzing

© Springer International Publishing AG 2016
L.A. Maciaszek and J. Filipe (Eds.): ENASE 2016, CCIS 703, pp. 201–221, 2016.
DOI: 10.1007/978-3-319-56390-9_10

software repositories. The term *mining software repositories (MSR)* describes investigations of software repositories using data mining [19].

To help the developers to identify the files to be changed during maintenance tasks, a mining software repositories approach has been proposed [33]. These files can be used to recommend coupled file changes. Couplings are defined as "the measure of the strength of association established by a connection from one module to another" [29]. Change couplings are described as files having the same commit time, author and modification description [12]. Frequently changed files can support developers in dealing with the large amount of information about the software product, especially if the developer is new on the project, the project started a long time ago or if the developer does not have much experience in software development.

1.1   Problem Statement

Several researchers have proposed approaches to identify coupled files to give recommendations to developers during a change [20,33,35]. Existing studies, however, focus on the presentation of the mining results and ignore the feedback of developers on the findings.

1.2   Research Objectives

The overall aim of our research is to support the developers in common maintenance tasks. In this paper, we concentrate on applying MSR to provide suggestions for likely changes so that we can investigate how interesting the suggestions are for the developers and what further information besides version histories might increase the interestingness.

We define *interestingness* as the subjective measure of the developers' opinion on how useful findings (here: coupled change suggestions) are for maintenance tasks.

1.3   Contribution

We present an industrial case study on the interestingness of coupled change suggestions. We identify frequent couplings between file changes based on the information gathered from three software project repositories. The version control system, the issue tracking system and the project documentation archives are used as data sources for additional repository attributes we join to the coupled changes we discover. In particular, we investigate the feedback of the developers about the interestingness of our findings by conducting a survey. We evaluate the answers by performing additional interviews and analyze them using the *Grounded Theory* method.

This paper is an extended version of our case study on interestingness of coupled file changes [23]. This extended version adds an additional research question investigating the influence of the involvement of the developers in the project on the interestingness of coupled change suggestions. We have also extended the discussion about the research questions and the related conclusions.

2   Interestingness

Coupled changes suggestions can be provided to the developers with an intention to help them by providing suggestions about other changes. There is no guarantee that they would like to use this kind of help.

Our approach is based on determining the interestingness of these coupled changes. We consider interestingness as a subjective measure which is derived from the user's beliefs or expectations [22]. Information is defined to be *interesting* if it is novel, useful and nontrivial to compute. Here, *useful* means that it can help to achieve a goal of the system or the user [11]. The interestingness of coupled changes is represented by the possibility that they will use it during their maintenance tasks. To determine the level of interestingness of the coupled changes and the repository attributes we conclude questionnaire and interviews to measure the feedback from the developers included in our case study.

We measure the interestingness using three levels: *interesting*, *neutral* and *not interesting*. Two categories of interestingness has been identified. The first category is the interestingness of coupled file changes. The second category is the interestingness of the repository attributes we extract from the version control system, the issue tracking system and the project documentation. We join this repository attributes to the coupled file changes.

3   Data Mining Background

To be able to extract coupled file changes by using data mining, we introduce the data technique that we employ in our study. One of the most popular data mining techniques is the discovery of frequent itemsets. To identify sets of items which occur together frequently in a given database is one of the most basic tasks in data mining [15]. Coupled changes describe a situation where someone changes a particular file and also changes another file afterwards.

Let us say that the developer changes file f_1 and then also frequently changes file f_3. By investigating the transactions of changed files in the version control system commits we identify a set of files that changed together. Let us have the following three transactions: $T_1 = \{f_1, f_2, f_3, f_7\}$, $T_2 = \{f_1, f_3, f_5, f_6\}$, $T_3 = \{f_1, f_2, f_3, f_8\}$. From these three transactions, we isolate the rule that files f_1 and f_3 are found together: f_1 and f_3 are coupled. This means that when the developers changed file f_1, they also changed file f_3. If these files are found together frequently, it can help other persons by suggesting that if they change f_1, they should also change f_3. Let $F = \{f_1, f_2, ..., f_d\}$ be the set of all items (files) f in a transaction and $T = \{t_1, t_2, ..., t_n\}$ be the set of all transactions t. As transactions, we define the commits consisting of different files. Each transaction contains a subset of chosen items from F called itemset.

An important property of an itemset is the support count δ which is the number of transactions containing an item. We call the itemsets frequent if they have a support threshold min_{sup} greater than a minimum specified by the user with

$$0 \leq \text{min}_{\text{sup}} \leq |F| \tag{1}$$

4   Related Work

Many studies investigated software repositories to find logically coupled changes, e.g. [3,9,12]. We identify two granularity levels, the first one [20,33] investigates the couplings based on the file level, the second [9,19,34,35] identifies coplings between parts of files like classes, methods or modules.

Most of the studies dealing with identifying coupled changes use some kind of data mining for this purpose [13,18,20,27,31,33,35]. Especially the association rules technique is often used to identify frequent changes [20,33,35]. This data mining technique uses various algorithms to determine the frequency of these changes. Most of them employ the Apriori algorithm [20,35], however other algorithms like the FP-Tree algorithm are also in use [33].

Most of the studies use a single data source where a kind of version control system is investigated, typically CVS or Subversion. To our knowledge there are few studies which investigate a Git version control system [4,6,17]. Other studies combine more than one data source to be investigated, like a version control system and an issue tracking system [5,7,8,32] where the data extracted from these two sources is analyzed and the link between the changed files and issues is determined.

To the best of our knowledge, there are only three studies investigating how couplings align with developers' opinions or feedbacks. Coupling metrics on the structural and the semantic level are investigated in [24]. The developers are asked if they find these metrics to be useful. They show that feature couplings on a higher level of abstraction than classes are useful. Here, the developers' perceptions of software couplings are investigated in [2]. Here the authors examine how class couplings captured by different coupling measures like semantic, logical and others align with the developers perception of couplings. The semantic couplings have received the best rating of all types of couplings. The interestingness of coupled changes is also studied in [33]. This study defines categorization of coupled changes interestingness according to the source code changes.

We focus on the interestingness of coupled file changes and attributes involving the developers' feedback on our findings using the following data sources: Two of the projects use Git[1] and the third one uses Mercurial.[2] The first industrial project uses JIRA as issue tracking system,[3] the open source project and the second industrial project use Redmine.[4] We use the available product documentation of the projects as additional source of information.

5   Case Study Design

The structure of our case study is based on existing guidelines [25].

---

[1] http://git-scm.com/.
[2] http://mercurial.selenic.com/.
[3] https://www.atlassian.com/software/jira.
[4] http://www.redmine.org/.

5.1   Research Questions

RQ1: How many coupled changes can we extract from software repositories? This research question provides the basis for our research. It is relevant to investigate for the reason that the number of coupled changes affects the outcome of the repository data analysis.

RQ2: How interesting are coupled change suggestions for developers? This is the central question of this study which decides if developers would like to use the suggested couplings.

RQ3: Does the experience of developers influences the interestingness of coupled changes? We expect that inexperienced developers would be more interested in coupled file suggestions considering their possible problems understanding the system [26]. Therefore, we investigate the developer's programming and project experience.

RQ4: Does the involvement in the project of developers influences the interestingness of coupled changes? We include both developers who were involved and those not involved in the development of the software products used in the case study. Although our goal is to support inexperienced or developers not involved in the projects, we expand the investigation on developers which were included in the software products, we want to get their feedback on the coupled changes.

RQ5: How interesting is additional information from other related project artifacts? After we determine the interestingness of the couplings, we will investigate if adding additional data sources influences the interestingness. First, we examine the version control system that is related to the changes, e.g. commit ids where the couplings were found, commit messages, commit dates and authors of the commits. Second, the information stored in the issue tracking system is investigated, attributes like issue description, issue date and issue status. Third, we look into the project documentation archive for information about the project structure and naming conventions.

RQ6: Does the experience of developers influences the interestingness of additional information from other related project artifacts? We investigate if the choice of the attributes from the version control system and the issue tracking system depends on the developer's programming experience.

5.2   Case Selection

The case selection is based on their availability and the suitability for our research. We select cases from industry as a part of our cooperation with our industrial partners as well as from the available open source projects developed at the University of Stuttgart. Hence, our subjects will be practitioners as well as students.

5.3   Data Collection Procedure

The case study uses two main data sources to investigate the coupled file changes. As first data source, we use the artifacts from the software product development archived in software repositories. We did not have any direct contact with the development process of the product. Instead, we examine the repositories of the software product being developed or maintained. The second data source consists of surveys and interviews with the project stakeholders providing direct information. We divide the data collection procedure into five parts.

Version Control System. The first unit of data we use is the log data from the version control system. Two software projects used Git, while the third project uses Mercurial as a control management tool. Both are distributed version control systems allowing the developers to maintain their local versions of source code.

The data collection from the version control system consists of four steps which lead to the extraction of the information we need.

- **Log Extraction:** We extract the information from the log file containing the committed file changes and the commit attributes. The log data is exported as text file.
- **Data Preprocessing**: After the text files with the log data have been generated, we continue with the preparation of the data for data mining. Various data mining frameworks use their own format, so the input for the data mining algorithm and framework needs to be adjusted.
- **Identifying Atomic Change Sets:** We divide the data into a collection of atomic change sets. Version control systems deal with this issue differently. In our case, the version control systems preserve the possibility to group changes into a single change set or a so-called *atomic commit.* It represents an atomic changeset regardless of the number of files changed. A commit snapshot represents the total set of modified files and directories [21]. We organize the data in a transaction form where every transaction represents a set of files which changed together in a single commit.
- **Data Filtering:** We filter the file names and the following commit attributes: *commit id, commit message, commit date* and *commit author.* We deal with empty entries and outliers and we prepare the log entries for data mining.
- **Change Grouping Heuristic:** There are different heuristics proposed for grouping file changes [20]. We use a heuristic considering the file changes done by a single committer as related. We group the transactions of files committed only by a particular author. We do not relate the changes done by other committers.

Issue Tracking System. Issue tracking systems store important information about the software changes or problems. In our case, the companies chose to use JIRA and Redmine as issue tracking systems. The students also track their issues using Redmine. We investigate the following issue attributes: *issue titles, issue descriptions* and *issue messages.* The issue tracking systems support spreadsheet export containing the considered issue attributes.

Project Documentation. The software documentation gathered during the development process represents a rich source of data. The documentation consists of file naming conventions, directory paths and the package structure description. From these documents, we discover the project structure.

For example in the last project, the subproject containing the files described by the path `astpa/controlstructure/figure/` contains the Java classes responsible for the control diagram figures of this software.

Joining Collected Data. After the mining process is finished and we have identified the coupled changes, we join them with the attributes from the version control system, the issue tracker and the project documentation. In [8], the authors create a release history database where they import the data from the version control systems and the issue tracking systems. Similarly, we create a database containing all file changes and the corresponding attributes from the repositories.

Every commit has it own hash value which represents the commit id. It is a unique value which identifies all the commits in the database. The issues are identified by their keys. We use the issue keys to follow down the commit where the change took place using the merge points of issues with the commit messages. We use the path information of the changed files to enlist the sub-projects. As a result we have a list of the most frequently changed files accompanied by the information about the commit attributes, issue attributes and the project structure.

Survey and Interviews. We investigate the developers' feedback on the interestingness of coupled changes and the additional attributes by conducting a survey and performing interviews[5] with the developers.

Survey: The developers answer a list of multiple-choice questions on-line. We investigate the background of the developers by asking their programming and project experience. The developers give us feedback on the concept of coupled changes, not on particular couplings. We choose this setup as a first means to get as many opinions as possible. Only few developers were available for in-depth interviews on specific findings. The developer can choose between: *interesting, neutral* and *not interesting* to evaluate the interestingness of coupled changes and repository attributes.

Interviews: We perform semi-structured interviews to get more in-depth feedback from the developers. This way, we ensure that the developers did not answer the surveys by randomly choosing the options. We ask the available developers who worked on the projects and other uninvolved developers about the interestingness of the file changes and the attributes. We present them actual coupled file changes extracted from the repositories.

---

[5] All questions are available on http://dx.doi.org/10.5281/zenodo.15065.

5.4   Ethical Considerations

The data delivered by the companies is confidential. Therefore, we preserve the anonymity of the stakeholders and the companies during this study. The confidentiality and the publication is regulated by a non-disclosure agreement between the researchers and the companies. All personal information extracted from the repositories, the survey and the interviews is anonymized and is not presented in the study.

5.5   Analysis Procedure

The data analysis is a combination of quantitative and qualitative methods. We use quantitative methods to find the number of couplings. We augment the results with a qualitative and quantitative analysis of the survey and the interviews with the developers.

Analysis of Repository Data. We analyze the repository data to answer RQ1. We run the mining algorithm to discover frequently coupled file changes. We investigate the additional attributes we gather from the commit logs, the issue tracking export and the project documentation.

Data Mining Algorithm: Various algorithms for mining frequent itemsets and association rules have been proposed in literature [1,14,16]. We use the FP-Tree-Growth algorithm to find the frequent change patterns. As opposed to the Apriori algorithm [1] which uses a bottom up generation of frequent itemset combinations, the FP-Tree algorithm uses partition and divide-and-conquer methods [14]. This algorithm is faster and more memory efficient than the Apriori algorithm used in other studies and allows frequent itemset discovery without candidate itemset generation.

Support Level: We analyze the coupled changes by defining the threshold value of the support for the frequent itemset algorithm. We use the thresholds that give us a frequent yet still manageable number of couplings. This threshold is normally defined by the user. We use the technique proposed by Fournier-Viger presented in [10] to identify the support level. These values vary from developer to developer, so we test the highest possible value that delivers frequent itemsets.

If for a particular developer, the support value does not bring any useful results, we continue dropping the value of the threshold. We did not consider itemsets with a support below 0.2 for the first two projects and 0.1 for the third project. There is a variety of commercial and open-source products offering data mining techniques and algorithms. For the analysis, we use an open-source framework specialized on mining frequent itemsets and association rules called the *SPMF-Framework*.[6] It consists of a large collection of algorithms supported by appropriate documentation.

---

[6] http://www.philippe-fournier-viger.com/spmf.

Analysis of Questionnaires and Interviews. To answer RQ2–RQ6, we analyze the questionnaires and the outcomes of the interviews.

Survey Analysis: We start by investigating the background of the developers by checking their answers about their programming and project experience. We analyze the answers from the questionnaire by calculating the distribution of the frequency of their answers. We put the main focus on the answers of the participants about the interestingness of coupled changes and the answers about the additional attributes.

Interview Analysis: We examine the interviews with the developers to validate the outcomes of the questionnaires and to understand the context of their answers. We analyze the interviews by using *Grounded Theory* [30]. The goal is to generate a theory that emerges from the data being comparatively analyzed.

To analyze the data and build the theory, we use the following types of coding activities in sequence: open, axial and selective coding [30]. After these codings, we perform the theoretical coding and create the conceptual model. We use the analysis software *Atlas.ti*[7] to link the codes and create a network diagram.

- **Open coding:** In the open coding we have a line-by-line examination of the interview transcripts to identify the main concepts and categories together with their dimensions and properties. We code the data from interview answers with a set of open codes derived from our research questions. Before we continue, we write a memo consisting of the hypotheses and ideas noted during the analysis.
- **Axial coding:** After the open coding is performed, we continue with the axial coding where we relate the categories, concepts and codes by identifying the relations among them. This is done using the paradigm model [30] and considering the relationships between contexts, interactions, conditions and consequences.
- **Selective coding:** The selective coding formulates a core category to which all other categories and codes can be related and includes all of the data.
- **Theoretical coding:** After finishing the open and axial coding, this coding involves the relationships between categories and subcategories and gives meaning to the theory.
- **Conceptual mapping and model:** We express the concepts of our theory and present their relations. We draw a category map which emerges from the analysis.

5.6   Validity Procedure

Internal Validity: We use widely known techniques and algorithms for repository mining. We extract data from a repository systems used among a high number of companies. We analyze the data from the software repository, perform a survey among the developers and we validate the answers given in the questionnaires by

---

[7] http://www.atlasti.com/index.html.

interviewing developers. We collect the answers and compare the results related to the research questions to identify if these reflect the investigated information [25]. This way we avoid to rely on a possible lack of precision in the answers on the questionnaires by the developers concerning the interestingness.

External Validity: We choose representative cases with high standards considering software development and standardized development techniques. We use an independent party to record the memos for the interviews and code the information to increase the objectivity of the analysis results.

6   Results and Discussion

We report the results of the analysis of the software repository data, the questionnaires and the interviews in relation to the interestingness of coupled changes and attributes.[8] We discuss the analysis outcomes and evaluate the validity of our results by taking into account the feedback from the developers.

6.1   Case Description

The cases in this study are three software projects. The first two projects were provided by IT companies from the area of Stuttgart, Germany. The third one is an open-source project developed at the University of Stuttgart.

The first project is a web-based software written in Java and supplied by an industrial partner. The repository of this project contains 1,610 commits performed by 26 developers during 2 years of development. The software changes are stored in Git and the issues are tracked using JIRA.

The second project is a C# software supplied by another partner from the IT industry. The repository contains 159 commits performed by 5 developers during 1 year of development. The project used Mercurial as version control tool and Redmine for issues management.

The third project is a Java open source software which was developed at the University of Stuttgart by student developers. The repository contains 752 commits, committed by 9 developers during 1 year. It uses Git for versioning and Redmine as issue tracking system. Certain project documentation archives of the projects were available from where we extract the information about the software structure and the naming conventions.

6.2   Number of Couplings (RQ 1)

In Table 1, we summarize the analyzed information from the repositories. Referring to the first project, the data from 22 out of 26 developers was relevant for the study. For the second project, the data from 4 out of 5 developers was taken into account. For the third project, the data committed by all 9 developers was

---

[8] The analysis results are available at http://dx.doi.org/10.5281/zenodo.15065.

Table 1. Results based on repository analysis, table reproduced from [23].

	Project1	Project2	Project3
No. of relev. dev	22	4	9
No. of commits	1610	138	752
No. of couplings	205	13	200
Freq. itemset supp	0.2	0.2	0.1

Table 2. Interestingness of coupled changes, table reproduced from [23].

	Involved	Not involved	All
Interesting	2	2	4
Neutral	9	10	19
Not interesting	0	0	0
Sum	11	12	23

suitable for analysis. The rest of the developers reported a low number of commits so we did not consider their change commits. We excluded their commits as unsuitable for the reason that they did not reach the minimum support for the frequency of the changes we defined previously.

The number of commits represents the size of the projects followed by the number of change couplings we have extracted. The number of coupled changes represents the basis of our analysis. We were able to extract 205 couplings from the first repository. From the second, a smaller repository, we report only 13 coupled changes. The third repository delivered 200 coupled changes. These results show that we need larger project repositories containing high number of commits to be able to deliver a high number of couplings.

6.3 Interestingness of Coupled Changes (RQ 2)

The participants were asked to give their feedback on how interesting coupled changes for maintenance tasks are. Most of the developers (19 of 23) reported a neutral opinion for the concept of coupled changes. A small group of four participants noted coupled changes as interesting. None of the developers rejected the idea as not interesting (Table 2).

The fact that the developers did not reject coupled changes allows us to continue our analysis. These results allow us to continue investigating the next research questions. We proceed our analysis and investigate how coupled changes is influenced by the developers' programming and project experience. Taking into account our small sample size, we refrain from formal hypotheses testing.

6.4 Influence of Developer Experience on Interestingness (RQ 3)

Both experienced and inexperienced developers were similarly interested in coupled changes which is in contrast to our expectations. In Table 3 we present the distribution of the interestingness of coupled changes in relation to the programming experience of the developers. What we can see is that regardless of their expertise level, none of the developers rejected the coupled changes. Very few developers have accepted the coupled changes as interesting, yet most of the developers took a neutral position toward the coupled change suggestions.

6.5 Influence of Developer Involvement in the Project on Interestingness (RQ 4)

The results in Table 2 show that there is no difference based on the involvement of the developers in the projects. Both involved and uninvolved developers did not reject coupled changes. Continuing with the developers involved in the project development, we group their answers based on their project experience. Table 4 shows the distribution of the developers by their programming experience. Again in all three groups from beginners to developers knowing the system, most of them have answered neutrally, not rejecting the coupled change suggestions.

6.6 Interestingness of Additional Information (RQ 5)

After the investigation of the coupled changes, we continued examining the interestingness of the repository attributes we have joined to the coupled files presented in Table 5. To support the coupled changes, we reported a set of common meta-data attributes [28] which allow us to find more information about the commits, the issues and the product itself. The repositories offer various attributes related to the committed changes, the issues found and the project structure.

Table 3. Couplings and developer's experience, table adapted from [23].

Programming experience	Freq	Freq. [%]	Interesting	Neutral	Not interesting
<1 year	2	9	0	2	0
1–3 years	4	17	2	2	0
3–5 years	9	39	1	8	0
>5 years	8	35	1	7	0

Table 4. Couplings and developer's project involvement.

Project involvement	Freq	Freq. [%]	Interesting	Neutral	Not interesting
<6 months–1 year	3	27	0	3	0
1–2 years	3	27	1	2	0
>2 years	5	46	1	4	0

Table 5. Interesting attributes, table reproduced from [23].

Attribute	Frequency	Frequency [%]
Commit message	22	95
File name	18	78
File type	9	39
Commit time	8	34
Commiter	6	26
Commit id	2	9
Issue title	21	91
Issue status	15	65
Issue type	14	60
Issue time	6	26
Project structure	20	86
Naming conv	15	65

We asked the participants about their feedback on the interestingness of each of the provided repository attributes. The results show that most of the offered attributes were rated by the developers as interesting.

Considering the commit related attributes, most of the developers found the commit message to be the most interesting attribute followed by the file name. The developers did not show much interest for the commit time, the committer and the file type. The commit id as attribute did not attract the developers' interest.

Regarding the issue related attributes, most of the developers were interested in the issue description. Some of the developers also found the issue status and type to be interesting. The issue time was not interesting for the developers.

From the documentation related attributes, the developers reported that both naming convention and the project structure information are interesting.

6.7 Influence of Developer Experience on Interestingness of Additional Information (RQ 6)

We examined the distribution of interestingness of the repository attributes according to developers' experience level. Based on this distribution we created two general groups of developers in this context: the first group called experienced, includes the developers having more than 5 years experience and the second group called inexperienced, includes developers having less than 5 years of experience. The results show that the experienced developers have a more clear picture of the set of interesting repository attributes. They have chosen a lower number of attributes compared to the inexperienced developers. The inexperienced developers have marked various commit and issue attributes being interesting for them. The more experienced developers' choice is more narrow

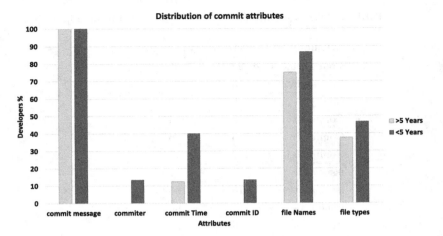

Fig. 1. Commit attributes and experience, figure reproduced from [23].

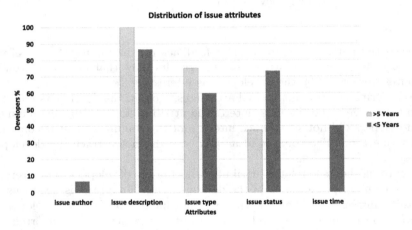

Fig. 2. Issue attributes and experience, figure reproduced from [23].

than the one for the inexperienced ones. The distribution of commit attributes is shown in Fig. 1. The distribution of issue attributes is presented in Fig. 2.

6.8 Validation and Theory

After the data mining analysis, we performed the interviews with developers who were active on the projects. For the first project, we managed to enlist 2 of the developers for interviewing. For the second project, we interviewed 2 developers and from the third project, we interviewed 4 out of 9 developers. They had been involved in the project from the beginning and have the most knowledge about the software. We also interviewed 4 developers not involved in any of the projects.

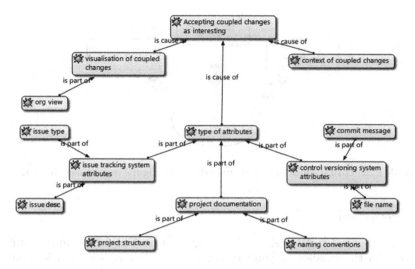

Fig. 3. Theoretical Framework, figure reproduced from [23].

Using Grounded Theory analysis on the interview transcripts, we derived a corresponding theory. We created the codes using an open coding procedure of the memos we created. They represent the answers of our participants to interview questions. We extracted the codes by identifying common issues in their answers.

We continued with the axial coding where we identified several categories as presented in Fig. 3. The core category we identified after the selective coding is *Interestingness of couplings and software repository information.* The results from the theoretical code show the core category, the subcategories and the relationships presented as a diagram in Fig. 3. We have categories covering the attributes we found to be interesting: version control attributes, issue attributes and project documentation. They are respectively divided in these subcategories: commit message, file names, issue titles, issue types, project structure and naming conventions. They represent the most interesting attributes which affect the interestingness of coupled changes.

The next categories are the visualization of coupled changes, consisting of the sub-category *organized view*, and the category *context of coupled changes.* The last two categories represent an additional feedback given by the interviewed developers where they would like to see an organized representation of changed files with a possibility to filter the information about them. They would also like to have information about the context of the changes. We present the key concepts of the theory together with their relations in Fig. 4. We see that the interestingness of the coupled changes also depends on the chosen repository attributes. Furthermore, it is also important to develop an organized presentation of coupled changes to the developers and to describe the context of these changes.

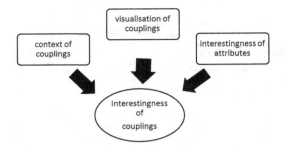

Fig. 4. Conceptual Model from grounded theory, figure reproduced from [23].

6.9 Discussion

The results related to RQ1 show that large repositories deliver more couplings compared to the smaller or younger repositories. Projects with a low number of commits do not provide enough data for a broader analysis. The number of commits and their size limit the output of our analysis. Our results lead to the conclusion that we need a relatively high number of couplings to be able to present a more exhaustive support for the developers in their tasks. Still, the setup of our analysis identifies a number of strongly coupled changes which limits the possibility they have happened by chance. We could reduce the support level of the data mining algorithm to provide a higher number of coupled changes, however, this could produce a threat for their accuracy.

The results for RQ2 report that the developers weakly support that coupled changes are interesting. The general concept of coupled changes was received mostly as neutral. The developers did not judged the coupled change suggestions very positive for the reason that they were not solving real maintenance tasks. We beleive that working with coupled change suggestions related to real maintenance tasks would increase the acceptance of coupled file changes.

The fact that none of the developers rejected the coupled changes, gave us an impulse to investigate other attributes related to the coupled changes. We proceeded with the analysis of the interestingness based on the developers' experience. During the interviews, actual examples of coupled changes were presented to the developers which increased their acceptance.

Considering RQ3, we expected that the coupled changes would be interesting for developers having a lack of programming experience. Our results at contrary show that also the experienced developers are similarly interested in coupled changes. The developers higher experience does not eliminate the possibility that the coupled suggestions could be helpful when working on an unknown source code, software structure or on an older project. The fact they did not reject the coupled changes reports that the benefit from them is not limited on novice developers which makes the coupled changes attractive for a broader audience.

About the results related to RQ4, both uninvolved developers in the project development of the investigated software products and those who worked on the projects provided a neutral feedback. They fact that they did not reject the coupled changes increases the target group for our coupled changes suggestions. These unexpected results show that also the developers working on a particular part of the source code could use some help when working on other parts of the system. These findings encourages us to include the coupled changes as a part of an integrated tool support for developers.

Answering RQ5, our results show that most of the attributes from the provided set were interesting for the developers. These results were also validated by the interviews. Using the commits, the questionnaire and the interviews, we reported that the commit message and the file names are the most interesting attributes. This shows that the developers found the information about the files being changed and the description of these changes to be interesting.

For the issue attributes, the developers reported that the issue description and the issue type are interesting, meaning that they were looking for the information which describes the problem to be solved and the importance of the issue.

For the documentation attributes, the project structure and the naming convention were both interesting for the developers. This shows that they were looking for the information that could help them to find the location in the system to begin with their source code changes.

We reported a set of repository attributes used by well known versioning and issue tracking systems involved in the projects. The attributes we defined are known and common in software development. During the analysis of the interviews, however, we found that the developers want a clear graphical representation of the coupled changes. They also reported that they would like to see the context of the coupled changes. This brings additional aspects to be considered in further research about coupled changes.

The results for RQ6 show that experienced developers know well what kind of repository attributes they want to see. Their choice is more precise compared to the inexperienced developers. The inexperienced developers did not have a clear picture which attributes to choose from the provided set. The fact that developers with different programming experience considered various attributes to be interesting brings us to the conclusion that we should not make a fixed choice of attributes for all developers. We can offer a flexible way for the developers to choose the attributes individually. This way, we support the developers which are not experienced and would like to have an overview of the provided set of repository attributes. On the other side we would like to offer the experienced developers to hide the unnecessary information including the not interesting attributes during maintenance tasks.

The results of the grounded theory show that the interestingness of coupled file changes is influenced by their presentation form and the related information such as the description of the change context. Providing a good visual concept is inevitable for a successful visual representation. Also the repository attributes influence their interestingness. Choosing wrong or not useful attributes can drop the acceptance of coupled change suggestions.

6.10   Evaluation of Validity

We validated the results of our study by checking all the steps in the procedure of gathering and transforming the data from the repository, the analysis methods and the results. In our study, we used a single data mining technique for the reason that the frequent itemsets technique is most appropriate for investigating frequent couplings. We investigated products built with common technologies and the repositories are maintained by well known and commonly used products.

We tested different threshold values for the support and the confidence of the algorithm to produce a sufficient number of frequent itemsets. The relatively low support threshold signalizes that there is not much space for a greater reduction of the value. However, it also reports a relatively low number of frequent couplings which reduces the possibility that these couplings happened by chance.

We validated the outcomes of the questionnaire answers by asking the developers again in the interviews about the interestingness of the couplings and attributes. The interview transcript was coded by two persons after we compared the notes. This way we checked whether we understood the developer's answers correctly. We interviewed both involved and not involved developers on the projects. We also performed double checks of the coding and the outcomes of the Grounded Theory analysis.

7   Conclusion and Future Work

7.1   Summary of Conclusions

The study results show that smaller software repositories do not provide a meaningful number of coupled file changes.

The feedback of developers on the interestingness of coupled changes is mostly neutral. Our results lead to the conclusion that the couplings were weakly accepted by developers having various programming experience and level of involvement in the project. Working on real maintenance tasks would increase the acceptance of coupled change suggestions.

The developers accepted most of the proposed software repository attributes joined to the couplings as interesting. Experienced developers report a narrower choice of attributes as opposed to the inexperienced developers.

The Grounded Theory shows that the our set of repository attributes influence the interestingness of coupled changes. Although we provided a number of repository attributes, the developers suggested additional aspects concerning the coupled change suggestions and the repository attributes. They would like to see more information about the change context and the visual presentation of the coupled changes. We conclude that the we have to develop a visualization concept for the coupled change suggestions and provide the possibility that the developers can individually adjust their choice of repository attributes.

7.2   Relation to Existing Evidence

Revelle et al. [24] investigated source code features coupling using structured and textual features. Here the developers are surveyed to determine if the metrics align with the developers' opinion. Their results show that the developers support the proposed coupling metrics. Our results show that the developers weakly accept the concept of coupled changes and the corresponding attributes from the repository.

Ying et al. [33] investigated the interestingness of coupled changes, whereby the authors used open-source projects and categorized the interestingness of couplings according to their criteria. We studied the coupled file changes in relatively small projects: two industrial projects and one open source project which reduces the number of couplings found. We used the developer's feedback to determine the interestingness of coupled changes instead of statically defining the interestingness of couplings.

7.3   Impact/Implications

This case study gives evidence that the coupled file changes are interesting to the developers during maintenance tasks. Yet, the interest is rather weak overall. Therefore, other contextual information should be investigated in future research to increase the interestingness. Using proper visualization, coupled file suggestions could be incorporated in a tool to support the developers during maintenance tasks.

7.4   Limitations

As it is case study research, we cannot guarantee the generalizability of the study. The data comes from two commercial and one open-source project. However, the procedure should be similar for other projects for the reason that we use well defined data mining techniques and commonly used repositories as data sources.

The number of coupled changes we found is limited by the support value of the frequent itemsets algorithm. Our results preserve relative small number of the most frequent and most valid couplings. The size of our sample limits the possibility for a deeper statistical analysis. Yet, our findings constitute a first insight into developers' opinions on coupled file changes.

7.5   Future Work

The next step is to perform an experiment to investigate coupled changes by directly observing their use for a real maintenance tasks. This could be visualized in a tool to present this changes to the developers. Furthermore, based on our findings, we believe more research should look into complementing the reporting of coupled changes with using additional context description.

Acknowledgment. The authors would like to thank Asim Abdulkhaleq for his help in the interview transcripts and coding for the Grounded Theory analysis.

References

1. Agrawal, R., Srikant, R.: Fast algorithms for mining association rules in large databases. In: Proceedings of the 20th International Conference on Very Large Data Bases, VLDB 1994, pp. 487–499 (1994)
2. Bavota, G., Dit, B., Oliveto, R., Di Penta, M., Poshyvanyk, D., De Lucia, A.: An empirical study on the developers perception of software coupling. In: Proceedings of the 2013 International Conference on Software Engineering, ICSE 2013, pp. 692–701 (2013)
3. Bieman, J., Andrews, A., Yang, H.: Understanding change-proneness in OO software through visualization. In: 11th IEEE International Workshop on Program Comprehension, pp. 44–53, May 2003
4. Bird, C., Rigby, P.C., Barr, E.T., Hamilton, D.J., Germán, D.M., Devanbu, P.T.: The promises and perils of mining git. In: MSR, pp. 1–10 (2009)
5. Canfora, G., Cerulo, L.: Impact analysis by mining software and change request repositories. In: 11th IEEE International Symposium on Software Metrics, p. 29, September 2005
6. Carlsson, E.: Mining git repositories: an introduction to repository mining (2013)
7. D'Ambros, M., Lanza, M., Robbes, R.: On the relationship between change coupling and software defects. In: WCRE, pp. 135–144 (2009)
8. Fischer, M., Pinzger, M., Gall, H.: Populating a release history database from version control and bug tracking systems. In: Proceedings of the International Conference on Software Maintenance, ICSM 2003, p. 23 (2003)
9. Fluri, B., Gall, H., Pinzger, M.: Fine-grained analysis of change couplings. In: Fifth IEEE International Workshop on Source Code Analysis and Manipulation, pp. 66–74, September 2005
10. Fournier-Viger, P.: How to auto-adjust the minimum support threshold according to the data size (2013). http://data-mining.philippe-fournier-viger.com/
11. Frawley, W.J., Piatetsky-shapiro, G., Matheus, C.J.: Knowledge discovery in databases: an overview (1992)
12. Gall, H., Jazayeri, M., Krajewski, J.: CVS release history data for detecting logical couplings. In: Proceedings of Sixth International Workshop on Principles of Software Evolution, pp. 13–23, September 2003
13. German, D.M.: Mining CVS repositories, the softchange experience. In: 1st International Workshop on Mining Software Repositories, pp. 17–21 (2004)
14. Győrödi, C., Győrödi, R.: A comparative study of association rules mining algorithms (2004)
15. Han, J., Mining, D.: Concepts and Techniques. Morgan Kaufmann Publishers Inc., San Francisco (2005)
16. Han, J., Pei, J., Yin, Y., Mao, R.: Mining frequent patterns without candidate generation: a frequent-pattern tree approach. Data Min. Knowl. Discov. **8**(1), 53–87 (2004)
17. Hassan, A.E., Holt, R.C.: Predicting change propagation in software systems. In: Proceedings of the 20th IEEE International Conference on Software Maintenance, ICSM 2004, pp. 284–293 (2004)
18. Hattori, L., dos Santos Jr., G., Cardoso, F., Sampaio, M.: Mining software repositories for software change impact analysis: a case study. In: Proceedings of the 23rd Brazilian Symposium on Databases, SBBD 2008, pp. 210–223 (2008)
19. Kagdi, H., Collard, M.L., Maletic, J.I.: A survey and taxonomy of approaches for mining software repositories in the context of software evolution. J. Softw. Maint. Evol. **19**(2), 77–131 (2007)

20. Kagdi, H., Yusuf, S., Maletic, J.I.: Mining sequences of changed-files from version histories. In: Proceedings of the 2006 International Workshop on Mining Software Repositories, MSR 2006, pp. 47–53 (2006)
21. Loeliger, J.: Version Control with Git - Powerful Techniques for Centralized and Distributed Project Management. O'Reilly, New York (2009)
22. McGarry, K.: A survey of interestingness measures for knowledge discovery. Knowl. Eng. Rev. **20**(1), 39–61 (2005)
23. Ramadani, J., Wagner, S.: Are suggestions of coupled file changes interesting? In: Proceedings of the 11th International Conference on Evaluation of Novel Software Approaches to Software Engineering, pp. 15–26 (2016)
24. Revelle, M., Gethers, M., Poshyvanyk, D.: Using structural and textual information to capture feature coupling in object-oriented software. Empirical Softw. Engg. **16**(6), 773–811 (2011)
25. Runeson, P., Höst, M.: Guidelines for conducting and reporting case study research in software engineering. Empirical Softw. Engg. **14**(2), 131–164 (2009)
26. Sayles, J., et al.: z/OS Traditional Application Maintenance and Support. IBM Redbooks (2011)
27. Shirabad, J., Lethbridge, T., Matwin, S.: Mining the maintenance history of a legacy software system. In: Proceedings of International Conference on Software Maintenance, ICSM 2003, pp. 95–104, September 2003
28. Steven, J., Zach, W.: Bad commit smells (2013). http://pages.cs.wisc.edu/~sjj/docs/commits.pdf
29. Stevens, W.P., Myers, G.J., Constantine, L.L.: Structured design. IBM Syst. J. **13**(2), 115–139 (1974)
30. Strauss, A., Corbin, J.M.: Basics of Qualitative Research: Techniques and Procedures for Developing Grounded Theory. SAGE Publications, USA (1998)
31. van Rysselberghe, F., Demeyer, S.: Mining version control systems for FACs (frequently applied changes). In: the International Workshop on Mining Repositories, Edinburgh, Scotland, UK (2004)
32. Wu, R., Zhang, H., Kim, S., Cheung, S.-C.: Relink: recovering links between bugs and changes. In: Proceedings of the 19th ACM SIGSOFT Symposium and the 13th European Conference on Foundations of Software Engineering, ESEC/FSE 2011, pp. 15–25 (2011)
33. Ying, A.T.T., Murphy, G.C., Ng, R.T., Chu-Carroll, M.: Predicting source code changes by mining change history. IEEE Trans. Softw. Eng. **30**(9), 574–586 (2004)
34. Zimmermann, T., Kim, S., Zeller, A., Whitehead, Jr., E.J.: Mining version archives for co-changed lines. In: Proceedings of the 2006 International Workshop on Mining Software Repositories, MSR 2006, pp. 72–75 (2006)
35. Zimmermann, T., Weisgerber, P., Diehl, S., Zeller, A.: Mining version histories to guide software changes. In: Proceedings of the 26th International Conference on Software Engineering, ICSE 2004, pp. 563–572 (2004)

A Systematic Literature Review on Cloud Computing Adoption and Migration

Antonio Carlos Marcelino de Paula and Glauco de Figueiredo de Carneiro[(✉)]

Salvador University, Salvador, Bahia, Brazil
{antonio.paula,glauco.carneiro}@unifacs.br

Abstract. *Context*: The appealing features of Cloud computing has attracted the attention of the research and the industry due to the possibility of providing a customizable and resourceful platform to deploy software. There is a myriad of competing providers and available services that can provide organizations the access to computing services without owning the corresponding infrastructure. *Goal*: Identify the opportunities to migrate to the cloud, the challenges, difficulties and factors that affect the cost-benefit relationship of such adoption. *Method*: In our previous work, we performed a systematic review to identify the approaches adopted by organizations to migrate to cloud computing and their perception of the cost-benefit of this migration. In this paper, we extended our previous work through a new search in the selected repositories to identify studies published from June 2015 to June 2016. *Results*: We concluded from the collected data that a significant part of the companies perceived inclination towards the innovative adoption process influenced by technological, organizational and environmental contexts. *Conclusion*: The results in this systematic literature review can help the development of guidelines to support newcomers companies to adopt and migrate to the cloud, how the cost-benefit relationship can be evaluated as well as the selection of providers.

Keywords: Cloud computing · Cloud migration · Provider selection · Cost-benefit relationship · Systematic literature review

1 Introduction

Cloud Computing (CC) is a paradigm shift in computing that has changed the way users deal and perceive computing [26]. This scenario has created opportunities for enterprises that have manifested perceived inclination toward cloud computing and the benefits reaped by them [4]. However, the identification of opportunities for migration, the reasoning of an attractive cost-benefit relationship and the selection of service providers that best fit their needs are not trivial tasks [16,17]. The selection of commercial cloud providers is a challenging task and depends on several variables and indicators. Among other reasons, cloud providers may continually upgrade their hardware and software infrastructures, and new commercial Cloud services, technologies and strategies may gradually

© Springer International Publishing AG 2016
L.A. Maciaszek and J. Filipe (Eds.): ENASE 2016, CCIS 703, pp. 222–243, 2016.
DOI: 10.1007/978-3-319-56390-9_11

enter the market [18]. Studies have shown that successful migration to the cloud are usually driven by a set of criteria to select providers that best fit their needs [7,14,17].

The reason for a Systematic Literature Review (SLR) is the necessity to identify, classify, and compare existing evidence on the strategies used by companies to identify scenarios of migration opportunities to the CC. To justify the adoption, a set of factors should be considered for the assessment of the cost-benefit relationship. Moreover, companies should be able to select a provider according to their needs and profile. The evidences collected and discussed in this SLR is intended to gain and share insight from the literature so that companies can decide towards cloud computing. This paper has three major contributions: (i) the identification of strategies and issues that companies have considered to migrate to the cloud; (ii) factors that should be considered in the cost-benefits relationship while adopting and migrating to the cloud; (iii) and finally aspects related to the selection of cloud computing service providers.

The rest of this paper is organized as follows: Sect. 2 provides background related to the research area and emphasizes the differences between this version of the systematic review and previous systematic reviews in the domain. Moreover, we also highlight the differences from the first version of this work published at [22]. In Sect. 3, we outline the research methodology; and in Sect. 4, we present and discuss the results of the SLR and its corresponding analysis. The concluding remarks directions for future research are discussed in Sect. 5.

2 Problem Statement and Scope

In this section, we present the concepts related to CC, the focus of this SLR. Based on a systematic search, we also link to existing secondary studies that discuss aspects related to the migration to the cloud and correlated factors.

Many enterprises have adopted the paradigm of CC where producers and consumers (of information) are not necessarily collocated [9,15,19]. Studies have reported that CC adoption by enterprises is primarily based on their perceptions about *cost reduction, ease of use* and *convenience, reliability, sharing* and *collaboration* and lastly but not the least, *security* and *privacy* [9].

Cloud computing comprises basically three services. Probably the most popular is the *Software-as-a-Service* (SaaS). It relies on the principle that instead of installing software on the client's machine and updating it with regular patches, the applications are available (hosted) over the web for the consumption of the end-user. This scenario enables the achievement of economy of scale [9]. The companies that provide SaaS most of the time hire the *Platform-as-a-Service* (PaaS). The main idea of PaaS is that instead of buying the software licenses for platforms like operating systems, databases and middleware, these platforms along with software development kits (SDKs) and the programming languages (such as Java, .NET) are made available over the web [9]. The last is the *Infrastructure-as-a-Service* (IaaS). It refers to the tangible physical devices (raw computing) like virtual computers, servers, storage devices, network transfer, which are physically located in one central place (data center) but they can be accessed remotely and used over the web using the login authentication systems and respective passwords [9].

These three services described above are deployed following four different models: (i) *Public cloud* is available from a third party service provider via web and is a very cost effective option to deploy IT solutions [20]; (ii) *Private cloud* is managed within an organization and is suitable for large enterprises (managed within the walls of the enterprises). Private clouds provide the advantages of public clouds, but still incur capital expenditures [20]; (iii) *Community cloud* is used and controlled by a group of enterprises, which have shared interests [20]; (iv) *Hybrid cloud* is a combination of public and private cloud [20]. This paper focuses on public cloud providers and the three types of CC services: SaaS, PaaS and IaaS.

This study has the goal to shed lights on the practices involved in the adoption of CC. The results of this study are expected to help different types of companies to decide for this adoption and how they can plan it. For this end, the study present different approaches, techniques and tools to overcome difficulties and challenges in the context of CC. The scope of this review is specific to identify strategies that can help organizations to migrate and adopt CC, their perception of the cost-benefit relationship of this adoption and how companies can select service providers that best fit their needs and profile. The scope and coverage of this systematic review differ significantly from previous reviews. During the conduction of this study, we found four systematic literature reviews (SLRs) focusing on the following themes: migration to the CC [10], service composition [11], service evaluation [18] and challenges and concerns when building cloud-based architectures [1]. Despite being relevant source of information for companies that plan to adopt the CC paradigm, none of these previous SLRs focused specifically on the relationship among the issues target in this paper. This relationship is indeed relevant for both the adoption and migration to the cloud. This is an extended version of a previous SLR conducted by the authors and published at [22]. We extended the search for primary studies published until July 2016, whereas the previous version of this SLR considered papers published until June 2015.

3   Research Methodology

In contrast to a non-structured review process, a Systematic Literature Review (SLR) [2,12] reduces bias and follows a precise and rigorous sequence of methodological steps to research literature. SLR rely on well-defined and evaluated review protocols to extract, analyze, and document results as the stages conveyed in Fig. 1. This section describes the methodology applied for the phases of planning, conducting and reporting the review.

3.1   Planning the Review

Identify the Needs for a Systematic Review. Search for evidences in the literature regarding how companies decide towards CC in terms of

(i) strategies to identify migration opportunities to the cloud, (ii) relevant factors for the assessment of the cost-benefit of this adoption of cloud and finally (iii) the selection of providers according to their needs and profile.

Specifying the Research Questions. We aim to answers the following questions by conducting a methodological review of existing research:

> **RQ1**. *Which strategies are used by companies to adopt and migrate to the cloud computing?* Identifying goals, proposals and motivations for the adoption of CC, help organizations to better characterize their needs and therefore provide conditions to a successful migration.
>
> **RQ2**. *Which factors companies consider to assess the cost-benefit relationship of adoption and migration to the cloud computing?* The knowledge of the costs and benefits of migration to the CC can be used as a support for its planning and reference for other companies.
>
> **RQ3**. *How companies select cloud computing service providers according to their needs and profile?* The knowledge of successful strategies and problems raised by inappropriate selection of CC providers allow organizations to be more confident to identify providers that best fit their needs.

These three research questions are somehow related to each other. However, studies could have discussed them separately. Regarding the cost-benefit relationship addressed by RQ2, it is possible that this relationship could be analyzed considering a specific provider. Moreover, there is the possibility of studies addressing this scenario comparing various providers with their respective characteristics analyzing to which extent they fit a company profile. This fact establish a close relationship between RQ2 and RQ3.

Publications Time Frame. We conducted a SLR in journals and conferences papers from January 2005 to June 2016. In a first version of this study, we performed the search from January 2005 to June 2015 and in this new version we extended it to June 2016 [22].

3.2 Conducting the Review

This phase is responsible for executing the review protocol.

Identification of Research. Based on the research questions, keywords were extracted and used to search the primary study sources in both versions of this study (with papers identified until June 2015 and until June 2016). The search string is presented as follows and used the same strategy cited in [3]:

> *(("Cloud Migration" OR "legacy-to-cloud migration" OR "Cloud adoption") OR ("Cost" OR "Return of investments" OR "ROI" OR "Cost-benefit")) OR (("Cloud Service" OR "Cloud Provider") AND ("Evaluation" OR "Selection")) AND ("Cloud Computing" OR "Cloud Services" OR "Cloud Interoperability").*

Table 1. Inclusion criteria [22].

Criterion	Description
IC1	The papers proposed OR discussed OR evaluated strategies OR methods OR techniques OR models OR tools OR frameworks applied by companies to adopt and migrate to the cloud computing OR to assess the cost-benefit relationship of such adoption OR to select cloud computing service providers according to their needs and profile
IC2	The publications should be journal or conference and written in English
IC3	Works involving an empirical study or have "lessons learned" (experience report)
IC4	If several journal articles reporting the same study the latest article will be included
IC5	The articles that address at least one of the research questions

Table 2. Exclusion criteria [22].

Criterion	Description
EC1	Studies not focused on cloud computing
EC2	Studies merely based on expert opinion without locating a specific experience, as well as editorials, prefaces, summaries of articles, interviews, news, analysis/reviews, readers letters, summaries of tutorials, workshops, panels, and poster sessions
EC3	Publications that are earlier versions of last published work
EC4	Publications that were published out of the period January 1st, 2005 to June 2016

Selection of Primary Studies. The following steps guided the selection of primary studies (Tables 1 and 2).

Stage 1 - Search string results automatically obtained from the engines - Submission of the search string to the following repositories: Digital Library ACM, IEEE Xplore, Science Direct and Google Scholar. The justification for the selection of these libraries is their relevance as sources in software engineering [27]. The search was performed using the specific syntax of each database, considering only the title, keywords, and abstract. The search was configured in each repository to select only papers carried out within the prescribed period. The automatic search was complemented by a manual search to obtain a list of studies from journals and conferences. The duplicates were discarded.

Stage 2 - Read titles & abstracts to identify potentially relevant studies - Identification of potentially relevant studies, based on the analysis of title and abstract, discarding studies that are clearly irrelevant to the search. If there was any doubt about whether a study should be included or not, it was included for consideration at a later stage.

Table 3. Quality criteria [6, 22].

Criterion	Description
QC1	Is the paper based on research (or is it merely a "lessons learned" report based on expert opinion)?
QC2	Is there a clear statement of the aims of the research?
QC3	Is there an adequate description of the context in which the research was carried out?
QC4	Was the research design appropriate to address the aims of the research?
QC5	Was the recruitment strategy appropriate to the aims of the research?
QC6	Was there a control group with which to compare treatments?
QC7	Was the data collected in a way that addressed the research issue?
QC8	Was the data analysis sufficiently rigorous?
QC9	Is there a clear statement of findings?

Stage 3 - Apply inclusion and exclusion criteria on reading the introduction, methods and conclusion - Selected studies in previous stages were reviewed, by reading the introduction, methodology section and conclusion. Afterwards, inclusion and exclusion criteria were applied. At this stage, in case of doubt preventing a conclusion, the study was read in its entirely.

Stage 4 - Obtain primary studies and make a critical assessment of them - A list of primary studies was obtained and later subjected to critical examination using the 11 quality criteria [6] set out in Table 3. We performed these four stages in the two versions of this study.

Data Extraction. All relevant information on each study was recorded on a spreadsheet. This information was helpful to summarize the data and map them with its source. The following data were extracted from the studies: (i) name and authors; (ii) type of article (journal, conference, workshop); (iii) aim of the study; (iv) research question; (v) scenario(s); (vi) results and conclusions; (vii) benefits; (viii) limitations and challenges.

Data Synthesis. This synthesis aimed at grouping findings from the studies in order to: identify the main concepts (organized in spreadsheet form), conduct a comparative analysis on the characteristics of the study, type of service adopted, cloud deployment model, and issues regarding three research questions (*RQ1, RQ2* and *RQ3*) from each study. Other information was synthesized when necessary. We used the meta-ethnography method [21] as a reference for the process of data synthesis.

Conducting the Review. We started the review with an automatic search followed by a manual search to identify potentially relevant studies and afterwards apply the inclusion/exclusion criteria. The first tests using automatic search began in March 2015. We had to adapt the the search string in some engines

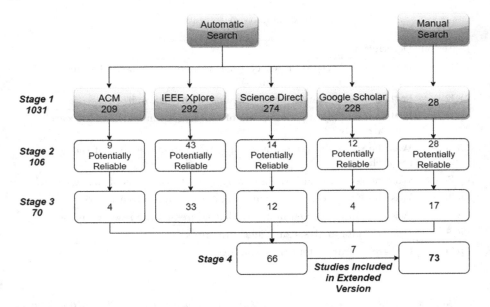

Fig. 1. Stages of the study selection process containing the Studies included in the extended Version of this SLR. Adapted from [22].

without losing its primary meaning and scope. The manual search consisted in studies published in conference proceedings and journals that were included by the authors while searching the theme in different repositories. These studies were equally analyzed regarding their titles and abstracts. Figure 1 conveys them as 28 studies. We tabulated everything on a spreadsheet so as to facilitate the subsequent phase of identifying potentially relevant studies. Figure 1 presents the results obtained from each electronic database used in the search, which resulted in 1003 articles considering all databases.

Potentially Relevant Studies. The results obtained from both the automatic and manual search were included on a single spreadsheet. Papers with identical title, author(s), year and abstract were discarded as redundant. At this stage, we registered an overall of 1031 articles, namely 1003 from the automated search plus 28 from the separate manual search *(Stage 1)*. We then read titles and abstracts to identify relevant studies resulting in 106 papers *(Stage 2)*. In *Stage 3*, we applied the quality criteria in each study and then we read introduction, methodology and conclusion to decide to consider 70 studies for the next stage. After applying the quality criteria, remained 66 articles to answer the three research questions - RQ1, RQ2 and RQ3 *(Stage 4)*. In the extended version of this SLR, we ended up with 73 studies as a result of the inclusion of 7 papers related to RQ1, RQ2 and RQ3. These papers followed the same four stages presented in Fig. 1, but their inclusion were represented only in Stage 4 in the same figure.

4   Results and Analysis

This section presents the results of this SLR to answer the research questions RQ1, RQ2 and RQ3 based on the 73 papers selected at Stage 4. Figure 2 conveys the selected studies and the respective research questions they focus on. As can be seen in the same Figure, 47 studies addressed issues related to RQ1, while 25 studies discussed RQ2 issues and, finally, 12 papers addressed RQ3 issues. All selected studies are listed in *Appendix* and referenced as *"S"* followed by the number of the paper. The papers included in the second version of this SLR are marked as '**' after their respective identification numbers.

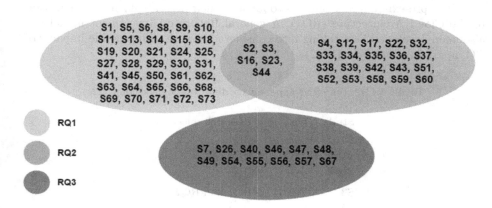

Fig. 2. Selected studies per research question (RQ) [22].

Table 4 presents the top ten papers included in the review according to Google Scholar citations. These papers are evidences of the relevance of the issues discussed in this SLR and the influence these papers exert on the literature as can be confirmed by their respective citation numbers. Table 4 shows an overview of the distribution of the most relevant papers according to the addressed research questions. In the following paragraphs we briefly describe these papers.

The paper [S41] that addresses RQ1 has the highest number of citations (594), according to data obtained in July 13rd, 2016. It is related to RQ1 and RQ2 and analyzes the use of CC in manufacturing business companies. It has been extensively used as a successful case of CC adoption having as a reference parameters of a cost-benefit relationship to guide such adoption. The paper [S55] has 571 citations according to Google Scholar and discusses issues related to RQ3. It describes the use of a tool called CloudCmp to perform benchmark suite for cloud platforms. This tool has been recognized as an important reference for benchmarking. To this end, it identifies a common set of services offered by cloud providers, including *elastic computing, persistent storage*, and *intra-cloud* and *wide-area networking*. The authors argue that CloudCmp enables predicting application performance without having to first port the application onto every cloud provider. The paper [S57] with 279 citations according to Google Scholar, proposes a framework and a mechanism to measure the quality and prioritize Cloud services providers. According to the authors, given the diversity of Cloud service offerings, an important challenge for customers is to find out appropriate Cloud providers that can satisfy their requirements (RQ3). This makes it difficult to evaluate service levels of different Cloud providers, justifying the use of a Analytical Hierarchical Process (AHP) based ranking mechanism to provide a quantitative basis for the ranking of Cloud services where the final ranking is based on the cost (RQ2) and quality [7]. The paper [S3] has 245 citations according to Google Scholar. The authors discuss how a proposed model can support companies to analyze several characteristics of their own business as well as pre-existing IT resources to identify their favorability in the migration to the Cloud Architecture (RQ1). A general Return on Investment model has also been developed here taking into consideration various intangible impacts of CC, apart from the cost (RQ2).

Table 4. Top ten cited papers according to google scholar [22].

Studies	Cited by	Research question
S41	594	RQ1
S55	571	RQ3
S57	279	RQ3
S3	245	RQ1 and RQ2
S65	226	RQ1
S4	208	RQ2
S2	182	RQ1 and RQ2
S54	145	RQ3
S59	136	RQ2

We have identified that eight (S38, S42, S51, S58, S60, S61, s63, S64) of the 73 selected studies reference the Technological Organizational Environmental (TOE) framework [24,25]. It is an organization-level theory aimed at supporting organizations in the adoption and implementation of innovations. Based on this framework, the innovation adoption process is influenced by three aspects of the enterprise [S64]: (i) *technological context*, which represents the internal and external technologies related to the organization; both technologies that are already in use at the firm, as well as those that are available in the marketplace but not currently in use; (ii) *organizational context* is related to the resources and the characteristics of the firm, e.g. size and managerial structure; (iii) *environmental context*, which refers to the arena in which a firm conducts its business; it can be related to surrounding elements such as industry, competitors and the presence of technology service providers. These papers are evidences that this framework is useful to guide organizations toward the adoption of CC.

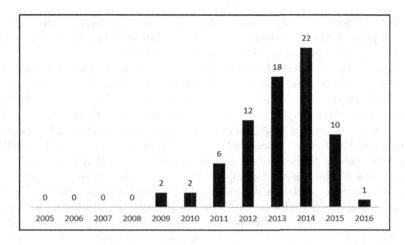

Fig. 3. Studies per year.

As can be seen in Fig. 3, the number of papers focused on the theme increased until 2014. No papers were found in this SLR before 2009. This is an evidence of the interest on migration and services provided by the cloud. We found 68 papers (93,15% of the total) between 2011 and 2015. The reason to have only 1 papers selected in 2016 is that in this year we considered only papers published until June.

4.1 Strategies for the Adoption and Migration to the Cloud (RQ1)

This subsection has the goal to discuss how selected papers addressed RQ1: *Which strategies are used by companies to identify scenarios of migration opportunities to the cloud computing?* **RQ1 Analysis**. We identified 25 papers that proposed and/or discussed processes, strategies and frameworks to support companies deciding for the adoption and migration to the cloud. We contextualize their contribution to RQ1 in the following sentences. The papers that present experience and case reports related to RQ1 are S11, S18, S24, S25, S30, S31, S41, S44, S45, S66, S71, and S73. The papers that present processes, strategies and frameworks related to the CC adoption and migration are S1, S3, S8, S9, S10, S14, S15, S16, S19, S20, S21, S23, S27, S28, S29, S50, S61, S62, S63, S64, S65, S68, S69, S70, and S72. Finally, four studies proposed the use of tools to support companies to identify and evaluate scenarios of migration opportunities to the cloud. The studies and the respective tools are listed as follows: [S2] describes a cloud Adoption Toolkit that uses Cost Modeling techniques to examine cost of deploying IT system to the cloud. [S5] describes an evaluation of the tools (CPTS, CSA STAR, C.A.RE and CloudTrust) to compare them. [S6] discusses the use of CloudMIG to support the migration of legacy software systems to the cloud. CloudMIG was also referenced in the following papers: S17, S1, S40, S62, S31. The Desktop-to-Cloud-Migration (D2CM) tool that supports transformation and migration of virtual machine images, deployment description and life-cycle management for applications to the cloud was described in [S13]. The Cloud Adoption Cloud Adoption Toolkit was referenced in papers S2, S69 and S26, whereas CDOsim was referenced in S7, S68 and S40.

A list of 25 of the selected studies proposed approaches to guide the migration to the cloud as described in the following setences. In [S1], the authors investigated the existing literature to classify the migration into five strategies as presented as follows: (i) migrate to IaaS, (ii) migrate to PaaS, (iii) replace by SaaS, (iv) revise based on SaaS, and (v) re-engineering to SaaS. They reviewed and compared the related researches on every migration strategy. In addition, related development tools were surveyed. The authors of [S3] performed an in-depth analysis of the financial perspective of CC. They discussed a model for both an objective as well as a subjective decision making tool to find the suitability of a company for adopting CC. In [S8] the authors conducted a synthesis study, for the choice of optimal Cloud structures, based on type of organizations. They focused on the main benefits, as well as on the various issues related to Cloud use. They performed a case study to demonstrate the migrating feasibility from a classic web service solution to the Cloud. [S9] proposed an initial conceptual approach of a cloud modernization assessment framework with the objective of measuring the impact of a potential migration to Cloud. The purpose was to advise software companies on the decision of what is more convenient, to migrate or to start from scratch, providing data about the required effort and cost as well as providing information about the organizational processes that will change as a consequence of the migration. This approach was comprised of 3 main steps: (1) the characterization of the legacy application from two points of view: technical and business, (2) a technical feasibility analysis and (3), an economic feasibility analysis. The authors of [S10] analyzed the different aspects of Cloud Services Brokerages (CSBs) and categorized them based on the data available on their websites. The authors enumerated a list of utilities a CSB should provide, which enlisted all the benefits of opting for a CSB, for both the consumer and the provider. The categories were used as an input to a four stage technique that shall help compare CSBs on preference and usability parameters. [S14] presented a step-by-step process to support cloud adoption and migration decisions in the enterprise. The authors demonstrated the use of cloudstep to support in the decision of business applications migration into the public cloud providers.

In [S15], the authors explained the multi-dimensional decision-making process carried out to migrate applications to cloud environments and how to formalise its effects in the cloud migration criteria. With the aim of helping organisations cope with these effects, the authors developed the InCLOUDer cloud migration decision support system which builds on top of the Analytic Hierarchy Process. In [S16], the authors discussed steps that need to be checked to determine the possibility as well as feasibility of application migration to the cloud. This was performed with a proposed compatibility checklist that is used to estimate the cost of application migration to PaaS. The authors also discussed general solutions to solve incompatibility issues of database migration.

The authors of [S19] proposed an approach to reverse engineer legacy software into models from which cloud-based software can be generated. [S20] proposed a migration process framework outlining major steps and their concerns. The authors identified through expert interviews the immaturity in terms of established procedures and availability of tools to support the architecture migration process. The study [S21] presented a generic framework to support the migration of live media streaming to a cloud platform, fundamental understandings on the practical feasibility and theoretical constraints in the migration are also discussed. According to the authors, extensive simulations driven by traces from both cloud service providers (Amazon EC2 and SpotCloud) as well as a live media streaming service provider (PPTV) to demonstrate the cost-effectiveness and superior streaming quality of CALMS, even with highly dynamic and globalized demands. [S23] proposed a set of migration patterns which span the continuum from legacy IT environment to the cloud is included as a common framework for aligning the various migration approaches developed. [S27] proposed three paradigms to support the migration to the cloud. The process paradigm refers to the jobs to be accomplished during cloud migration in terms of the examination of current processes, the development of new processes under cloud context, and the determination of the KPIs and KEIs for new processes. The system paradigm focuses on the review and migration of the infrastructure, platforms, databases and applications of an organization. And finally, the organizational paradigm that describes the strategies and concerns of the whole transformation of an organization to cloud environment. [S28] proposed a framework to support the migration of legacy systems to the cloud based on security and trust concerns.

In [S61], the authors proposed a research model to integrate the diffusion of innovation (DOI) theory and the technology-organization-environment (TOE) framework. It was used to compare the adoption of CC in two distinct sectors, namely manufacturing and services. The [S62] study presented an extensible architecture for detecting software system's violations against limited access to the underlying file system or enforced restrictions regarding provided standard APIs. The authors presented results concerning a quantitative evaluation regarding the detected constraint violations of five open-source systems. The applications were validated against the modeled PaaS cloud environment Google App Engine for Java. [S63] combined the theoretical approach from scientifically recognized literature with a practical evaluation of influences on the diffusion and acceptance of CC among SMEs. [S64] discussed the main factors that were identified as playing a significant role in SME adoption of cloud services: relative advantage, uncertainty, geo-restriction, compatibility, size, top management support, prior experience, innovativeness, industry, market scope, supplier efforts and external computing support. [S65] empirically examined main drivers and inhibiting factors of SaaS-adoption for different application types. The analysis showed that social influence, the pre-existing attitude toward SaaS-adoption, adoption uncertainty, and strategic value are the most consistent drivers. [S68] discussed the challenges found during the migration of an existing system to a cloud solution and based on a set of quality requirements that includes the vendor Lock-in factor and also present a set of assessment activities and guidelines to support migration to the Cloud by adopting SOA and Cloud modeling standards and tools. [S69] proposed a framework called CloudGenius to automate the decision-making process based on a model and factors specifically for Web server migration to the Cloud. The CloudGenius framework defines a Cloud migration process that offers a model and methods to determine the best combined choice of a Cloud VM image and a Cloud infrastructure service. [S70] Analyzes and identifies relevant technical, economical, and organizational factors. This is performed as exploratory research consisting of performing (a) a literature review and (b) multiple case-studies with 17 organizations, who have adopted or plan to adopt cloud-based services. Also, as these factors are not mutually exclusive, this paper discusses interrelations of these factors and its complexity. [S72] presented ToscaMart, a method to support developers to specify individual components in their application topologies, and illustrates how to match, adapt, and reuse existing fragments of applications to implement these components while fulfilling all their compliance requirements.

Finally, 12 studies discussed case studies to illustrate the migration process. The [S11] summarized potential benefits and risks to migrate traditional applications to the cloud using CloudFTP on Windows Azure along with the auto-scaling feature. [S18] discussed the motivation, requirements, feasibility of migrating CiteSeerX digital library to provide an IaaS model in a private cloud. In [S24] the authors combine legacy system migration solutions and virtualization technology with the application of cloudstack to build an enterprise private cloud platform. [S25] presents an overview of major requirements that must be considered when migrating e-health systems to the cloud. Study [S30] discusses some of the characteristics to consider when migrating testing to the cloud from the application point of view. The paper [S31] explores early implementations of cloud enterprise systems and compares them to the academic literature. In [S41] two types of CC adoptions were suggested, manufacturing with direct adoption of CC technologies and cloud manufacturing. [S44] used small case study to show that application performance doesn't deteriorate when migrating applications to the cloud. [S45] abstracts from current market prices and investigates the interaction of cloud provider and clients from an analytical perspective. A general understanding of how providers and clients potentially benefit financially from Infrastructure-as-a-Service (IaaS) can help clients to appraise price uncertainty in strategic resource planning decisions. [S66] examine CC adoption preparation and reasons for non adoption among Small and Medium Enterprises (SMEs) in Ireland. [S71] proposed a design of a private IaaS Cloud adopted for a university IT infrastructure. The authors proposed two solutions to improve its security; especially the isolation of data in the IaaS Cloud, and the isolation of networks within the university by adopting the Tree-Rule Firewall approach. [S73] reported a study focusing on relevant issues enterprises are confronted with when making CC adoption decisions. The findings indicated that security, strategy and legal/ethical issues were the most relevant from the perspective of the companies.

4.2   The Cost-Benefits Relationship in the Adoption and Migration (RQ2)

This subsection discusses how selected papers addressed **RQ2**: *Which factors are considered by companies to assess the cost-benefit relationship of adoption and migration to the cloud computing?*

During the analysis of **RQ2**, we identified a myriad of factors related to the cost-benefit relationship of cloud computing adoption. Based on the evidences collected from the papers, there is no consensus on a minimum set of factors that should be used for this end. In [S3], the authors argue that CC has been viewed mainly from the cost perspective. The paper proposed a model that helps not just identify the suitability of a company for the cloud by clearly spelling out all the factors that need to be considered for the same, but also gives a certain profitability valuation of the benefits associated with CC. An approach to detect performance anti-patterns before migrating to CC based on static analysis was presented in [S12]. In [S4], the architectural features of CC are explored and classified according to the requirements of end-users, enterprises, and cloud providers themselves to support the cloud adoption. The [S2] study described the Cloud Adoption Toolkit that provides a framework and a cost modelling tool to support decision makers. In [S16], the authors presented a compatibility checklist that is used to estimate the cost of application migration to PaaS. The migration of legacy applications to CC was discussed in [S17], whose focus was on the application performance analysis and providers characteristics. The authors of [S22] discussed the migration of agile projects to the cloud in terms of cost, time and quality. [S23] discussed potential issues and challenges that organizations may face while considering to migrate workloads to the cloud: efficiency, agility, quality, security, governance and standardization in the delivery, consumption and operation of IT services, all at reduced capital and operational expense. In [S32], an analysis of the difficulties of company's traditional accounting system was investigated. The factors affecting migration and adoption were studied and models for the cloud deployment and service complying with the company requirements were proposed. The paper [S33] investigated the migration costs of several deployment options using benchmarks and concluded that application characteristics such as workload intensity, growth rate, storage capacity, and S/W licensing costs produce complex combined effects on overall costs. In [S34], a critical review and impact of vendor lock-in for enterprise adoption from a technical, business and legal viewpoint was presented. The study [S35] evaluated the decision to migrate to cloud storage against the alternative to buy the storage devices and facilities under a probabilistic model for the evolution of storage characteristics, disk failures, and prices.

[S36] proposed the use of a real option model to help companies think and decide when to switch to cloud based on the expected benefits, uncertainties and the value a company puts on money. [S37] investigated different approaches to reduce both cost and task completion time of computations using Amazon EC2's spot instances for resource provisioning. In the case of [S38], the authors focused on the following factors: availability, portability, integration, migration complexity, data privacy and security. Hypotheses regarding the relevance of each barrier/difficulty, the adoption decision and a hypothesis at the integrated level, were evaluated. The study [S39] identified and investigated cognitive factors that contribute to shaping user perceptions of and attitude toward mobile CC services by integrating these factors with the technology acceptance model. A framework based on the structural equation modeling analysis was employed and results revealed that user acceptance of mobile cloud services was largely affected by perceived mobility, connectedness, security, quality of service and system, and satisfaction. A literature review on technological innovation characteristics was conducted by the authors to identify potential gaps in ongoing research. The review also provided an overview of relevant empirical studies on CC that were based on the Diffusion of Innovation (DoI) theory [23] and the Technology Acceptance Model (TAM) [5]. As a result, the focus was set on the examination of the following factors: compatibility, relative advantage, complexity, image and security & trust [S42]. The authors of [S43] listed best practices for efficiently managing the resources required for the mobile cloud model, namely energy, bandwidth and cloud computing resources. The best practice approaches for implementations were applied to existing works in the area, along with the Context Aware Mobile Cloud Services (CAMCS) cloud middleware and the Cloud Personal Assistant (CPA), the representative of the user within the middleware. In [S44], the authors discussed the cloud model in five perspectives: on-demand self-service, broad network access, resource pooling, rapid elasticity, and measured service. A case study was used to demonstrate that application performance does not deteriorate when migrating applications to the cloud. [S51] proposed a tripod model of SaaS readiness that suggests that for organizational users to adopt SaaS, they need to get ready from technological, organizational and environmental aspects. [S52] presented a taxonomy to help profile and standardize the details of performance evaluation of commercial Cloud services. In [S53], the authors proposed a set of *de facto* metrics adopted in the existing Cloud services evaluation work to collect and arrange different Cloud service features to be evaluated. They ended up with an evaluation metrics catalogue. In [S58], the TOE (Technology-Organization-Environment) framework and HOT-fit (Human-Organization-Technology fit) model were used to investigate the critical factors affecting hospitals? decisions regarding the adoption of CC technology. Data was collected through a questionnaire research designed to hospital CIOs in Taiwan. In the study [S59], the authors investigated a set of five factors (ease of use, convenience, security, privacy and cost reduction) that influence cloud usage by business community, whose needs and business requirements are very different from large enterprises. The study [S60] discussed how cloud adoption intention, pricing and deployment options are derived from the TOE framework.

Regarding **RQ2**, the paper S44 presented an experience report. The following list of papers were identified as discussing processes, strategies and frameworks: S2, S3, S4, S12, S14, S16, S17, S22, S23, S32, S33, S34, S35, S36, S37, S38, S39, S43. The Cost Modeling tool (Cloud Adoption Toolkit) was also classified in the **RQ2** scope.

4.3   Selecting Cloud Computing Service Providers (RQ3)

This subsection discusses how selected papers addressed RQ3: *How companies select cloud computing service providers according to their needs and profile?* According to Fig. 2, twelve papers discuss issues related to RQ3. In the following paragraphs we contextualize how each of these papers contributes to RQ3.

Regarding **RQ3**, the paper S56 presented an experience report when followed the Cloud Evaluation Experiment Methodology (CEEM) to benchmark GCE and also compare it with Amazon EC2. The following list of papers were identified as discussing processes, strategies and frameworks: S40, S46, S47, S48, S49, S54, S57, S67. In the case of the paper S26, it proposes a migration decision support system that incorporates both offering matching and cost calculation, combining features from various approaches. The tools related to **RQ3** were referenced in S7 (CDOSim) and S55 (CloudCmp).

According to [8], IT-related success is described through three categories of derived benefits: strategic, economic and technological. Strategic refers to an organization's renewed focus on its core business activities that can accompany a move to cloud computing when its IT functions, whole or in part, are hosted and/or managed by a cloud vendor. Economic refers to an organization's ability to tap the cloud vendor's expertise and technological resources to reduce in-house IT expenses. Technological refers to an organization's access to state-of-the-art technology and skilled personnel, eliminating the risk and cost of in-house technological obsolescence. Deployment is defined in terms of the strategic, economic, and technological benefits realized through cloud computing, which can set the organization apart from its competitors.

[S56] followed the Cloud Evaluation Experiment Methodology (CEEM) to benchmark Google Compute Engine (GCE) and Amazon EC2. The goal was to help understanding the elementary capability of GCE to deal with scientific problems. [S26] proposed a migration decision support system (MDSS) to select providers. In addition, it also provided a matching and migration cost calculation. [S40] proposed an approach to support customer decision making for selecting the most suitable cloud configuration-in terms of infrastructural requirements and cost. [S46] proposed a framework to incorporate a modelling language and also provided a structured process to support elicitation of security and privacy requirements. The goal was to select a cloud provider based on the suitability of the service provider to the relevant security and privacy requirements. The authors of paper [S47] performed a survey to obtain Cloud service selection approaches from companies considering five perspectives: decision-making techniques; data representation models; parameters and characteristics of Cloud services; contexts, purposes. [S48] highlighted the importance of an informed choice of a Cloud Service Provider (CSP) in minimising one's exposure to the insecurity of a cloud context and proposed a well-defined approach, known as the Complete-Auditable-Reportable (C.A.RE) to this end. Paper [S49] presented the FAGI model, whose goal was to identify the security controls needed by an organization and guided the organization in the selection of a trusted service provider. The [S54] study proposed a taxonomy that identified and classified eight important elements that characterise Cloud computing infrastructures: service type, resource deployment, hardware, runtime tuning, security, business model, middleware, and performance [S57] proposed a framework and a mechanism called SMICloud to measure specific quality attributes and prioritize Cloud services. The goal was to compares different CSPs and measure QoS attributes defined by Cloud Service Measurement Index Consortium (CSMIC). In [S67], the authors identified five main performance criteria considered relevant to measure QoS for cloud users: Availability, Reliability, Performance, Cost and Security. Under each main criteria, subcritera, which are directly measurable from cloud provider premises, were defined.

In the following, we presented studies that also presented tools. [S7] presented a simulation tool called CDOSim whose goal is to simulate cost and performance attributes in CDOs. The tool is build upon and significantly extends the cloud simulator CloudSim and integrates into the cloud migration framework Cloud-MIG. [S55] the tool CloudCmp to systematically compare the performance and cost of cloud providers along dimensions that matter to customers. This systematic review provided evidences of strategies used by companies to identify opportunities to migrate and adopt cloud computing, how they assess the cost-benefit relationship and strategies behind the rationale to select providers. A spectrum of techniques and approaches has been identified that cope with various concerns, i.e., security and trustworthiness, elasticity, portability and interoperability, and cloud resilience. In addition, many studies look into reference architectures and cloud-based architecture design methods as well.

4.4 Implications for Research and Practice

From Fig. 4, it is possible to conclude about the importance of the process to select the strategy to be adopted by a company (RQ1), the cost-benefit relationship (RQ2) and in the selection of providers (RQ3). In this case, they confirm the relevance of process in the support of cloud computing adoption [13].

Fig. 4. Types of support for the adoption of cloud computing.

The following validity issues were considered in the analysis of the data from this SLR. The first is related to bias in the extraction of data. We addressed this issue through the definition of a data extraction criteria to guarantee consistent extraction of data to related to the research questions. The findings and implications are based on the extracted data. Another possible threat is the way data was selected, that may have caused another bias. We addressed this threat during the selection step of the review, i.e. the studies included in this review were identified through a thorough selection process which was comprised of multiple stages. The papers selected in this systematic review were collected from different literature repositories covering relevant journals and proceedings. One possible threat is bias in the selection of publications. This is addressed through the specification of a research protocol that defines the research questions and objectives of the study, inclusion and exclusion criteria, search strings, as well as the search strategy and the strategy for data extraction.

5   Conclusions

In this Systematic Literature Review (SLR), we selected evidences from the literature to describe, characterize and highlight differences and commonalities among strategies adopted by companies to decide for the migration to the cloud. In this scenario, we also focused in the identification of evidences related to the cost-benefit relationship of this migration and selection of cloud service providers. Our goal was to systematically analyze data from the selected papers to draw a clear picture from what has been registered in the literature regarding how companies decide towards cloud computing. One of the main contribution of this paper was also the discussion of a list of approaches published in the literature that deal with the cost-benefit relationship and the rationale behind the selection of providers and their respective services. We are already investigating how providers have perceived the clients adoption and migration to the cloud computing paradigm and how they tailor their strategies to meet the needs of customers. We have already performed the snowballing technique considering the selected papers of this SLR to increase the list of papers that discuss the aforementioned research questions.

Appendix

See Table 5.

Table 5. Studies included in the review.

ID	Author, Title	Venue	Year
S1	J.-F. Zhao and J.-T. Zhou, **Strategies and Methods for Cloud Migration.**	IJAC	2014
S2	A. Khajeh-Hosseini, D. Greenwood, J. W. Smith and I. Sommerville, **The Cloud Adoption Toolkit: Supporting Cloud Adoption Decisions in the Enterprise.** *Top Ten Cited Paper According to Google Scholar*	SPE	2012
S3	S. C. Misra and A. Mondal, **Identification of a Companys Suitability for the Adoption of Cloud Computing and Modelling Its Corresponding Return on Investment.** *Top Ten Cited Paper According to Google Scholar*	MCM	2011
S4	B. Rimal, A. Jukan, D. Katsaros and Y. Goeleven. **Architectural requirements for cloud computing systems: an enterprise cloud approach.** *Top Ten Cited Paper According to Google Scholar*	JGC	2011
S5	M. I. M. Almanea **A Survey and Evaluation of the Existing Tools that Support Adoption of Cloud Computing and Selection of Trustworthy and Transparent Cloud Providers.**	INCoS	2014
S6	S. Frey and W. Hasselbring **An Extensible Architecture for Detecting Violations of a Cloud Environments Constraints during Legacy Software System Migration.**	CSMR	2011
S7	F. Fittkau, S. Frey and W. Hasselbring, **CDOSim: Simulating cloud deployment options for software migration support.**	MESOCA	2012
S8	O. Sefraoui, M. Aissaoui and M. Eleuldj, **Cloud computing migration and IT resources rationalization.**	ICMCS	2014
S9	J. Alonso, L. Orue-Echevarria, M. Escalante, J. Gorronogoitia and D. Presenza, **Cloud modernization assessment framework: Analyzing the impact of a potential migration to Cloud.**	MESOCA	2013
S10	B. Wadhwa, A. Jaitly, and B. Suri, **Cloud Service Brokers: An Emerging Trend in Cloud Adoption and Migration.**	APSEC	2013
S11	L. Zhou, **CloudFTP: A Case Study of Migrating Traditional Applications to the Cloud.**	ISDEA	2013
S12	V. S. Sharma and S. Anwer, **Detecting Performance Antipatterns before Migrating to the Cloud.**	CloudCom	2013
S13	S. N. Srirama, V. Ivanistsev, P. Jakovits, and C. Willmore, **Direct migration of scientific computing experiments to the cloud.**	HPCSim	2013
S14	P. R. M. Andrade, R. G. Araujo, J. C. Filho, T. R. Pereira, A. B. Albuquerque, and N. C. Mendonca, **Improving Business by Migrating Applications to the Cloud Using Cloudstep.**	WAINA	2015
S15	A. Juan-Verdejo, S. Zschaler, B. Surajbali, H. Baars, and H.-G. Kemper, **InCLOUDer: A Formalised Decision Support Modelling Approach to Migrate Applications to Cloud Environments.**	SEAA	2014
S16	Q. H. Vu and R. Asal, **Legacy Application Migration to the Cloud: Practicability and Methodology.**	SERVICES	2012
S17	G. Kousiouris and D. Kyriazis, **Legacy applications on the cloud: Challenges and enablers focusing on application performance analysis and providers characteristics.**	SERVICES	2012
S18	J. Wu, P. Teregowda, K. Williams, M. Khabsa, D. Jordan, E. Treece, C. L. Giles, **Migrating a Digital Library to a Private Cloud.**	IC2E	2014
S19	A. Bergmayr, H. Bruneliere, J. L. C. Izquierdo, J. Gorroogoitia, G. Kousiouris, D. Kyriazis, M. Wimmer, **Migrating legacy software to the cloud with ARTIST.**	CSMR	2013
S20	C. Pahl, and H. Xiong, **Migration to PaaS clouds - Migration process and architectural concerns.**	MESOCA	2013
S21	F. Wang, J. Liu, M. Chen and H. Wang, **Migration Towards Cloud-Assisted Live Media Streaming.**	TNET	2014
S22	M. Manuja, **Moving agile based projects on Cloud.**	IAdCC	2014
S23	J. Banerjee, **Moving to the cloud: Workload migration techniques and approaches.**	HiPC	2012
S24	B. Cai, F. Xu, F. Ye and W. Zhou, **Research and application of migrating legacy systems to the private cloud platform with cloudstack.**	ICAL	2012
S25	A. Michalas, N. Paladi and C. Gehrmann, **Security aspects of e-Health systems migration to the cloud.**	HealthCom	2014
S26	V. Andrikopoulos, Z. Song and F. Leymann, **Supporting the migration of applications to the cloud through a decision support system.**	CLOUD	2013
S27	H.-I. Wang, and C. Hsu, **The paradigm framework of cloud migration based on BPR and gBPR.**	ICAwST	2013
S28	S. Saadat and H. R. Shahriari, **Towards a process-oriented framework for improving trust and security in migration to cloud.**	ISCISC	2014
S29	B. P. Peddigari, **Unified Cloud Migration Framework Using factory based approach.**	INDCON	2014
S30	T. Parveen and S. Tilley, **When to Migrate Software Testing to the Cloud?**	ICSTW	2010
S31	T. Boillat and C. Legner, **Why Do Companies Migrate Towards Cloud Enterprise Systems? A Post-Implementation Perspective.**	CBI	2014
S32	M. Sadighi, **Accounting System on Cloud: A Case Study.**	ITNG	2014
S33	B. C. Tak, B. Urgaonkar and A. Sivasubramaniam, **Cloudy with a Chance of Cost Savings.**	TPDS	2012
S34	J. Opara-Martins, R. Sahandi and F. Tian, **Critical review of vendor lock-in and its impact on adoption of cloud computing.**	i-Society	2014
S35	L. Mastroeni and M. Naldi, **Long-range Evaluation of Risk in the Migration to Cloud Storage.**	CBC	2011
S36	C. -Y. Yam, A. Baldwin, S. Shiu and C. Ioannidis **Migration to Cloud as Real Option: Investment Decision under Uncertainty.**	TrustCom	2011

Table 5. *(Continued)*

ID	Author, Title	Venue	Year
S37	S. Yi, A. Andrzejak and D. Kondo Monetary Cost-Aware Checkpointing and Migration on Amazon Cloud Spot Instances.	TSC	2011
S38	N. Phaphoom, X. Wang, S. Samuel, S. Helmer and P. AbrahamssonA survey study on major technical barriers affecting the decision to adopt cloud services.	JSS	2015
S39	E. Park and K. J. KimAn Integrated Adoption Model of Mobile Cloud Services: Exploration of Key Determinants and Extension of Technology Acceptance Model.	TELE	2014
S40	J. Garca-Galn, P. Trinidad, O. F. Rana and A. Ruiz-CortsAutomated configuration support for infrastructure migration to the cloud.	FGCS	2015
S41	X. Xu From cloud computing to cloud manufacturing. *Top Ten Cited Paper According to Google Scholar*	RCIM	2012
S42	M. Stieninger, D. Nedbal, W. Wetzlinger, G. Wagner and M. A. Erskine Impacts on the Organizational Adoption of Cloud Computing: A Reconceptualization of Influencing Factors.	PROTCY	2014
S43	M. J. OSullivan and D. Grigoras Integrating mobile and cloud resources management using the cloud personal assistant.	SIMPAT	2014
S44	P. J. P. da Costa and A. M. R. da Cruz. Migration to Windows Azure Analysis and Comparison.	PROTCY	2012
S45	J. Knsemller and H. Karl A game-theoretic approach to the financial benefits of infrastructure-as-a-service.	FGCS	2014
S46	H. Mouratidis, S. Islam, C. Kalloniatis and S. Gritzalis. A framework to support selection of cloud providers based on security and privacy requirements.	JSS	2013
S47	S. Le, H. Dong, F. K. Hussain, O. K. Hussain, E. Chang, L. Sun, E. Chang.Cloud service selection: State-of-the-art and future research directions.	JNCA	2014
S48	M. Ouedraogo and H. Mouratidis Selecting a Cloud Service Provider in the age of cybercrime.	COSE	2013
S49	C. Tang and J. Liu.Selecting a trusted cloud service provider for your SaaS program.	COSE	2015
S50	F. CRowe, J. Brinkley and N. Tabrizi.Migrating Legacy Applications to the Cloud.	CLOUDCOM	2013
S51	Z. Yang, J. Sun, Y. Zhang and Y. Wang.Understanding SaaS adoption from the perspective of organizational users: A tripod readiness model.	CHB	2014
S52	Z. Li, L. OBrien, R. Cai and H. Zhang. Towards a Taxonomy of Performance Evaluation of Commercial Cloud Services.	CLOUD	2012
S53	Z. Li, L. OBrien, H. Zhang and R. Cai. On a Catalogue of Metrics for Evaluating Commercial Cloud Services.	IWGC	2012
S54	R. Prodan and S. Ostermann. A Survey and Taxonomy of Infrastructure as a Service and Web Hosting Cloud Providers. *Top Ten Cited Paper According to Google Scholar*	IWGC	2009
S55	A. Li, X. Yang, S. Kandula and M. Zhang. CloudCmp: Comparing Public Cloud Providers. *Top Ten Cited Paper According to Google Scholar*	IMC	2010
S56	Z. Li, L. OBrien, R. Ranjan and M. Zhang. Early Observations on Performance of Google Compute Engine for Scientific Computing.	CLOUDCOM	2013
S57	S. K. Garg, S. Versteeg and R. Buyya. A framework for ranking of cloud computing services. *Top Ten Cited Paper According to Google Scholar*	FGCS	2013
S58	J. W. Lian, D. C. Yen, Y. T. WangAn exploratory study to understand the critical factors affecting the decision to adopt cloud computing in Taiwan hospital.	IJIM	2014
S59	P. Gupta, A. Seetharaman, and J. R. Raj. The usage and adoption of cloud computing by small and medium businesses. *Top Ten Cited Paper According to Google Scholar*	IJIM	2013
S60	P. F. Hsu, S. Ray and Y. Y. Li-Hsieh. Examining cloud computing adoption intention, pricing mechanism, and deployment model.	IJIM	2014
S61	T. Oliveira, M. Thomas and M. Espadanal. Assessing the determinants of cloud computing adoption: An analysis of the manufacturing and services sectors.	IM	2014
S62	S. Frey, W. Hasselbring and B. Schnoor. Automatic conformance checking for migrating software systems to cloud infrastructures and platforms.	JSEP	2013
S63	M. Stieninger and D. Nedbal. Diffusion and Acceptance of Cloud Computing in SMEs Towards a Valence Model of Relevant Factors.	HICSS	2014
S64	Y. Alshamaila, S. Papagiannidis and F. Li. Cloud computing adoption by SMEs in the north east of England. *Top Ten Cited Paper According to Google Scholar*	JEIM	2013
S65	A. Benlian, T. Hess and P. Buxmann. Drivers of SaaS-Adoption An Empirical Study of Different Application Types. *Top Ten Cited Paper According to Google Scholar*	BISE	2009
S66	M. Carcary, E. Doherty and G. Conway. The Adoption of Cloud Computing by Irish SMEs an Exploratory Study.	EJISE	2014
S67**	S. S. Wagle, M. Guzek, P. Bouvry, and R. Bisdorff An Evaluation Model for Selecting Cloud Services from Commercially Available Cloud Providers.	CLOUDCOM	2015
S68**	P. Scandurra, G. Psaila, R. Capilla, and R. Mirandola Challenges and assessment in migrating IT legacy applications to the cloud.	MESOCA	2015
S69**	M. Menzel, and R. Ranjan CloudGenius: decision support for web server cloud migration.	WWW	2012
S70**	R. Garg and B. StillerFactors Affecting Cloud Adoption and Their Interrelations.	CLOSER	2015
S71**	I. H. Mohamed, A. Karim and A. Ahmed The migration of the university IT infrastructure toward a secure IaaS Cloud.	ICEIT	2015
S72**	J. Soldani, T. Binz, U. Breitenbcher, F. Leymann and A. Brogi TOSCA-MART: A method for adapting and reusing cloud applications.	JSS	2015
S73**	R. El-Gazzar, E. Hustad and D. H. Olsen Understanding cloud computing adoption issues: A Delphi study approach.	JSS	2016

**Papers included in the extended version of this SLR.

References

1. Breivold, H.P., Crnkovic, I., Radosevic, I., Balatinac, I.: Architecting for the cloud: a systematic review. In: 2014 IEEE 17th International Conference on Computational Science and Engineering (CSE), pp. 312–318. IEEE (2014)
2. Brereton, P., Kitchenham, B.A., Budgen, D., Turner, M., Khalil, M.: Lessons from applying the systematic literature review process within the software engineering domain. J. Syst. Softw. **80**(4), 571–583 (2007)
3. Chen, L., Babar, M.A.: A systematic review of evaluation of variability management approaches in software product lines. Inf. Softw. Technol. **53**(4), 344–362 (2011)
4. Buyya, R., Yeo, C.S., Venugopal, S., Broberg, J., Brandic, I.: Cloud computing and emerging it platforms: vision, hype, and reality for delivering computing as the 5th utility. Fut. Gener. Comput. Syst. **25**(6), 599–616 (2009)
5. Davis, F.D.: User acceptance of information systems: the technology acceptance model (TAM) (1987)
6. Dyba, T., Dingsoyr, T.: Empirical studies of agile software development: a systematic review. Inf. Softw. Technol. **50**(9–10), 833–859 (2008)
7. Garg, S.K., Versteeg, S., Buyya, R.: A framework for ranking of cloud computing services. Fut. Gener. Comput. Syst. **29**(4), 1012–1023 (2013)
8. Garrison, G., Kim, S., Wakefield, R.L.: Success factors for deploying cloud computing. Commun. ACM **55**(9), 62–68 (2012)
9. Gupta, P., Seetharaman, A., Raj, J.R.: The usage, adoption of cloud computing by small, medium businesses. Int. J. Inf. Manag. **33**(5), 861–874 (2013)
10. Jamshidi, P., Ahmad, A., Pahl, C.: Cloud migration research: a systematic review. IEEE Trans. Cloud Comput. **1**(2), 142–157 (2013)
11. Jula, A., Sundararajan, E., Othman, Z.: Cloud computing service composition: a systematic literature review. Expert Syst. Appl. **41**(8), 3809–3824 (2014)
12. Kitchenham, B., Charters, S.: Guidelines for performing systematic literature reviews in software engineering. In: Technical report, Version. 2.3 EBSE Technical Report. EBSE (2007)
13. KPMG: The cloud takes shape. Global cloud survey: the implementation challenge (2013)
14. Li, A., Yang, X., Kandula, S., Zhang, M.: CloudCmp: comparing public cloud providers. In: Proceedings of the 10th ACM SIGCOMM Conference on Internet Measurement, pp. 1–14. ACM (2010)
15. Li, Q., Wang, C., Wu, J., Li, J., Wang, Z.-Y.: Towards the businessinformation technology alignment in cloud computing environment: an approach based on collaboration points and agents. Int. J. Comput. Integr. Manuf. **24**(11), 1038–1057 (2011)
16. Li, Z., O'Brien, L., Cai, R., Zhang, H.: Towards a taxonomy of performance evaluation of commercial cloud services. In: 2012 IEEE 5th International Conference on Cloud Computing (CLOUD), pp. 344–351. IEEE (2012)
17. Li, Z., O'Brien, L., Zhang, H., Cai, R.: On a catalogue of metrics for evaluating commercial cloud services. In: Proceedings of the 2012 ACM/IEEE 13th International Conference on Grid Computing, pp. 164–173. IEEE Computer Society (2012)
18. Li, Z., Zhang, H., O'Brien, L., Cai, R., Flint, S.: On evaluating commercial cloud services: a systematic review. J. Syst. Softw. **86**(9), 2371–2393 (2013)

19. Mahesh, S., Landry, B.J., Sridhar, T., Walsh, K.R.: A decision table for the cloud computing decision in small business. In: Managing Information Resources and Technology: Emerging Applications and Theories, p. 159 (2013)
20. Mell, P., Grance, T.: The NIST definition of cloud computing (2011)
21. Noblit, G.W., Hare, R.D.: Meta-ethnography: Synthesizing Qualitative Studies, vol. 11. Sage, USA (1988)
22. Paula, A., Carneiro, G.: Cloud computing adoption, cost-benefit relationship and strategies for selecting providers: a systematic review. In: Proceedings of the 11th International Conference on Evaluation of Novel Approaches to Software Engineering (ENASE 2016), pp. 12–23. SCITEPRESS (2016)
23. Rogers, E.: Diffusion of Innovations, 5th edn. Free Press, New York (2003)
24. Tornatzky, L., Fleischer, M.: The Process of Technology Innovation. Lexington Books, Lexington (1990)
25. Trott, P.: The role of market research in the development of discontinuous new products. Eur. J. Innov. Manag. 4, 117–125 (2001)
26. Weiss, A.: Computing in the clouds. netWorker 11(4), 16–25 (2007)
27. Zhang, H., Babar, M.A., Tell, P.: Identifying relevant studies in software engineering. Inf. Softw. Technol. 53(6), 625–637 (2011)

Author Index

Printed in the United States
By Bookmasters